I0674297

Carelle Stein

The Sixth Spoon:
The Tale of a Probate Lawyer Gone Weird

3rd Printing

Copyright: 2015 by Carelle Jean Muellner Stein

The moral right of the author has been asserted.

This is a work of fiction. All characters in this book are fictionalized, even if loosely based on historical or public figures. Some of the places described in this book exist now or have actually existed in the past. All characters and places have been selected or created by the author for her unknown purposes. Any resemblance to persons (whether living or dead) and references to personalities or statements made by any particular historical or public figure may not reflect any actual basis in truth or fact. The characters are constructed simply to benefit the story line and reflect the imaginary musings of the author who has worked too long and hard and who hasn't had enough time off lately.

All rights reserved. No part of this book may be used, reproduced or transmitted in any form or by any means, electronic or mechanical, including photocopying, recording, or by any information storage and retrieval system, without permission in writing from the copyright owner.

Cover Design © Susan Mrosek, Pondering Pool, Inc.
Editor: Debbie Nelsen

Trade Paperback 13-ISBN: 978-0-9966899-1-5
Library of Congress Control Number: 2015918622

This book was published at Oakdale, Minnesota,
in the United States of America.

This novel is dedicated to Ted,
who has cherished and encouraged
my own fulfillment as an individual,
though all the changes of our lives.

This is a novel about a probate lawyer gone weird.
It is a parable about life at its worst and life at its best.
A mystery.
It contains wonder, despair, and hope.
It is about life, and events that transcend and
transform.

Table of Contents

Our ancient stories tell us that certain places can be a focus of life-changing events. Places where there are surges of energy or passion; sometimes uncontrolled, uninvited, and totally unexpected. Places of power, outside of time, that change everything...

Prologue

July.

The Cabin

I discovered this rental cabin years ago, under some very peculiar circumstances. Not scary circumstances you understand, it's just that some odd and unusual events led me here to begin with. Having found this place, I kept coming back year after year. You could say I was drawn here. Compelled even. I wondered about that.

The surprising thing, though, is that when I arrive here each summer, nothing has changed. I mean NOTHING, as in NOT-ONE-THING. The cabin is precisely as I left it. Even the plastic wine glasses I purchased years ago are on the exact same shelf. How can this be? No cracks; no chips; no dust. Too weird. Two glasses sitting there, on the same shelf, in a silent plea for someone special to share wine with.

Looking up, I gaze at the knot in the old wooden ceiling. It is not merely a comfort; it is a thing of reverie, the last piece of the grand puzzle of life. A concentric circle. A pure shade of brown within a darker shade of brown. Perhaps the knot was part of some old, grand oak (or maybe chestnut) tree, harvested a century ago, with the essence of the earth still clinging to its roots. A loving, connected, ancient tree. Connected to me, today, by this amazing knot in the ceiling of MY rental cabin. Maybe the rest of the tree was even used to panel the entire cabin, with its wide boards and darkened patina. In my world, today, a knotted ceiling would be made of some old, gnarled buckthorn tree, or worse yet, a picture of some old gnarled buckthorn tree, laminated between two sheets of plastic.

My eyes are drawn again to the small warped door to the right of the hand-laid stone fireplace. I've always wondered what lay behind that locked, misshapen door with the curiously small round window in it. A seriously dirty window. A window so glazed over with dirt, that even spit can't penetrate the grime. The truth is, I've wanted to open that door SO bad. In fact, for the past two summers, I've engaged in an internal debate as to whether my rental rights include the right to open the suspect closet door - you know, Property Law 101. Don't I have the right to open every door and every drawer when I rent a piece of real estate? "Of course I do," my inner voice argues! Don't

I have adverse possession rights if I rent the cabin for the same week every year - my week - for at least 15 years? You betcha! Damn straight. Wait. Maybe I have to pay the real estate taxes too? Alas, I can't remember. But I've waited long enough to open that door, my inner voice wails! I realize this is my nemesis. For I know with certainty that I will never be truly fulfilled in life until I find out what's behind that goddamn closet door!

Every year, I leave the closet door alone. Every year I ponder the mystery of the closet door. Or, more likely, the "mustery" of the closet door. Yuk. The debate continues, but sanity prevails. I leave the closet door alone again this year and begin to pack up.

...The storm came up suddenly, like a blinding headache or a cold. Totally unexpected. Some kind of virus of the air currents. Psychic dust devils? I wondered about that too.

In a burst of high-tension energy, the rain began to sheet down in torrents. As the wind rose, the sky was illuminated by colors only an artist or a three-year old could imagine. It was a streaked curtain of color - a muted watercolor - greenish in the middle with the edges turning shades of coral, purple and then vibrant blue. Wow! Like a rainbow on its side, with every part of it reflected in the wild and uncontrolled waves bashing the shore.

In my dreams, storms and water have always been harbingers of change. All New Age, dream-interpretation, metaphysical literature will corroborate this idea. You know, the winds of change, the water of re-birth, etc., and yada yada. This storm was not symbolic in any sense though; it was a very real and lively 3-dimensional experience. This storm involved REAL water. Multiple gallons of it. Real wind too. The kind of wind that blows your hat off and joyfully raises your skirt. This storm had it all. Yet, in some funny, inexplicable way, this storm felt different. What was different, I wondered?

Well, for one thing, this storm had a finite, perverse glamour about it. It was much more dramatic and tangible than any human-controlled act.[1]

But the extraordinarily scary part, I finally realized, was that this storm was meant for me. I knew it. There was a connection here, somehow. I felt this storm intimately. It shocked me; moved me. It was in my face and in my bones. Yikes! How is that even possible? Was some kind of change imminent? Did this storm symbolize the coming of a dynamic, amazing, powerful change? All this water! It had to mean something!

Get a grip! I told myself.

---

[1] It's important to understand that I'm not a Storm Queen or anything as exotic as that. And, just for the record, I am very familiar with drama in human-controlled situations. So I know the difference.

Change? So, what's the big deal? Why did that bother me at all, I wondered? I knew that life could change all on its own, without storms or even showers. Sometimes all it took were harsh words or a whimper. And, just like the physical reality of this violent, virulent, powerful storm outside of my window, I recognized that some people are storms too, even unwittingly. Chaos seems to surround them. Aha! So, what if this amazing storm and I, being somehow connected, could change everything? Hum. Change emerging from a single convergence point in time and space? Like Dorothy and the tornado? Is it even possible?

I shook my head to clear the bats out.

So, I tried to ignore it. The storm, that is. But this storm was so wild that I couldn't ignore it or pretend it wasn't happening either. On the other hand, it's easy to ignore life on a daily basis. You know what I mean. You get the cup of coffee on the way to work; you work the work, and play the play. There might be a niggling sense of "duh, why am I doing this?" from time to time. But, essentially, unless some event triggers a change, life just tends to continue on its own momentum. Day by day. That's why we need storms, I guess, in real life or even in dreams, to show us the path of change.

Then the lights went out, of course.

It was hard to read anything after the first hour, since the sky was nearly black in the middle of the day and there was no electricity. My arm got tired from holding the flashlight. Worse yet, the ice cream in the freezer melted. I knew for certain that I would have to leave if the beer got warm. I had visions of driving over downed power lines, charged with electricity. Do cars get electrified I wondered? I heard one time that if a person's body doesn't touch the ground, there is no danger of electrocution. I should have paid more attention to physics and the practical things in life, I suppose. Then I would be able to answer my "should-I-leave-now" or "wait-till-morning?" questions. Better stay put, I decided.

Sitting in a cabin alone in the dark may be fun for some; a kind of peaceful solitude with just enough ambiance to make a nature-communer feel satisfied. For a city girl like me (well, maybe a "small city" girl) it was just a little spooky. The darkness made me think of God, the Goddess, the force, the universe, nature, and good and evil. Yeah. There was always the concept of evil to think about; pervasive evil. But, all shivering aside, I do not buy into the traditional definition of evil, at least not in the mainstream or religious sense at all.

I must have fallen asleep. In that place between awake and asleep, Harrison Ford (it felt like Harrison) was just about to kiss me, and well, hopefully a little bit more...

The sound of the refrigerator kicking back-in startled me awake. Damn! Just a few minutes too soon. What a dumb sound anyway! The silence had been so absolute. Next, the ceramic teapot on top of the refrigerator began bumping against the half-empty wine bottle, vibrating to the tune of the motor. Ah, the miracle of modern technology! Things would soon be back to normal, or so it seemed. But, something had changed. Something still felt a little "off." Just a whisper; a premonition. Something different coming; something a little more.

The rain subsided. My feet hit the cold floor. Old cabin; old screens; old floor; old ceiling with a knot in it. Sand hidden in the corners. Spiders taking every opportunity to rebuild and re-arm their webs for the coming days. No matter. I began to open the windows. The curtains moved only slightly now, with the ever-most gentlest breeze tickling my face. I told myself that I was just imaging this "new" thing on the horizon. This "something else coming" thing. Then, with intent, I decided it was time to move on. Having decided, I actually felt better.

I stepped outside. It was dawn, and the air smelled green and fresh. A new day; a new awakening. It was time to go.

But... wait. I don't want to go back! It feels like home here. The home of my heart. It could be my home, I consider. Maybe I'll check out the Cass County Courthouse in Walker. Maybe they need a new lawyer in town - a good probate lawyer - to take care of all the dead peoples' families. Yeah, sure. All fifty of them each century. I just might be able to make a living here if I give up every amenity in life. Beans, biscuits, blue jeans and water. Yep. That's all I really need; along with, well, maybe some moisturizer and a new lipstick every now and then.

Well, no matter. I'll be back next year, and the year after that I vow. And, maybe next year I'll explore the "older" path; the one behind the "old" path. Maybe I'll even sew some new, heavier curtains to keep the sound of the rain out when the next storm comes. Better yet, I'll open up the closet door next year. Yeah! That's what I'll do! Sure thing.

I hit the road back to the Twin Cities.

One duck among millions, again.

Chapter 1

The Courtroom

If I walk through the Courthouse door with my eyes closed, will anything have changed? Will there have been some incredible, unbelievable, brilliant metamorphosis due to weather, politics, taxpayer revolt, or even natural disaster - since yesterday? I'm easy. I'll take anything. Even a small, wondrous change will do.

I close my eyes and cross my fingers, hoping for the best. Let's see, is the onyx Indian[2] still two stories high? Are the marble floors and intricate brass railings all still there? I open my eyes. Yep. Nothing's changed. No matter. This is my Courthouse anyway. Mine, mine, mine! Just like it should be, a temple of reason, truth, faith, and delivered justice.

---

[2] Sorry, Native American, I mean.

The elevator doors open and about ten people squeeze in, including me. We all look around, but not directly at each other. This would violate the Minnesota-nice rule. We certainly would not want to talk to one another and inadvertently disclose a secret longing or acknowledge our proximity. We try not to smell each other either.

I study the brass workings on the doors of the elevator, free associating: Could not be duplicated today… renovated brilliance… perfectly redone. Who cares about taxpayer dollars when the alternative would be sheet-rocked trusses and eight stories of plate glass? Besides, you don't freeze your ass off in this building in the winter, I muse. It's so easy to forget about air conditioning and summer when you live in Minnesota. Likewise, it's also easy to ignore the metal detectors once your pockets are resupplied and your briefcase returned. As Tracy Luther says, "it is what it is."

Despite its modernized efficiency, I move my lips in silent prayer that the elevator won't act up again. The last time the elevator misbehaved, I had somehow convinced myself that I could easily walk down sixteen floors to ground level rather than risk getting stuck in the elevator with a judge, a bailiff or another, God forbid, lawyer. For, in my opinion, the only thing worse than being married to a lawyer would be getting stuck in an elevator with one. Still single and not wanting to tempt fate, sixteen floors shouldn't be too bad, I had misguidedly reasoned. I'm physically fit. My tummy is flat. So, down I went. And, just twenty heart-pounding minutes later, breathing heavily and sweating like a pig, I reached the main floor. Who am I trying to kid? Down is always worse than up! I'm not twenty-seven anymore. I'm not a ballet dancer or even a power walker. Not such a smart idea was it, girl? Next time, I had decided, I'd just let myself be rescued, stuck in the elevator, all alone, or at least with someone who smells good, after two hours or so of strict Zen time. That wouldn't be too bad either would it? So, trusting in the universe, I had decided to be brave and take the elevator today. After all, nothing has changed here. Everything looks normal, right? A regular day. Things generally happen the way you expect them to, don't they? Well, maybe not always, and maybe not today.

Thankfully, the elevator doors open and close without incident. Sixteen times. People tended to exit the elevator at an alarming speed. Each person bounding forward to the life they had chosen, juggling some critical timetable to make all the pieces fit. Clock time. Each time the doors open, I move aside to let both the powerful and the hopeful pass, waiting for my turn. I am finally alone as the doors open up on the 16th Floor. I step out, looking for my client. One old man in an old-looking suit sitting on the old wooden bench, alone. Nope. Not my client. No one waiting for me. OK then.

I look around. The yellow cast of the marble walls does nothing to help my eyes focus. The subdued lighting and the old style benches contribute to the time-warped hush that encompasses everything. You could almost believe that you had stepped back in time at least eighty years. Ah, yes. I recognize the "good old days" analysis. The days when gaslights illuminated the interiors, and when courthouses were treated with respect and reverence. Sanctuaries of the rule of law. But I knew it was all camouflage.

My heels click as I walk down the hall toward the assigned courtroom. A definitely female power sound not present in 1920 Kansas and not in Munchkin-Land either. Never mind, I knew exactly where I was. I was most certainly present at the Ramsey County Courthouse in Saint Paul, Minnesota, in the cold, cold nort-land. But no bailiffs, no wheelchairs, no clerks to be seen. Where was everybody today? I glanced at my watch - thirty minutes early. Wow, what was I thinking? As I turn to go back down to the basement to get some powdered coffee, the elevator doors open and my client pauses on the threshold.

The hallway lighting did not flatter her. In reality, there was no way that any lighting, shadows, cosmetics or hair color could improve my client's appearance. She was ugly and old. Not evil, just ugly and old, in the modern-day sense of not being attractive or sexy at all. But she was a good woman. She was simply a kind, old, demented woman, and she needed my help. Accompanying her was an equally old woman, my client's sister, but I knew that she, at least, had a driver's license. I smiled at the ladies and took my client's hand. We shuffled over to the docket posted on the Courtroom door. My case was listed as #6, on a calendar of fifteen other cases all scheduled at the same time. Oh yeah! We'll be out of here in less than twenty minutes for once. We moved into the courtroom, took our seats, and waited for our case to be called.

"Counsel, note your appearance." Prompted by the words of Judge Henderson, opposing counsel responds, "Samuel Smith, on behalf of Petitioner, Social Services for the Elderly." Following Sam's cue, I note my appearance, "Gracie... Grace Swan, your Honor, court-appointed attorney on behalf of the proposed Ward, Dolores Anderson. Also present in the Courtroom is Mrs. Anderson's sister, Lorraine Larson." Lorraine nods at me from the spectator's gallery. Sam and I sit at counsel table, with my client Dolores next to me, gripping her cane. Business as usual.

Sam directs his client's representative, a youngish woman with long blonde hair, to take the witness stand. She raises her right hand to be sworn in. The Judge's clerk asks the witness to state her name and spell her last name.

"Annie Shepard, S-H-E-P-A-R-D." She replies.

Sam asked, "Who do you work for Ms. Shepard?"

The witness replies, "Social Services for the Elderly."

"Are you familiar with this case?" He continues. I inwardly groan. Oh, come on, Sam, lay the proper foundation. This young woman can't be more than twenty-two years old; she looks like a Macy's model, not a social worker. As usual, I do not raise any objection, and the testimony continues.

"Yes. I am one of the case workers assigned to help Mrs. Anderson," the perky former cheerleader replies. Yeah, right, I ruminate, for at least the last two weeks since you graduated from high school.

"Are you asking the Court to appoint Social Services for the Elderly, Inc. as Guardian for Mrs. Anderson?" Sam continues.

"Yes, I am," Ms. Shepherd replies. The one-sentence tit for tat continues until all the legal bases for the case are touched upon - just barely. No tears, no trauma. Thankfully, my client, poor, elderly, ugly Dolores, will not remember the testimony twenty minutes after she leaves the courtroom.

"Dolores needs protection, blah, blah, blah... Dolores is not thinking clearly, blah, blah, blah... Dolores has dementia, hypertension, diabetes, has lost one kidney and has curly hair..." No. Stop. Wait a minute, that's me! I'm the one with curly hair, not Dolores! I look over at Dolores just to be sure that she is still breathing. I note that she is a little red in her face, but no curly hair. I notice that Dolores' cane is wiggling, just a little. Hum. Judge Henderson looks down at me and asks, "Ms. Swan, do you have a statement?"

"Yes, your Honor," I say as I rise and turn toward the bench. I tell the Court that I have reviewed the medical records, that I have spoken with the hospital's social worker and with Dolores on two occasions, and that I agree Dolores needs a Guardian. I hear the heavy breathing of Dolores next to me, but I fearlessly press on. I tell the Court how Dolores has no children, that her husband died some years ago, and that she now lives alone in a small apartment in downtown Saint Paul. Picking up speed, I rapidly continue, "Dolores wants me to tell you that she has worked very hard her whole life, your Honor, and that she has earned every penny herself, without help from anyone." Dolores' breathing slows down slightly, and the Judge turns to speak to her.

Judge Henderson was good-looking as judges go; slender, dark haired, not too old, not too young, and he looked good in black. He had a winning smile and an easy presence which made the old folks trust him. But, never be deceived! The Judge's mild and personable demeanor hides a very astute, critically analytical legal mind. He knows the probate code like the back of his hand, probably better than the back of his hand. Best of all, though, he knows how to be "judgy," when he needs to be. He knows how to maintain order and manage his courtroom, another big plus. Part of those management skills includes settling down confused, old persons, and placating angry family members. Thankfully, Judge Henderson can usually tell a con a mile away. Once, years ago, during a particularly litigious trial, he had winked at me from the bench, and I almost fell over backwards at counsel table. I think he just wanted to see if I was paying attention. He hasn't winked at me since, but I pay extra good attention these days anyway, just in case.

The Judge asks Dolores a few questions to make a good record, fixing the poor testimony. Dolores willingly tells him that she is fifty-nine years old, that she works at Donaldson Company, that she can manage just fine on her own without any help, that Nixon is President, and that she lives in a little house in Brainerd with her husband who likes to shave in the kitchen sink. Of course, the legal file clearly shows that Dolores is eighty-three years old; that she has been waiting for a Guardian to be appointed before the County will release her from Regions Hospital after a hip fracture; and that her husband has been dead for almost 20 years.

When the Judge had almost completed his inquiry, I turn to face Dolores and notice that she is lowering her cane from the strike position. Geez, that was a close one! Dolores is smiling in a dreamy sort of way as she responds to the Judge, "Yes, of course, I heard everything. I'm not sure why I'm here. I'm just fine. You don't have to worry about me. Sure, I talked to this nice lady here next to me.

She's my insurance agent. Where'd you say I got I all that money from again?"

No objections. The Court does its job, takes away Dolores' civil rights, and orders Social Services for the Elderly, Inc. to be Guardian for Dolores. One more person controlled by an artificial entity and politics, with a smattering of due process. Everything done right and perfectly legal.

I leave the Court room wishing for a beer, and realizing that I have at least seven hours to go before I can have one. I wonder about Dolores. Where did the spark go? Is this a natural process occurring here? And, was she really planning to hit me with her cane? I did my job, in the most perfect and least controversial way. No intrusion, no light show, just business as usual.

Is this what will happen to me in the end? To end up like Dolores in a perfectly warm, protected, sheltered, and controlled world? In a locked ward with 24-hour cable available so I won't miss any exercise shows or special jewelry deals? Is this loving, nurturing imprisonment preferable to the iceberg floating away, at a slow pace, toward the inevitable conclusion of life? Will I die while watching re-runs of **I Love Lucy?**

I walk three blocks through the 2nd floor skyway to my office. With my briefcase in one hand and my Starbucks cup in the other, I push open the door to the reception area of my office. Natalie, the receptionist, my friend, and my sometime assistant, is sitting at her desk, on the telephone, of course. She gives me a nod and terminates the call. "Here's your messages, Gracie," she says. "The social worker on your new case called a few minutes ago, and she wants you to call her back right away. She sounded worried. And, oh yeah, Harvey scheduled an appointment for you to meet with a Ms. Strong tonight at 6:00 p.m."

"Who is Ms. Strong," I ask, "and why so late?"

Natalie responds, in her usual manner, "New client; don't know; talk to Harvey; Davy and I had good sex last night." The phone rings, Natalie takes the call. I move on down the hall to my office. Geez. I'm glad somebody had good sex last night.

Well, to be honest, Natalie always has good sex with Davy or Sam, Jocko, or Phil. Hopefully, not all at the same time. You get the idea. Looking at Natalie is like looking at a miniature version of the computer-generated Laura Croft. They shared the same attitude, for sure; the same pouty lips and pointy nipples. I'm pretty sure that Lady Croft wasn't a Minnesota Rollergirl with dreads, though. I wonder if Natalie and Laura might actually share the same tattoo artist? Of course, all is hidden, until the right time. I look down at my own disobedient nipples. Oh, well, one can only hope.

I walk down the hall to my office on the right, next to the law library. Tom, my boss, has the corner office, of course, the office farthest away from the reception area. The office of power. Me, well, I have the office of, the office of... of... chaos. I look at my desk. Stacks of paper everywhere. At least three different case files opened and in process: working on a pleading for a guardianship case, drafting a Will, a Supplemental Needs Trust, and reviewing the notes from my last scheduling conference. Oh boy. If Professor Gerster saw this mess, I'd find myself writing a brief on a lawyer's legal liability to third party beneficiaries for allowing an incapacitated person to sign her neighbor's Will, leaving everything to the Cat Society.

My mail is already opened and stacked high, purportedly in order of priority. I flip through the pile, hoping for "THE LETTER." You know, "THE LETTER" which changes your life forever. Nothing resembling "THE LETTER" appears to be in my pile of goodies. Darn. On my way through the pile I find a Notice of Appointment of Attorney - me - for my new client, a fellow named Franklin DuBois. A guardianship hearing scheduled for about five weeks in the future, concerning the probable incapacity of Mr. DuBois. And, of course, the phone message from Amy Tucker, a social worker at the nursing home where Mr. DuBois is currently a resident. She wanted a call-back right away. Um. My inner voice says, "crisis." I try to ignore it. But I glance at my watch anyway, and compulsively pick up the phone to dial Ms. Tucker. Maybe I can squeeze a meeting in with Mr. DuBois before lunch. Oh yeah, I remember, a late meeting scheduled with Ms. Strong too. Suddenly I have a premonition, a feeling that I have learned to call in my private vernacular, a "twiggle." A very powerful twiggle, in fact. A type of hysteria really, I had convinced myself. The physical feeling was a cross between a twinge and a giggle. Voila! A "twiggle." I've had this feeling a few times before. Well, maybe a lot lately if I cared to admit it to myself. There was no doubt about it now, it was going to be a very, very long day.

Finally.... today's the day! I get to see her; to meet her in person at last! My Gracie!

... I wonder if she'll like my new hair ...

I will tell her about everything. About why she's so different; about how we are connected. I will tell her about her mother.

Then, I'll be able to move on. Finally. My work will be done. Well. Almost. There's still that NSA thing ....

I have to remember to give her my journal. That's important, or she won't understand anything.

Chapter 2

The New Clients

He was little; he was weird-looking, and he wasn't where he was supposed to be. Furthermore, he seemed to be bothering everyone. Our conversation took us back and forth in time and space; from his father's garden shed, to the broken computer at his home located on 46th Street in South Minneapolis - the house he had sold five years ago after his wife died. He eventually told me that he was part-Seminole Indian, but that didn't explain why he was weird-looking or why I finally located him, my client, Franklin DuBois, on the 4th floor of the Hennepin County Medical Center later that morning. In our phone conference, Ms. Tucker, the social worker, had informed me that Mr. DuBois had "brain atrophy" - whatever that is. [Note: Just for the record, there are days when I'm convinced that I have "brain atrophy."] She also explained that Mr. DuBois had broken his hip and suffered a heart attack; that he was in constant pain, hallucinating, and unable to communicate. Sounds pretty bad, but even that wasn't the whole story. After my brief conversation with Mr. DuBois himself, it became crystal clear that he was at HCMC mainly because he wanted a smoke. A simple thing. He wanted to smoke a goddamn cigarette. It was the biggest deal in his life. He had no family or friends that he could remember; he had no permanent residence. Smoking was a simple comfort at the end of his life. The essential problem was, however, that Mr. DuBois could not sit up because of his broken hip. So, every time he had demanded a cigarette at the care center[3], the staff had to wheel his hospital bed outdoors so he could light up. "State regulations, you know," the social worker had advised me. When my client's head had finally cleared (probably because of the frigid air in November), he finally agreed to be treated. Hurrah! Now that I understood the basic dynamic involved, it seemed like a simple case. So, why did I need to become involved? In other words, why did Mr. DuBois need an attorney to represent him in a guardianship case if he had already consented to treatment?

It's always a bad sign when a lawyer shows up at a hospital and the hospital staff is already assembled. Especially when they say, in unison: "Thank God you're here!" Yikes.

---

[3] The politically-correct version of "nursing home."

Medical staff told me that my client had a blood clot in his hip, and that his chance of a good outcome was steadily declining. In other words, he would die. I said, "Well, do something about it." The chorus told me that they had been trying. They had scheduled surgery two times, and my client had withdrawn consent both times after the operating forum had been prepared for him. In other words, each time Mr. DuBois had been wheeled into surgery, he had freaked out and refused treatment. The chorus then launched into the costs of preparing the operating forum... blah, blah, blah... resistant to cares... blah, blah, blah... refused to sign papers for hospice... blah, blah, blah... Ethics Board... blah, blah, blah... capacity to consent, etc. Everyone knew my client had the right to refuse treatment. The legal dilemma at this point was clear. Mr. DuBois couldn't make a medical care decision for himself because he was scared and confused. I was his court-appointed advocate. What could I do?

Shit. Now I needed two beers.

The worst part about being in a service profession and trying to do good in the world is that you rarely get any guidance or feedback. An occasional hug, a pat on the back, or the words "good job," or "you tried your best," or even "that was a stupid fuck-up - don't do it again" isn't really sufficient for behavior modification. And, with all the resources seemingly attributed to infinity, it seems to me the universe should provide something more concrete than organized religion to provide the correct framework for meritorious action. We all know how political every human act can become, especially when public or religious institutions are involved (or purportedly independent judiciaries for that matter). All kinds of abuses and influences inflame our world every day. We can easily spin our wheels, in an eternal quandary, if we ask foundational questions, such as: Do I have the right to intervene? Am I making the right decision? Is it important for the truth to come out? Does evil really exist? If I don't have sex for two years will I forget how to do it? Or, the essential and most immediate question (lacking any feedback from the universe at all) is: Will the Judge be pissed if I request an emergency ex parte guardianship hearing this afternoon?

I call Natalie. "Nat," I say. "Drop everything. I need you to pull the last emergency guardianship petition we did and conform it for my new case, you know, Franklin DuBois. Get it drafted as best you can. I'll fill in the details later when I get back to the office. Can you get it done, say, in an hour? Pretty please?"

"Gracie, geez, Tom's got me on this brief he wants out by Friday." Natalie replied breathlessly.

"Yeah, I know. I'll deal with Tom. Just do it. It's important."

"Does this mean dinner at Whistle Binkies on the Lake?" Natalie asked.

"Natalie, don't you remember what happened the last time I took you to Whistle Binkies? Do you really want to repeat that experience?"

"Sure do. He had rock-hard shoulders and…"

"OK. OK. Don't remind me! Call Judge Henderson and ask if he can hear an emergency petition at 4:00 p.m."

"You betcha. Ya heh." Natalie disconnected.

I had to be out of my mind. Pre-empt Tom's brief? Whistle Binkies? Judge Henderson at 4:00? Oh my.

My next call was to the best professional fiduciary in town, Jim Watkins. Since Mr. DuBois had no family who could help, maybe Jim could figure out what Franklin DuBois really wanted to do. That is, if Jim was willing to take on another case - to act as Mr. DuBois' legal guardian - then he could authorize the surgery or not. Jim had worked with old codgers before; he certainly would be able to understand and decide for Mr. DuBois. Better yet, Jim was not weird-looking in any sense, but he was definitely short. So, maybe Jim could even possibly look like a Seminole Indian to a person with "brain atrophy." This might help Mr. DuBois' comfort level. Always a plus.

After twenty minutes on the phone on the way back to the office, Jim agreed to be appointed as emergency guardian if the Court granted my petition. Jim was close to retirement and very busy, so he really did not want to take the case at all at first. I knew this. However, we both knew that an emergency guardian has limited powers and is only required to act for a short period of time. So it was a short-term job, but a critical one. After outlining Mr. DuBois' predicament, Jim took up the charge because he is one of the good guys. Thank God for good guys with big hearts. Jim would be on standby that afternoon while I met with the Judge. If everything went the way I hoped, I would owe Jim big-time for this one.

By 4:00 p.m., I was ready to do battle. The battle was accomplished in Judge Henderson's chambers.

"Good afternoon, your Honor." I started.

"Hello, Ms Swan. What's this all about?" Judge Henderson stated, nodding for me to sit down at the table in his office.

"Well, your Honor. I was just assigned this case…" and I outlined Mr. DuBois' situation in some detail.

"Why can't it wait until the hearing next month?" the Judge reasonably asked.

"According to the treating physician, Mr. DuBois will be dead before the hearing comes up." I said.

Raising his eyebrows, the Judge reads through my Affidavit. "It's very unusual for court-appointed counsel to bring this kind of petition. Why didn't the Petitioner's attorney bring this emergency action?" Judge Henderson inquired.

"I asked him to do it. He said he was tied up on another case this afternoon, your Honor. But, he's not objecting. I asked the County Attorney's Office to bring the emergency petition too. They said they couldn't do it until next week. It can't wait until next week. So, I guess I get to do everybody's job today." I replied.

Shuffling papers and making grimacing faces all the while, Judge Henderson finally looked up. "All right, Ms. Swan. The only reason I am granting this Emergency Petition is because you are bringing it on behalf of Mr. DuBois himself."

I breathed a sigh of relief. "I get it, your Honor. Thank you very much."

"Just one more thing, Ms. Swan - Gracie."

I held my breath. What now, I wonder?

"How is it that you always wind up with these odd cases?" Judge Henderson asked.

"I really don't understand why, your Honor. It's like I've got a neon sign plastered on my forehead proclaiming 'exceptionally odd cases and/or obscure points of law preferred' isn't it?" I asked the Judge. He just smirked. I honestly couldn't tell if Judge Henderson was amused, pissed, or just astonished. No feedback.

I really need feedback from some source. Currently, in my quest for feedback, I am examining the idea of angels[4]. Specifically, whether or not angels truly exist. Having been raised and schooled in the Catholic tradition (and having

---

[4] Defined as messengers of God··· or messengers of the universe, depending on your point of view.

fallen astray), doctrinally this type of question would normally consign me straight to hell without any further argument at all. Doctrine only works, however, if a person believes in hell to begin with. Another problem in my analysis. I gave up the idea of hell and eternal damnation a long time ago. Too many shades of gray. Today's question then, for purposes of the argument with myself, is "Maybe angelic events are supposed to provide feedback for the human race?" Yeah, feedback. And, I really need feedback, right? Answering, my lawyer-self says: "Unfortunately, Gracie, you must believe in angels to recognize angelic contacts as valid." My hopeful-self answers my lawyer-self: "But, even if actual angels don't exist, could an insightful book, the way a person says 'thank you,' a child's shy smile, or a wink from a colleague…. couldn't those things possibly be the feedback I am looking for? In other words, is it possible for 'good' events or unexpected outcomes in a person's life to be characterized as angelic events? And what about all that other weird stuff?" All of a sudden, I become aware that I am talking to myself, out loud. I also then notice that the argument is becoming more and more convoluted, with the possibility of mania, depression, or just an old-fashioned headache lurking in the near future. Not to mention "brain atrophy." And so I stop. For now.

Looking back, however, it seems to me that certain individuals, from time to time, whether they are aware of it or not, may become mouthpieces for the universe. And, as such, provide needed feedback.

I wish to note that the old lady who hobbled into my office at 5:30 p.m. that afternoon (thirty minutes early, of course) definitely did not look like an angel. But her face was wrinkled in a somewhat wizened manner, which at first glance seemed to reflect some kind of ageless wisdom. Or maybe my eyes are getting funny, I thought. On second glance, it was obvious she had not used Oil of Olay in a long, long time. She did look a bit familiar, but I couldn't place her. She had orange hair. The lines on her face increased upward like contour lines on a territorial map. Some of the lines might have started out as laugh lines in the distant past, but her body movements did not reflect any joyfulness, humor, or delight with life. Her body posture expressed what I would term "resolve." She had something to say to me, and I had a premonition that I wasn't going to like what she had to say. I also knew there was no way to stop her from saying it.

I introduce myself, and offer her a seat across from my desk. She selects the chair closest to the window, a purple chair, where the last glimmers of late afternoon sun stream in on her face. The shimmery radiance settles on her like a blanket. I rub my eyes to try and focus better. She is shivering. She places a large Cub grocery bag on the floor beside the chair. Her direct gaze does not pause on my credentials, framed in burgundy wood, hanging behind my desk on the office walls. My wall of fame, or infamy as the case may be. Instead, the old woman openly studies me - my demeanor, my hair, my clothing, my expression - seeming to gauge my worthiness by inspection alone. Have I just grown another nose or something, I wonder? Maybe I am just imagining this scrutiny? I push aside my streaked curly hair (sometimes red, sometimes brown, sometimes gold - right now a combination of all three), and gaze back at her with my ice-blue colored eyes, though my eyes are only curious, not cold. It seems to me that in those few moments we arrive at some kind of silent understanding and acceptance. As I look at her, she looks at me: I, a woman who is not young, who had never even really felt young, but who seems to muster strength, when necessary, from some source within. I understand that my client, too, musters strength from within, when necessary. I am uncertain if either one of us knows where our hidden strengths come from, but we can sense it in each other. Whatever unspoken communication passes between us, it is fleeting, over in a moment. I also recognize humor and… something else. I exhale sharply and take a deep cleansing breath. I feel like I have passed an important test. As I finally exhale, the old lady begins to speak.

"Gracie… you do not know who I am. But I am as old as this world, and part of time itself; a part of you. You sense certain things because we are connected, you and I. We live simultaneously in the past, present, and future."

Uh-oh. Here it comes, the looney bird part. But I'm ready for it now.

"Because my work takes me through dimensional space, I can see things that other people do not see, and I know things that other people do not know. So, some people in your world will call me 'crazy'."

Yeah, me too.

She continues, "All the answers are contained in my work; the journal of my work. With the help of your young man, you will attain knowledge of the true workings of the universe. Use this knowledge only for the good of all - to shield, protect, and guide!"

Startled, I raise my hand in a stop motion and reply, "OK, let's slow down just a bit. Can I ask you a few questions?" She nods. Truly looney tunes. Gone completely, I think. Another one. Oh well.

I continue, "Tell me what your name is, and who referred you to my office." As if we were old friends, the old woman replies without hesitation, "Well, he named me 'Anna' in your present - Anna Strong. That's why I'm here today. I took a chance in meeting you. Harvey told me it would be dangerous right now, but there was no choice about it. I wish I had more time to fill you in on the details, but he'll have to do it."

Wow. Harvey told her... what? Maybe I made a mistake about wanting some feedback from the universe! I try to remain calm and respectful. She continues, "I'm so glad to see you and finally meet you here - today! Wow! You're quite pretty, if a little bit strange. It looks to me like you need more sleep, a little worn out at the edges, aren't you, dear? I didn't expect that." Then she smiles as if she is satisfied. She has two upper teeth missing.

This is pretty significant, I am thinking. I've just received a vote of approval from my latest, and perhaps my most odd client to date. And she has a very interesting occupation - an alternate realty, inter-dimensional what? Journalist! Can this day get any stranger?[5] And, further, who is the "young man" she is referring to? The one who will tell me all? I wonder whether Anna has been time traveling in a medieval circus.

My body had a definite physical reaction to all of this unexpected strangeness though; my skin felt tight, and again I felt goose bumps rising. The back of my neck began to tingle. I wonder if my hair is rising like a cat's?

Despite my sick expression, Anna goes on. "You already know that the path is not always clear until the moment reveals itself." She pauses, blinks, and with a surprised expression on her face, continues, "Well, my dear, it appears the time has come. Our paths are now convergent. What a miracle, as the wheel turns again and again!

---

[5] DEAR READER. Never, ever, ask that kind of question, even of yourself, at any time. The prior statement is simply begging for an application of Murphy's Law, with immediate consequences.

Blessings upon you and your life in this dimensional space. Listen to me now! Read my journal carefully and don't try to change the rules like before - like you always do!"

Before what? What journal? I ask myself. Yikes, this lady is creeping me out. "Hold up, wait, what do you mean about..." I start to reply. But before I can finish my sentence, with a surprisingly quick motion, the old woman stands up, reaches over my desk, and grasps my hand in a vice-like grip. Immediately, I feel a surge of heat like liquid fire shoot from her hand into my body piercing my very core. At once, I become very disoriented and dizzy, and my ears start ringing. My body is pulsing and tingling all over. What's going on? Did she zap me with a hand buzzer? Am I dying? Am I drugged? Maybe I shouldn't have had that extra glass of wine at lunch. Even as the world goes black, I see Anna collapse, falling onto the floor next to my purple chair.

I don't know how long I was out. It could have been seconds, minutes, or even hours. Time had no meaning. The interlude was simple dreamless non-existence.

When I was finally able to rouse myself, I stood and thought, what an outrageous dream! My brain was foggy and my ears were still ringing. Suddenly I recall the old woman. I try to move quickly around my desk, my knees still wobbly, and there she is, sprawled on the floor! I grasp the edge of the desk to steady myself and yell for Natalie. Natalie comes rushing into the office. She says, "Jeez,

Louise. Where's the fire? I'm on my way..." as she follows my gaze to the floor. "What happened? Did your client pass out?" Still swaying, I reply, "I don't know what happened. Is she breathing?" With a smirk on her face, Natalie says, "Gracie, you're kidding, right? There's really only one rule in this office! You're not supposed to kill the clients! Tom's gonna be really pissed, and I don't think Harvey will be sending you any more business either." But when she sees the look on my face, she at once understands that the matter is very serious indeed. I stammer, "Call 911," and Natalie leaves the room running to call for help. Adrenaline rushing, I crouch at the old woman's side, cautiously taking her hand into my own. I can't find a pulse.

I've lost clients before. Thankfully, they do not usually die in my presence. There have been a few times, however, when it's been a close call. Once, arriving during a blizzard at a potential client's home, a young woman answered the door, showing me into a small vestibule where I started taking off my boots. I assumed this was my potential client's daughter. I started to introduce myself. But the young woman interrupted, "I know who you are. We called you. My mother is dying." I said, "I know, that's why I'm here." "No. You don't understand," the daughter stated, her voice rising in volume, "my mother is dying right now." Then, she took off running, leaving me in the vestibule. One boot on; one boot off. Diddle, diddle dumpling... I was speechless. Within minutes, all of the [then dead]

35

woman's children came rushing out of the bedroom, each person trying to squeeze into the tiny vestibule already crammed full of people, wet boots, and cat hair. All I wanted to do was leave, even it if it meant abandoning one boot, and jumping into a snowbank to get away. The bereaved children began arguing about who got the house and informing me as to what each one of them expected to get as an inheritance from their dead mother. Struggling back into my one boot and backing quickly out the door, I politely expressed my sympathy and asked them to schedule an office conference after the funeral. That was one bad day.

Another client wanted to update his estate plan. I appreciated his wry, kindly sense of humor. He was a widower, and somewhat of a financial wizard. He checked me out thoroughly to be sure that I met his standards of competency (I was female after all). Then, shortly after we completed his estate planning work, he made an appointment for his girlfriend to meet with me to complete her estate planning work as well. The old guy was very adamant that his girlfriend should be buried in the grave next to the one allocated for him, and he was to be buried next to his beloved dead wife. Somewhat of a twist on the ménage à trois theme, I thought at the time. Harmless wish. No problem. I made sure that his girlfriend got rights to the allocated grave as he requested, among other things. After the girlfriend's estate planning work was completed, my client paid my bill, her bill, all his other bills, including his 2nd quarter estimated taxes (in advance), walked out into his backyard and blew his brains out with a hand gun. I later learned that he'd had a recurrence of bone cancer, and he didn't want to go through the pain again. I did not suspect what he had planned to do. I never had a clue. Another bad day.

This was the worst day yet.

Chapter 3

Practicing Law

There are many odd things about a lawyer's life. One constant requirement is the "temporary suspension of disbelief." Stated another way, a lawyer should try not to make moral judgments about a client's behavior. We are, after all, advocates. We practice law in today's modern world. Unreality and disconnection are just one part of the job. You could call them occupational hazards. Strictly speaking, though, "unreality" is not quite the precise word to describe a lawyer's life, and preciseness is everything when you're in the law. It may be that the mere act of being precise helps all lawyers convince themselves that shades of gray are OK. In other words, all the nuances make sense in the overall analysis. The disconnect part allows us to survive and thrive. Let me explain.

From the first day at law school, you are told that you are the best of the best, the cream of the cream of the crop. (Disconnect #1, we are not like everybody else.) On my first day of law school, for example, the Dean explained in a huge assembly hall packed with 200 ideologues that we were all selected (by his own hand, no doubt) because of our elite status. We were all meant for greater and perhaps, glorious things. He knew this for certain because of our GPAs, our LSAT scores, and our personal essays. Perhaps the Dean even had a message from God, the Goddess, the force, or the universe, who knows? In any case, we all excelled; our intellect far exceeded the norm. We would be stimulated, challenged and fulfill dreams and expectations beyond a mere mortal's ken. What the Dean didn't say is that we would be badgered, brain-washed and disillusioned before even the first semester was completed. It is important to note, however, that this disconnection was critical to convince us to put up with the unreality of the law school experience in the first place. There were many other omissions and imprecise statements in the Dean's dissertation. His impreciseness may have hidden many truths, but it helped us get through it all. For example, if the Dean had been speaking precisely (and truthfully), he would have explained that all of the female law students would begin to lose their hair before the end of the first semester.

It goes something like this. Even stellar human beings have to pee. So, one day, while sneaking into the bathroom sanctuary to pee out your last three cups of coffee, you will comb your hair, out of habit, and notice that there are several extra strands of hair on the comb. You will then wonder, a little, if you are using the wrong shampoo. The next time, streaking to the ladies room, you will again notice that there are a few more hairs on your comb. This will give rise to a modicum of disquiet. One extra worry to push aside. However, at semester's end, just before your one and only exam for torts or civil procedure (the maker or breaker of all academic lawyers) when you are in the stall, you will hear a female law student say, "My God, I'm losing my hair." Then, worse yet, you will hear another law student chime in, "I am too!" Then, rushing out of the stall, you will come face to face with two stunningly beautiful, younger, and very worried women, each holding a comb; each comb full of hairs. As an experienced and sophisticated woman of the world, however, you say, "Oh yeah, I guess women really do lose their hair when under stress." You commiserate with them a bit; everyone is astonished that such a truism could possibly be true, and then everyone rushes to their exam, wondering if a score of 15 or 16 will be worth it, when their boyfriends find out that they had to have a hair transplant to recover from law school.

My disconnect button was engaged, big time, as I watched the coroner remove Anna's body from my office. I couldn't connect the event of our meeting and Anna's death with reality. What had actually transpired? I didn't kill her, did I? Did she kill herself? What had happened to me, and why did I black out? I'm tried and true. In other words, I don't usually bite the dust when I meet old, odd clients. When the EMTs arrived, I did not know how to explain what had happened to the old woman. I could barely utter any comprehensible words at all. What had transpired? Objectively, I knew that at one moment in time, I was interviewing a potential new client, and at the very next moment, she was dead on the floor in my office. Yikes. This was too weird. And, would there be death cooties all over my favorite purple chair? I would have to google that for sure.

Natalie came into my office. She noticed that my face was ashen and my hands were shaking. "Hey, Gracie," she said, "you going to be OK? If you want, you can come home with me for the night. Davy will behave if you're around. We'll just hang. How about it?"

"No, Natalie," I said. "I'm good. I'll be OK. I just need to blank out for awhile. Anyway, you and Davy have plans. Go home. I'll see you in the morning."

"You sure?"

"Yeah. Oh, did you get ahold of Tom?"

"No, I wasn't able to reach him. He's at some kind of puffed-up political thing tonight. It can wait. Wha?" She said as I made a face at her. "It's no big deal-e-o. People die around here all the time." She grinned impishly and winked. "Besides, the look on his face when I tell him will be priceless, and I don't want to miss it!"

41

"How can you joke about this? It's a disaster!"

"Chill. I'll fill him in tomorrow. It'll be fine."

"OK. If you're sure." I said, chewing on my lip nervously but a little relieved at her lame attempt at humor. At least Natalie was OK. "Go on home, Natalie. Good night. I'll close up."

"OK, see you then. Call me if you need anything."

"All right. Thanks."

Natalie left then. I looked around my office one last time and noticed the grocery bag in the corner of the room. Wait. Oh no! That's Ms. Strong's bag. Oh, God! The EMTs left her bag here. What the hell am I supposed to do with it? Isn't there some kind of chain-of-command for this type of thing, I wondered. For personal effects? I remembered that the old woman had set her grocery bag next to my purple chair when she arrived. The EMT people must have moved it when they started to work on her. Oh this is great! Just great! I walked over to the bag and picked it up. It was heavy. I looked inside. What? Holy Toledo! The bag was stuffed full of stock certificates, notes, and old papers. What have I gotten myself into, I wondered? The safe was locked, Natalie had the key. I couldn't just leave this stuff here overnight. I grabbed the grocery bag and my purse. I shut all the office lights off, locked the main door, and left the building.

As I put the keys in the Jeep's ignition, my mind raced back over the day. Some days never seem to end. And this day surely should have ended seven hours ago. As I drove down the street, I could not shake a sense of what? Foreboding? Well, not exactly. More like a feeling that I was on the threshold of something. Something important. That same feeling I'd had back at the cabin last summer. Some kind of change. But what? A black swan? Again, a twiggle. Yeah. Something's coming. Something totally unexpected, totally unpredictable, and it will change everything. I shook my head then, to erase the disturbing thoughts floating there. I did not then comprehend my role in the strange events that had transpired that day, or that would unfold in the next few days. I simply dragged my tired feet home and put myself into bed. A White Russian would have been nice just then - either the liquid kind or the male kind - but, oh well. I could only hope for some clarity tomorrow, since nothing made sense tonight. I thought of the seriously dirty window in the door of the closet at the cabin as I drifted off to sleep, reaching for the door knob.

Chapter 4

The Next Morning

The day begins with a lavender sky. "How can a sky be lavender?" I am thinking. Well, maybe the air looks lavender because the air *IS* lavender. Maybe my eyes create the color of the sky to simply coordinate the reality of my senses with my somewhat awkward fashion sense. Why not? Something is nagging at me... but I am unconcerned. And, furthermore, I just know in my bones that something really big, big, big, and good, good, good is going to happen today! I am full of hope and joy. And to kick-start it all, I have a lavender sky! Wow. Now all I need is a doughnut. Well, maybe two doughnuts. And, of course, coffee. Yep. Coffee and gluten - it was good to be alive!

I step into my living room, strewn with magazines and stacked mail, all unopened. I turn slowly around, appreciating all the green plants shimmering in the lavender light streaming in through the uncurtained windows. I reverently step into the smallish kitchen (from

IKEA of course), grind the beans, and add filtered water to the silver streamlined urn of life. It makes that happy sound of water swishing in an old pot, and the room fills with an aroma worth waking up for. I pour my first cup, adding as much cream to the coffee as I can without disturbing the exquisite hotness of it. Then I reverently stir the cup with one of my favorite old spoons. My spoon. One of five antique spoons, with floral embellishments, discovered and purchased up North, to the amazement of the store's proprietor. ("Who wants only five spoons? Maybe I should have charged her more!") So, OK, you say. I have a collection of five precious antique spoons. Big deal! But where is number six? I'm sure it's behind a bookcase somewhere, dusty and abandoned. But someday, maybe today, I'll find the Sixth Spoon, and I will reunite it with its five siblings. On that day, I know my life's work will be completed.

The caffeine begins to kick in. Again, some little voice in the back of my mind. SOMETHING BIG. TODAY. Wa?? Oh my God! That's right. The old lady at the office. Finally, after two cups of coffee and two doughnuts, I could remember it all! I leapt from the chair and promptly tripped over the brown paper bag belonging to the poor, weird old woman who had died. After she ZAPPED me! How did she do that?? I wonder what she wanted to tell me, before she DIED! Not "passed away;" she really died. In MY office. In front of ME! I could feel my heart pounding as I reached for the old lady's bag and began to search for something, anything, to explain the actual feeling of doom that had descended upon that bright, sunny, lavender Friday morning.

After thirty minutes, I had a pretty good idea about Ms. Strong's net worth. Hundreds of stock certificates, the actual negotiable paper, correctly registered to my (almost) client. Thousands of shares of stock. At least fifty different offerings, all recognizable and still in existence; blue chip: IBM, AT&T, Honeywell, Minnesota Mining and Manufacturing (a/k/a 3M), plus shares of all those bailed-out bank stocks, you know, US Bank, Wells Fargo, and so on. There was a fortune here, with a capital "F." There were other words that came to mind, starting with a capital "F," but I had sworn (bad choice of words) not to indulge my frustrations or aggravate the people around me by continuing to talk like a longshoreman. It should be noted, however, that in my state of mind at that particular moment, I was seriously in danger of losing my resolve with respect to the "F" word.

I continue my inventory of the Cub bag: Keys. Lots of keys. Colorful keys: one red, one blue, one orange Tweety Bird key. What was that all about? An address book. Candy. Bank statements. Candy (wrapped in that yellow stuff). More bank statements. More candy (orange - probably cause rashes). Social Security Card. No driver's license. Um. I wonder if the EMTs had taken Ms. Strong's purse when they took her body last night? An Xcel bill for a house on North Fourth Street in Stillwater - probably her house; a Menards credit card. Why did she come to see me? Wait, Natalie said that Harvey had made the appointment. Maybe Harvey knows something! Dressing quickly in my normal uniform consisting of black everything, I pop a yellow-wrapped candy into my mouth. Ick! I am not brave enough to try one of the orange ones, even though orange is one of my favorite colors. I grab my car keys and Anna's Cub bag, and bolt for the door.

I usually park my Jeep in the garage, but last night, I remember, I was too tired and I couldn't find the controller to operate the garage door. In all the confusion, I must have left the controller at the office in my other coat. So, I ended up parking in the driveway like I've done a million times before.

I live in a suburb of Saint Paul called Oakdale. It's a community of just under 20,000 people, mostly blue collar, about ten minutes from downtown. Most of my neighbors don't know that I'm a lawyer, and I'm not sure they would like it if they knew my occupation anyway. A few years ago, I discovered that there was a rumor going around that I worked for "the government." This statement is technically true since the Court does appoint me, from time to time, to work on some difficult cases. So, if necessary, I correct my neighbors' beliefs without an actual statement of fact. Unfortunately, because of these "small corrections," it turns out that most of my neighbors think I am a spy or that I work for the Army Corps of Engineers. Since I have no legal duty to clarify or correct their impressions, and because I don't ever want to be invited to the neighborhood block party, I have made a decision to continue to be the "mystery neighbor." Let's be perfectly clear however, if any neighbor asked me straight out if I was a lawyer, I wouldn't lie about it. Being an officer of the Court, I am compelled to tell the truth, as you know. However, even if I told them the truth about my occupation, they probably wouldn't believe me anyway since I have curly hair.

I run to the Jeep, with the lavender sky just turning to gold on the edges, fading fast. With horror, I note that my right front tire is flat. I never get a flat tire. How can this be? I close my eyes and visualize the tire round and firm. I add a little prayer with a quiver in my voice. They say there is power in prayer, you know. I open my eyes, hoping that my reality has changed. Guess what! The goddamn tire is still flat. I need to work on this "making your own reality" stuff. Obviously, I don't have the hang of it yet. I am now resolved to more complications than I am prepared to handle this morning. The doughnuts and the coffee, joyfully eaten just minutes before, begin to feel like mashed potatoes and okra in my stomach. I don't have time for this. The lavender sky is now a kind of routine gray, with just a smidgen of gold around the edges.

Just as I turn to go back into my apartment to find the telephone number for a cab, a midnight blue "Yellow Cab" pulls up to the curb. Wow, that was fast. How did I do that? I open up the passenger door and slide in. "I need to get to the Wells Fargo Bank Building fast. Do you know...?" As I glance up, I lose the power of speech and gulp air. I also experience the distinct feeling that this is... no coincidence. That this is... something. Maybe the "something more" that I was halfway expecting? No. It couldn't be. That would be too easy. All of a sudden, everything was all jumbled around. My hormones; this feeling of knowing. I actually felt faint. I had never had this kind of physical reaction to a male of our species before - or a male of any species for that matter. Instinctively, I check my vital signs wondering if I'd experienced a mini stroke or had been struck by lightening. Nope. Everything checked out OK.

Just for the record, it's not like I've never seen a cute guy before. But, this guy, he goes beyond cute straight to "stud muffin." By my definition, a cute guy is usually a guy who knows he's attractive and desirable - but he thinks you want to sleep with him no matter where you are and even if you haven't shaved your legs in two weeks. (That's why opaque tights are so popular these days by the way.) In other words, your basic model of "cute guy" is typically and obnoxiously self-aware; he is conscious of what he wears, what he says, who he goes out with, etc. No romance. On the other hand, a "stud muffin," albeit a variation on the cute guy model, usually doesn't even know that he's something special. And, more important, his body language oozes romance. This particular stud muffin had longish streaky blonde hair, blue eyes that matched the color of the leather seats, and half a day's growth of beard at 7:30 in the morning. Um, gotta love that testosterone.

I cleared my throat and began again, "I need to get to the Wells Fargo building asap."

"Sure enough," he said, "but you're probably going to need your cell."

"My cell phone? Of course, it's right here," I say as I reach into my coat pocket. What? No cell phone. How did he know that I didn't have my cell? "Sure. Thanks. Can you wait a minute while I run up to get it? I must have left it on the hall table."

"Take as much time as you need. I'm all yours today," he answers.

"Yeah, I wish," I mutter under my breath as I run back into the house to retrieve my cell. A stud muffin and a cell phone, that's all I really need to make me happy. No, that's not quite right. I instantly revise my wish list, as follows: Two weeks at the cabin with this particular stud muffin, and no cell phone. Can't go wrong with that kind of wish list. Can't go wrong at all.

His name was Quinn. Actually, his name is Quinlan Anatoly Molnår, Ph.D. It said so on his cabbie identification card posted on the dashboard. He was easy to talk to. He told me his parents had managed to escape from Hungary after the failed revolution against the communist occupation in 1956. His father had been an engineer and his mother had been a teacher. No surprise that science and education were very important to him. He told me about the Ph.D. part as we whizzed through spaghetti junction and took the turn onto 6th street, headed for Kellogg Boulevard. It turns out he got his doctorate in physics from Stanford about ten years ago. He was currently working on some kind of biogravitational project. Since his grant funds had dried up, he drove cab by day, taught classes at the U at night, and then morphed into "Lab Man." It appears that he is currently funding his research with his temporary "new" career, that of a stud muffin gypsy cabbie, of course. (He didn't tell me that part - I figured it out all by myself.) I flash on the image of Clark Kent transforming into Superman by stripping his clothes off in a telephone booth. My body temperature begins to rise. OK then.

We arrive at the Wells Fargo Building at exactly 7:59 a.m., of course. If a physicist can't be on time, who can? As I pay Quinn, he says, "I'll pick you up at 10:57 a.m. right here."

Wait a minute, I start to say. But, no time to dally. I humor him and nod, "Sure," I say, knowing I will probably still be in Court at 10:57 am. Regretfully, I think, in a city of three million people, I'll probably never see him again. Glancing at him one last time, I can hardly manage to tear myself away from the blue/blue combination (blue eyes, blue leather seats). But, I force myself out of the cab, seriously wondering about my ability to transition from love-struck or at least hormonally-affected almost-human female to probate lawyer. I find myself hoping that there will be no Jeep tires available anywhere in the Twin Cities for the next few years, justifying the economics of continual cab rides. Simultaneously, I pray there will never be any grant money available again in my lifetime, anywhere, so that Quinn will have to continue being my cab-driving slave. Shaking my head and pushing an errant curl back into place, I again wonder what he means about picking me up at 10:57 a.m. I try to move on. Maybe he means he hopes he will see me again? A small glimmer of lavender light in my day, even if it is just wishful thinking. Oh well, another cryptic statement to add to my ever-expanding list of cryptic statements to ponder later. Much later.

Chapter 5

The Reading of the Will

Again, I find myself in the skyway. My theory is that skyways were invented primarily to manipulate the psyche of Minnesota residents, causing them to engage in unnatural acts. An experiment in social engineering actually. Some genius figured out that if Minnesotans did not have a method to travel from one building to another without continually waging war against the elements, no one would leave their home or office between Halloween and Mother's Day. As it turns out, no one leaves their home or office between Halloween and Mother's Day anyway. This is either due to our northern European work ethic or our sun-deprived burrowing instincts. In either case we don't have to put our boots on if we stay put. After Mother's Day, however, all bets are off, and no one goes inside until the evening of Labor Day. We eat, sleep, hike, bike, some of us make love, and we fanatically garden until the first snow falls, usually around Halloween, and the cycle begins again.

For the record, each skyway system has its own distinct character, similar to ethnic neighborhoods. Accordingly, the skyways in Saint Paul are totally unlike the skyways in Minneapolis, similar to the differences between the residents of Saint Paul and Minneapolis. In Saint Paul, the people are not hustling, bustling, or Chicago-like. There are typically no jostling crowds, no interesting shops, and no kick-ass footwear. More to the point, Saint Paul's skyways are used as serviceable pathways only. They accommodate travel without weather effects, but also without any art or design gimmicks to distract anyone passing through. My office, of course, is in Saint Paul.

I note that the skyway seems quiet, almost deserted today, as I stride toward the elevator banks. Charlie, the guard, nods good morning to me, as he usually does. But, like the skyway, even Charlie seems subdued. He glances at me, then past me, in a worried sort of way. Does everyone know, already, I wonder? I glance at my watch, it's only 8:03 a.m. "Good morning, Charlie," I say. He responds, "How you doing, Gracie? Lots of action in your office this morning. What'd you guys do, kill somebody?" My stomach sinks even further, the dread growing. I slink to the bank of elevators, take the first one up to the 9th floor, anxiously glance right and left as I move down the hallway, cross my fingers, and turn the door knob to the right for good luck. I step into the waiting room just as Natalie rounds the corner. She hisses, "Tom's in a state. Better get in there right now, and turn on the charm. The cops were here already this morning. They were asking for you."

Yikes. "Asking for me?" I swallow.

"Yeah, they said there was something funny between you and the old lady, and you had a lot to gain from her death. They want to question you."

"A lot to gain from Ms. Strong's death? ME? How could that possibly be? I only knew her for five minutes. She didn't even sign a retainer agreement!"

"Well, who knows? They were in with Tom for about twenty minutes, and then all hell broke loose. I tell you, I heard a lot of growling noises coming from both sides of the room. I thought there was a zombie war going on." Nonchalantly Natalie examined her fingernail for any sign of deterioration. I noted she had half-moons painted on each nail, in contrasting red and white. She looked back up at me. "So, anyway, Tom was having a choking fit and started howling his head off as as soon as they left. Then he got Harvey on the phone, then the Lawyer's Board called, and he's been on the goddamn phone ever since, baying like a basset hound."

Before I had a chance to respond in any coherent way, Natalie babbled on, "You know, I got a feeling that old lady was loaded! Big probate... yada, yada, yada." Natalie's words stop making sense (if they ever did) as I moved down the hall to my office.

My cell began ringing. I picked up. "Gracie, this is Harvey. We need to talk, right away. Anna wasn't supposed to die in your office; she told me she just wanted to meet you. The probability curve's screwed. Get on down here, now." The phone line went dead.

Just for the record, Harvey is not Jimmy Stewart's six foot tall pooka[6], he is my ex-neighbor, former law professor, and friend. My parents died when I was quite young, and Harvey lived next door to the woman who raised me. It's seems like I've always known Harvey. Every time I needed help, there he was. A great guy. He taught Wills and Trusts 101. He wrote the book on probate law, literally. He is about seventy years old, he's been a widower as long as I've known him, and he's retired now. He's a rotund guy, usually pretty jolly, with a big, red scotch nose. Sometimes I fantasize that if God were male, he would look exactly like Harvey.

Harvey's law office, when he decides to come in, is on the 6th floor of my building. He mostly does pro bono work these days, just to keep his hand in. He likes to write

---

[6] "A pooka is a deft shape shifter, capable of assuming a variety of terrifying or pleasing forms, and may appear as a horse, rabbit, goat, goblin, or dog, to be respected or feared by those who believe in it. The origin of the name may come from the Scandinavian word for 'nature spirit.' From Wikipedia, the Free Encyclopedia of our time. In the 1940s film, Harvey, Jimmy Stewart's pooka was a giant invisible 6 foot rabbit named, of course, Harvey.

about the charitable gifting and generation-skipping stuff. Yuk. I think he's working on some kind of perpetual trust legislation at the moment, trying to defeat the Rule Against Perpetuities in Minnesota. If anyone can figure it out, Harvey can. Tom is also Harvey's former student, and they have an on-again and off-again collegial relationship. They must have been getting on pretty well when Tom hired me, based on Harvey's recommendation. Today, however, I sense that they're definitely in the "off" mode.

Harvey likes to joke around, but I had the distinct impression that he wasn't joking around with me when he hung up the telephone. He was dead serious. Ouch. Poor choice of words. I had a direct order to show up at his office, pronto. What did he mean about Anna wanting to meet me, and that bit about screwing something up, or was it some... one? Grasping for understanding, did Harvey mean that Anna's death screwed something up? Probability curve? What? Inter-gravitational fields, or was that something that the cabbie, Quinn, had said? Or did I screw something or some... one up, again? All in one morning? I felt goose bumps begin to rise on my arms. Great, all I needed right now was a panic attack. Something is seriously wrong, I thought. What am I saying? Of course, something is seriously wrong. Grasping for known facts, I begin my litany: For beginners, Anna Strong is dead; she died in my office; she wanted to meet me, and I don't know why. Before she died, she zapped me, and I am clueless as to why I passed out. I met the cutest guy, but he's a cab driver/physicist. (And what kind of occupation is that anyway?) I have just experienced the weirdest eighteen hours of my life; and I am scheduled to appear in Court on the 10 o'clock calendar. Oh hell.

I take a deep breath. "I'm going down to talk to Harvey for a few minutes." I streak out of my office headed for the door. "You can't go now!" Natalie screeches. Before I have a chance to escape, Tom's voice bellows through the office wall: "Is that you Gracie? Get in here, now!"

I am cornered. No way out. I make a face at Natalie and move toward Tom's office. "What's up, boss?" I ask. Tom motions to the chair in front of his desk. "Sit down, Gracie. You're in deep kimshee."

Now, perhaps a moment is needed to define "deep kimshee." This is an expression generally used in my office in place of "deep shit." You get the idea.

Most of the time I don't mind sitting in Tom's office. It feels like a real lawyer's office, with all the accoutrements of wealth and power. He even has a statue of "blind justice" in the corner. A female form, with one breast bared, blindfolded, holding the scales of justice. A symbol for all lawyers everywhere. All the chairs are from Gabberts, covered in wine-colored leather; his desk is massive and (somehow) uncluttered. Law books are tidily shelved on bookcases purchased at auction from Sotheby's. Retainer agreements are stacked and on stand-by, ready to be signed upon a moment's notice. Tom's office even smells like a sanctuary of law; no lingering cigar smoke in this decade, but the slight aroma of men's cologne, expensive whiskey and rare brandy. Even without the outward trappings, people would assume that Tom is a lawyer, they would never think he worked for the Army Corps of Engineers: perfect shave, perfect haircut, pinstripes, expensive watch, attitude. His hair is chestnut brown, and he has a million dollar smile, literally. He likes expensive wine, expensive women, status and prestige. He shares joint legal and physical custody of his two beautiful daughters with his heiress ex-wife.

I like Tom, and, even if I won't sleep with him, he usually likes me. Tom is not well-liked or understood by many. Even so, he's a legal scholar, a well-respected litigator, and my boss. What the general public does not know is that on weekends Tom comes to the office dressed in a black polo shirt with a pirate logo on the right shoulder. It is his trademark shirt because it exemplifies the main focus of his personality. He is a shark.

"Well, Gracie, you've been a busy girl haven't you?" Tom starts speaking before I even settle into my favorite chair in front of his desk, next to the window. I glance out; the snow had begun to fall.

"Oh, you mean about Anna Strong?" I cautiously reply, hoping to keep the conversation on a professional level. "You know, we never even had a chance to get acquainted before she, well, before she…"

"You could begin there." He said, heating up. "But what I really want to know is why the hell you drafted her Will naming yourself as her principal beneficiary? Christ, Gracie, you know better than that! You can't name yourself as any kind of beneficiary under the Will unless you are related to her. It's a direct violation of the ethical rules. You told me that you didn't have any living relatives."

He glared at me and continued, "So what's the story, Gracie? The cops want to talk to you and the Lawyer's Board is already on my ass about this. It looks really bad for the firm. Our reputation will be irreparably damaged unless you can explain the terms of the Will. So…"

"What do you mean I drafted Anna's Will? I never drafted Anna's Will! How could I? I just met her last night, a few minutes before she died," I choked, suddenly confused and beginning to hyperventilate.

"Stop playing games! Your name is on her Will, as the drafter." He shoved a packet of bound papers across the desk. It was obvious that what he was showing me was a photocopy of a Will. The first page of the document said "Last Will and Testament of Anna Strong" in large, bold, old English-style type. I quickly flipped to the end of the Will and noted the date, November 11, 2014. Two days ago. Signed in front of two witnesses: Quinlan A. Molnår, and Harvey L. Waterston. Harvey? My Harvey. Quinn? The cab driver? My ears began to ring - again.

Thankfully, in times of stress, my lawyer training kicks in. So, arching my eyebrows (in an exercise of will, so to speak), I calmly turn back to the first page. With deliberation, I force myself to read each word. I need to understand the implications of this Will, and what Anna intended to do. The air in the room seemed to thicken, magnifying the importance of what was to come.

As if I were construing Anna's Will for the Court, I summarize the Will out loud: "The first paragraph identifies Anna as a resident of St. Louis County, Minnesota, and revokes all former Wills." Wait, Stillwater is in Washington County, not St. Louis County. St. Louis County - that's Duluth! How did I get the idea that Anna lived in Stillwater, I wonder? Continuing out loud, "Article One directs the Executor to pay all Anna's debts and taxes, and expenses of settling her estate. Article Two directs the Executor to look for a list of personal property items and to give those items to the persons designated on Anna's list. All items not on Anna's list are to go to…. Grace L. Swan." ME! Wait a minute! Wow, what's going on here? I put aside my emotional response and continue to read in a measured voice. "Article Two continues with other special gifts: certain stocks to a woman's shelter; certain bonds to the Cat Society in Woodbury; a cash gift to a church; Anna's house to… Grace L. Swan." ME! Again. My lower lip begins to tremble, just a little. What is going on here? Why is she leaving all this stuff to me? I force myself to continue, but my voice quivers: "Article Three leaves the rest, residue and remainder of Anna's estate to Grace L. Swan." Of course. "Article Four appoints... Grace L. Swan as Executor. All of the rest of the Will is boilerplate, listing powers of the Executor, as usual." I was definitely having trouble breathing now, but I forced myself to continue. "Tom, there has to be some mistake. I didn't even know Anna. Why would she leave everything to me?"

Tom said nothing.

I noted once again that Anna signed the Will in front of two witness who also signed the Will: my fantasy cab driver and my law professor. Under Minnesota law, it only takes two witnesses to make the document legal.

I look up and find Tom staring at me with a sharp, unreadable expression on his face. "Continue reading, Gracie" he commands. Mesmerized with incredulity, I stutter, "Anna, Quinn and Harvey signed the Will in front of Analiese Johnson, a Notary Public for Ramsey County, Minnesota." But the final, and damning, notation at the very bottom of the Will clearly sets out the scrivener: "This Instrument was drafted by: Grace W. Swan, Attorney at Law." Oh God, I thought, this can't be happening. I don't remember drafting this Will. "Wait. No. I'm Grace 'L.' Swan. Not Grace 'W.' Swan. My middle name is Lorraine! I always use my middle initial in the drafter's block on any document I draft. It's the wrong middle initial! So, I couldn't have possibly drafted this Will! Somebody else must have done it!"

"Scrivener's error." Tom yells. "Typo."

"I didn't draft this Will!" I yell at the universe in general, and more particularly at Tom. "Who drafted this Will? It's got to be fraud." By the time I finish reading the Will, despite my attempt at professional detachment, I am blinking my eyes rapidly, wondering if I am experiencing the first stages of an epileptic fit. "I need a drink of water," I say to Tom as I look up at the ceiling and again out the window at the snow now coming down in plate-sized flakes. Tom is watching me carefully.

Sensing that I am on overload, maybe questioning my sanity, perhaps even wondering if I could be telling the truth, he stands. "I think you need something stronger than water," Tom says, as he pulls out the bourbon, at 8:35 a.m. in the morning. "It's going to be a long day." That's the mother of all under-statements, I think, as I gulp down the liquid fire and wonder what all these events are leading up to. Still searching my ashen face, Tom shifts to counselor mode, "Gracie, I didn't think you were hurting financially. Have you been drinking or using illicit... BLAH, BLAH, BLAH?"

"Well, got to go," I state as I rise from the chair, a livid blush adding color to my face. "Places to go; people to see; things to do. You know - situations; circumstances; shoes.

Court at 10:00 o'clock." Tom glances up, astonished, and starts to rise from his chair, but I can't understand a word he is saying. I rush out of his office. Harvey better the hell know what's going on, I am thinking. As I race through the hall, Natalie says, "You got a call holding on Line 2, a reporter from Channel 11 about your Jorgensen case at 10 o'clock. And the Lawyer's Board wants a call back. There's also a cute guy in the waiting room. He wants to know if..."

"Are you nuts?" I reply. "I can't talk to anyone now!" Natalie just continued to smile her contented smile and lets me rave on. "Did Davy screw your brains out last night or what? Is everyone nuts here today or is it just me?" I turn and race out of the office into the hallway. Even as I flee, I understand that I have transitioned into self-preservation mode. As I hit the elevator button to go down to the 6th floor, I have faith that Harvey will explain the whole deal, because if he can't, my legal career is over.

Chapter 6

The Meeting In Harvey's Office

Harvey was wearing white pants today. Huh? A little odd looking for a person of his age. Not hip at all. How 1960s. Harvey saw the fashion police expression on my face, shrugged his shoulders, handed me a cup of coffee in my favorite "Brandeis Travel Service" brown mug, and we started to cross the room to sit on the sofa facing the gas fireplace where fake logs burned brightly. Without any warning, we both watched in horror as the coffee cup handle (which, I thought, I had saved by gluing) disintegrated. I jerked as the scalding coffee immediately burned my hand and began soaking through my skirt to my very tender thighs. (Never having been exposed to direct sunlight for more than twenty minutes each summer, what do you expect?) Reflexively, I flung the broken cup away from me, and its remaining contents landed on Harvey's white pants. Oh my. The look on Harvey's face as the brown stain spread across the front of his pants and simultaneously soaked into my court skirt! We looked at each other and immediately burst into laughter. Hysterical laughter.

As you may know, hysterical laughter is a phenomenon that begins with one person. It then travels, like a virus, throughout a room until every person in the room is laughing uncontrollably. The essential problem, however, is that no one can stop. Laughing, that is. Hysterical laughter is real. It is the kind of laughter that shuts down schools in India for several days at a stretch. Under the circumstances, apparently this was the only kind of laughter that was outrageous enough to apply to our present conundrum, and we both knew it. Harvey and I laughed so hard that tears flowed down our cheeks and my stomach began to hurt. I wondered how much longer I could stand here, laughing like a lunatic? I became concerned about bladder control. I considered laying down flat on the floor before I said, "It was only a coincidence, right, Harvey? The universe really isn't out to get me, is it?" I questioned. Harvey's choked response wasn't very helpful: "Well, Gracie, I'm not so sure just now," causing us to laugh even harder. Finally, Harvey looked on helplessly as I excused myself to the Ladies' Room to try to clean up and gain control of myself. Harvey was reaching for the Kleenex box as I left his office. The time was 8:52 a.m.

I had to pinch myself, but I finally managed to stop laughing! Wow, what an incredible emotional release!

Could there be any better way to begin a search for understanding and enlightenment? I felt like on some inner level each and every atom of my body had participated in that wild, instinctual, primal laughter. Amazingly, I had a flash that, somehow, everything was really going to turn out OK. Starting right now. The panic subsided.

When I returned from the Ladies Room exactly ten minutes later, Harvey was gone. He had simply vanished. The only evidence that he had ever even been in the room with me was the coffee-soaked Kleenex in the trash can, a broken coffee mug lying on the rug in front of the fireplace, and a scrawled message that Harvey had left for me on his desk. Written on the yellow legal pad were only four words and an address: "Carnegie's. Saturday. 10:00 o'clock a.m.. 101 W. 2nd Street, Duluth."

I was speechless. I began to notice the rhythm of my own heart, beating wildly. Anticipating.

I seriously wanted to go to Duluth today! Yup. Right now! In winter! Why not? Tomorrow is Saturday and I have the day off. Besides, I need a little vacation, don't I? Duluth in the middle of winter is such a fairy tale city. Frost-covered trees, lovely big, slippery hills, and, of course, Lake Superior, Minnesota's largest lake - really an inland sea. Wouldn't want to miss those lovely November gales, would I? Of course, a three hour drive in a Jeep with a flat tire might be an issue. Of course, if the tourists have already booked all of the hotel rooms over the weekend that might be an issue. No problem. I could always just find some nice longshoreman to shack up with. Why, I might even be able to squeeze in a long, long walk on the boardwalk with the wind whipping across my face and icicles forming on my coat. Wouldn't want to miss all those lovely frozen waves, would I? Besides, I desperately needed to freeze at least five pounds off my ass by Christmas anyway. Why, I can hardly wait! All in all, my kind of weekend. YOU THINK? Actually, I really was planning to visit Duluth in the spring anyway. But, for sure, I needed to go to Duluth NOW, just to kill Harvey.

OK. Three minutes of deep breathing. 9:12 a.m. Harvey's gone. Anna's dead. Tom's on a rampage. The cops want to talk to me. The Lawyer's Board is looking for me. My office is a war zone and I've got to be in Court in forty-five minutes. My skirt is wet and ruined. Natalie's wearing a black skirt. Black goes with everything. Yeah! Thank God for black.

I leave Harvey's office and race back down the hallway. The elevator doors are beginning to close and I manage to squeeze myself in, just in time. I nod politely to the other passenger in the elevator, a rather startled-looking gentleman, in his late 30s, maybe early 40s. Glancing at him quickly, he seems familiar, somehow. Actually, he seems a little blurry to me. My eyes can't seem to focus right. I shake my head and tell myself to get a grip. He steps quickly back from the door to give me more room. Great, now I'm scaring myself AND the other tenants in the building. My shoes are squishing and I know I look like a crazy woman. The other passenger in the elevator gives me a tentative, gentle smile and says in a strangely muffled voice, "Got a lot on your mind?"

"Well, sir," I reply, thankful that he can't actually read my mind, "There's so much going on up there right now that I just might have to delay my visit to the funny farm for a few days, and that wouldn't be so good for anyone." He looks at me in a sympathetic sort of way, raising his eyebrows. The elevator doors open, and I rush out in a flash.

I wail as I burst back into the reception area of my office. "Natalie, I need your skirt. Fifty bucks if you can whip it off in the next five minutes." Natalie replies, "$75 and you got a deal." At my nod, she begins unzipping her skirt. "Wait, wait," I say. "Isn't there somewhere… you can go to change into… something? You keep some exercise clothes here at the office, don't you?"

"Nope, took 'em home to be washed a couple of days ago. But, Davy was there and he started touching me the minute I walked in the door and I…"

"Stop," I say, and I notice that I'm beginning to sweat, again. "Tom keeps some gym shorts here doesn't he?"

"Yeah."

"Good, good, OK. Do you know where he keeps them?" I look frantically around the office, ready to take off at a run before Natalie strips down to her VS panties and one of our clients walks in. I can already see the jewel in her navel. We certainly don't need a second death in the office within twenty-four hours. Natalie replies, "Sure thing - in the coffee bar."

"The coffee bar?"

"Yeah, in the coffee bar - on the shelf behind those little individual cups."

Oh. At this point, my mind is blank. I've lost my edge. I know there is some good reason why Tom shouldn't keep his sweaty gym pants on a shelf behind the individual cups of coffee in the coffee bar. Maybe it's an OSHA thing. Maybe it's just a little kinky. At this point, I simply can't muster the mental discipline to understand the appropriate rationale to determine why this behavior is not acceptable. I rush to the coffee bar, find Tom's gym shorts, hand them to Natalie, just as she finishes whipping her skirt off. "Thanks, Nat. I owe you one," I state as I grab her skirt and run to my office and slam the door. I immediately rip off the now cold, smelly black skirt. Wow, I never knew this kind of wool smells like a cat when it's wet. Maybe that's why it is labeled "dry clean only." So, nobody will ever know it's really made out of cat fur rather than real wool. Except for the teenage minimum wage dry cleaning attendants, that is. And they don't talk; they only text.

I wiggle into Natalie's size 6 skirt and manage to zip it up. Since I am four inches taller than Natalie, my guess is that the Judge will only ream me out at the bench rather than holding me in contempt for letting my ass hang out in open Court. No time. I have to prepare for my 10:00 o'clock hearing on the Jorgensen Emergency Guardianship Petition. Oh yeah, I think, Natalie said something about a reporter on the Jorgensen case. What's that all about? Um. I buzz Natalie and ask her to come into my office.

I notice that my coffee mug is empty, and that's just fine with me.

Chapter 7

The Infernal Machine

"Counsel, note your appearance for the record." Judge Henderson commands.

I rise and reply, "Grace Swan, your Honor, representing Linda Jorgensen, the Respondent. My client is present in the Courtroom today, seated at my left." I touch my client's arm lightly. The judge nods at me, and then turns to look at opposing counsel.

"Your Honor, I'm John Rigby, attorney for the Petitioner, Rhonda Albertson. My client is Ms. Jorgensen's daughter." He nods to a handsome woman in her middle 50s, wearing lots of sparkly jewelry (probably real), seated next to him. This is the first time I have set eyes on my client's daughter. Ah, so you're Rhonda, I think. She glances at me; well, actually looks right through me. Just as if she knew my skirt was four inches too short and my checking account balance was $10.57. She immediately

72

glances back at Rigby, a well-known attorney from a large, influential law firm. She sniffs. I am obviously an unworthy adversary. Well, Rhonda, here I am girly, and I'm not going away. I re-name you 'Rhonda the Bitc...' No, I'm a professional. I hereby re-name you 'Rhonda the Rich'. As a character study, of course. With this silent interchange, I begin to get an inkling of the dynamic underlying the emergency petition brought by Rhonda the Rich.

"Welcome. Mr. Rigby, Ms. Swan. Counsel, are there any interested persons present in the Courtroom?" The Judge again glances at Rigby and then at me, looking for a response. Since I do not know the answer to the Judge's question, I too look at Rigby inquiringly, and he answers the Judge: "Three of Ms. Jorgensen's other children, Thomas, Bryan and Katherine, are seated at the back of the Courtroom, Your Honor."

The Judge looks into the audience, and everyone present at counsel table turns around to look at the three well-dressed, obviously wealthy people seated together in the back of the Courtroom. All of their faces are impassive, in a measured and aristocratic way, showing no emotion whatsoever. Fancy suits; fancy jewelry. I was willing to bet that none of their shoes squished when they walked and that the hem of the woman's skirt fell well-below her ass, unlike my borrowed skirt, which I again tried, albeit unsuccessfully, to stretch further down my thighs.

Glancing around the audience, the Judge scratches notes on his legal pad, and then looks up: "All right, thank you." Then, nodding to Rigby and me, the Judge announces, "You may be seated." We all sit down.

Show time.

The Judge continues for the record, "Before the Court is a Petition for the appointment of an Emergency Guardian for Linda Jorgensen. I have reviewed the Court's file, including all pleadings, affidavits, and responsive documents, so let's keep it short. Mr. Rigby, you represent the Petitioner, please proceed."

"Thank you, Judge. As I said, the Petitioner is Linda Jorgensen's daughter. She is concerned that her mother is not taking care of herself; she is not eating properly; she is losing weight, and she is depressed. Ms. Jorgensen has fired all of the help that my client has hired for her, and she refuses any and all aid from her family. She won't take the medication her doctor has prescribed. Linda Jorgensen needs a Guardian to make personal and medical decisions for her."

I am ready to burst. The Judge looks at me, "Ms. Swan?"

I reply in a slightly shaky voice, "This is an emergency petition, your Honor, but there is no emergency. Nothing in the documents Mr. Rigby filed support the argument that my client's legal rights should be transferred to a Guardian. It's all hearsay, arguments, and innuendo. There is no factual basis for bringing this extraordinary procedure!" Calming down and catching my breath, I continue, "There is no evidence to support the allegation that my client will suffer imminent harm or that she is in any personal danger whatsoever. Furthermore, my client is a resident of Oregon. She is just here temporarily for the purpose of visiting her daughter. I am handling this case only because her Oregon attorney is currently out of the country. He'll be back in the United States in three days. What's the rush? There is no clear showing of necessity for this Court to shift any of my client's legal rights to her daughter or to anyone else on an emergency basis."

I look at my client, and she is nodding vigorously. Linda, my client, is short and a little skinny, with permed blonde hair. She looks a little older than her seventy-seven years. No surprise, since her eighty year old ex-husband had apparently experienced male menopause and divorced her after six children and fifty-four years of marriage. In our interview, Linda told me that the divorce had been hard on her, of course, and she was clinically depressed at first. But, she also told me that once she stopped planning to murder her husband and his trophy wife and got off the meds, things got better. Also, since she was a devout Catholic girl, she knew God was on her side because she was the wronged one, and He would punish her husband eventually. Pretty good coping technique. She didn't have to seek retribution, since the Big Guy would do it for her.

In any case, her belief system helped her make a new life for herself. A good use of religion. The Court system had helped too, since Linda became the beneficiary of a $10 million trust fund as a part of the divorce settlement. Maybe the Big Guy had already played his cards.

The facts suggested that Linda had been living independently and successfully on her own for the last five years. In other words, I knew she had to have been eating - at least occasionally - or she would be dead already. So what was really going on here?

Linda told me that her children lived all over the United States and that she usually had a pretty good relationship with each of them. However, it was clear that Linda was frustrated because, in her opinion, the kids had too much contact with her evil ex-husband. So it seems, in retaliation, she had developed a pretty good pattern of harmless harassment, taking great pride in her ability to aggravate and frustrate her children since they were so good at aggravating and frustrating her. She would simply make arrangements to rent an apartment close by a child's home and stay just long enough to make them all crazy. Kind of like payback for getting too cozy with her ex.

In most circumstances, this would be a pretty healthy arrangement. Except for the money part, that is. The money adds another angle. I've found that, every now and then, when a legal action concerns guardianship of an extremely wealthy mom, the real issue underlying the case is who gets guardianship of mom's money. I predict that the legal battles for the next few decades will revolve around "substitute decision-making" as the baby boomers fall into old age and want to control their parents' money. Especially with the economic downturn. But their parents are just too darn healthy to die! So, this case is just a forerunner of the many to come, variations on a theme.

I write down one sentence on my note pad. "Follow the money. Who will control Linda's trust fund if she is found to be legally incapacitated?" I underline the question twice. I need to get a copy of the Trust.

I had stopped speaking.

The Judge's voice interrupts my reverie, "Ms. Swan? Did you have anything else?"

"Sorry, your Honor. The bottom line is that my client's life is not in any danger. And, although my client is fashionably slender, she most likely will not die of malnutrition within the next three days. There is no emergency. The Petitioner has not met her burden of proof. She isn't able to show by clear and convincing..." Before I can finish my brief summary of the legal standard the Judge must apply under these circumstances, Rhonda the Rich stands up and explodes, "But, your Honor, she's depressed - her doctor says she's unstable, and she's not eating! She's lost 47 pounds in the last month! There's absolutely nothing in her refrigerator..."

I quickly rise, "Objection, your Honor. No doctor's reports have been admitted into evidence…"

The Judge holds his hand up in a stop gesture, looking directly at me, then at Rhonda the Rich. Then, looking directly at Rigby with a raised eyebrow, he asks, "Do you wish to call your witness?" Shit, I think, Pandora's box. It must be the skirt or the goddamn Infernal Machine.[7] "Yep. The goddamn Infernal Machine," I mutter under my breath. I'm sure Rigby coached her on how to manage a perfect outburst in the Courtroom.

Simply put, Rhonda the Rich was not supposed to get the chance to give any testimony or to tell her story at all. Only the Judge and the attorneys were supposed to talk at this hearing. Because the statements in the Petition were very weak, the Judge would normally have dismissed Rhonda the Rich's Petition without testimony because the potential danger to my client was clearly not serious enough. There was no medical emergency. But, because of Rhonda's emotional outburst, the Judge was pulled into her story. Now he wonders whether or not Linda really needs help. The basic trouble right now (the wild card) is that the

---

[7] To clarify, an infernal machine is a complex machine that is doing something, but it is not doing what you anticipated that it was going to do. Anything can be an infernal machine depending on what is going on. And, as such, it will require much thought and effort to get it properly aligned. In other words, to make it do what it is supposed to do. To make it behave.

Court is genuinely concerned about and is charged with the duty of protecting vulnerable persons. So, being pulled-in, the Judge will now allow some limited inquiry into Linda's situation. He will allow Rhonda some leeway to raise her concerns on the record. My job is to get Rhonda the Rich to hang herself.

"Yes, your Honor," Mr. Rigby replies, smirking. "I call the Petitioner, Rhonda Albertson, to the stand." He motions for his client to rise and step up into the witness stand to be sworn in.

The clerk steps forward, "Please raise your right hand." Rhonda raises her right hand.

"Do you swear to tell the truth, the whole truth, and nothing but the truth, so help you God?"

"I do," she replies.

The clerk continues, "Please state your name, and spell your last name."

"Oh. Rhonda Albertson, A-L-B-E-R-T-S-O-N."

"Counsel, you may proceed," Judge Henderson says.

Rigby starts, "Ms. Albertson, please tell the Court why you are concerned about your mother's weight loss?"

"Objection, your Honor. Mr. Rigby is leading the witness."

"Sustained. Mr. Rigby, please refrain from leading the witness."

"Sorry, your Honor. Let me rephrase. Ms. Albertson, please tell the Court why you believe your mother is unable to meet her needs for food, clothing, shelter and safety."

The Judge makes a face at Rigby, I groan, but do not object.

Rhonda the Rich brightens up and answers, "Well, she isn't eating. She has no food in the refrigerator... She was 167 pounds when she left Portland, she's now down to 120 pounds.... Her doctor says..."

"Objection, your Honor. There is no medical testimony...," I start.

"Sustained. Any other testimony, Mr. Rigby?"

"No, your Honor."

"Ms. Swan, any questions for Ms. Albertson?"

"Yes, your Honor."

"You may proceed."

"Ms. Albertson, do you live with your mother?"

"No, of course, not. I have my own family." Rhonda's face begins to get a little red.

"If you don't live with your mother, how do you know how much food she has in her refrigerator?" I ask.

"The last time I was at her apartment, I sneaked a look in mom's refrigerator when she was in the bathroom. I was worried about her because she was looking so skinny. So, I checked, and the refrigerator was empty. There was absolutely..."

I quickly interrupted Rhonda, "Your mother eats at restaurants doesn't she?"

"Sure, but she just picks at her food. I don't know the last time that she ate..."

I look straight at the Judge and say, "Your Honor, could you please instruct the witness to answer the questions with a simple 'yes' or 'no?'" I request.

Judge Henderson nods, and with an exasperated sigh says, "Ms. Albertson, please refrain from any narrative. Just answer counsel's questions with a simple 'yes' or 'no'."

"OK, but my mother is in real trouble," Rhonda the Rich replies, and starts to cry.

Geez, Louise, I am thinking. But, too late, the damage is done.

I put my client on the stand. One last chance.

"Ms. Jorgensen, please tell the Court what you had for breakfast today."

"Well, now, there wasn't time to eat this morning."

"What do you generally eat for lunch?" A whole turkey, I was praying.

"I don't like lunch much, so I normally skip it." Oh brother, I silently moan, what's going on here?

"You do eat don't you?"

"Well, of course, I eat. I eat all the time. My refrigerator is full of food."

With an audible, frustrated groan the Judge interrupts, "You know, sometimes I get kind of judgy," his forehead was definitely wrinkled and his bushy black eyebrows had almost met in the middle of his forehead, giving him a vulcan-like appearance. Judge Henderson shook his head and frowned. This was not a good sign. "I'll tell you what I'm going to do. Swan. Rigby. Both of you go straight over to Ms. Jorgensen's apartment right now. I want you to inventory her refrigerator and report back to me Tuesday morning at 10:00 a.m. Court dismissed." Before I could shut my mouth, he was gone.

Wow. Damn. Wish I was a Judge.

Chapter 8

The Infernal Machine II

As I step out into the cold, cold wind in front of the Wells Fargo Building, yes, indeed, Quinn's cab pulls up. Hesitating only slightly, I yank open the door to the front seat and crawl in. With a determined look on my face, I ask, "How did you know I would need a cab at 10:57 a.m.? Are you and Judge Henderson in collusion somehow?" At the blank look on Quinn's face, I knew there was no collusion. "Well, then, how?" I persisted.

Quinn reached over to turn the heater up. "It's kind of complicated," he said.

If you only knew, I thought. "I'm all ears. I could use some explanation for all the weird stuff that's been happening around me lately. And how the hell did you end up witnessing Anna Strong's Will? The one I didn't draft? Don't tell me that you're providing feedback for the

83

universe, and don't tell me that you're an angel. For the record, I don't believe in angels or devils, so don't bother with that one either. Well?"

"Ah, a bit testy, are we?" Quinn pulled out into the traffic and headed for 35E North. It looked like he was smiling. I was pissed with my general situation, and he was the only one around to be pissed off at. He had to have some answers.

"And don't give me that killer smile. Wait, you're not a killer are you?" Now, he was really smiling. "No, Gracie, I'm not a killer or a stalker. I'm just here to help you, and I think that, somehow, you'll end up being able to help me."

"What in the world could I possibly do to help you?" I blurted out. He looked me over. My nose was red and cold, my hair was standing up, and I was wearing a skirt 2 sizes too small. I'm positive I did not appear to the general public as any kind of wonder woman at any time. Or, for that matter, as any sort of sexual object at this particular moment. Where did that come from, I wondered? Well, even if I was attracted to smart good looking men, in general, and even if my undisciplined brain seemed to move in that certain direction where Quinn was concerned, we were in a cab, for God's sake, and it was winter in Minnesota after all.

"Well, have you ever heard of something called an infernal machine?" Quinn started.

Oh, my God, what was going on? How does he know about the infernal machine? My eyes grew wider. Quinn must have interpreted my astonishment as a lack of knowledge, and he began to explain his interpretation of the infernal machine concept.

"See, anything can potentially become an infernal machine depending on what is going on. So, for example, if your Jeep lurched sideways every time you backed up, and your headlights flashed on every time you touched the radio, it would be an infernal machine. It's not doing what it supposed to be doing, right? Follow me so far?"

"OK." I nod, following. "Been there. Done that."

"In my situation, Gracie," he swallowed, shook his head, and then rushed on, as if he had a hard time believing his own words. "I have this device called a synchrotron in the basement of my research lab." Another considered pause. "Let's just say that when I got into the lab yesterday afternoon, I discovered that the synchrotron was directing particles to a particular place in space∞time; say, like, it became aligned, linked, to a particular event point - or person - and it was working in a loop. We could say its output relates to a certain event point that cannot be modified or changed no matter what I do. My students have been working on it 24/7. In other words, it's stuck…"

"Stuck? What do you mean, stuck?"

"What I mean is that we're trying to reprogram it. We're having a hard time redirecting it."

"You can't redirect it? Like, it's out of control?" I interjected, close to panic. Three questions in a row, without taking a breath. Not a good sign.

"Something like that. It's behaving erratically. It's misguided, and it acts in a somewhat, well, seemingly personal way."

"What do you mean 'personal'?" I said with great foreboding. I knew the answer already, but I just did not want to admit it to myself, and I needed to hear the answer out loud.

"Well, Gracie, it seems to be linked to you, somehow, and to a series of events that began about 3:00 o'clock yesterday afternoon."

My brain began working a hundred miles a minute. "Whoa, wait. Give me a minute." How could Quinn's infernal machine problem have anything to do with me? 3:00 o'clock yesterday afternoon? *Thursday.* That would be a couple of hours before Anna died in my office, I thought. Just about the time she would have been signing her Will. The Will that I didn't draft. Oh, man, did I say I wanted feedback from the universe? What was I thinking?

"So, the person is me. And, let me guess, the place is somewhere in Duluth, right?"

A pause. "Yes. How did you know that?"

"We'll have to discuss it later on the way to Duluth, after I inventory my client's refrigerator for the Judge," I reply, in my stand-by snippy court voice.

Quinn raises an eyebrow and starts working his mouth to speak, trying to form words, and then apparently changes his mind. I think he was fairly certain, and so was I, that any particular words or explanation that came out of my mouth, just at that moment, would be gibberish.

"Just get me to Roseville pronto." I say. He nods, and pulls into traffic.

I'm not sure why, but I got the distinct impression then that Quinn was relieved. After the screwy explanation of his "situation with the infernal machine," he probably thought I was going to call the paramedics to have him admitted to the Psych Ward at St. Joe's Hospital on a 72-hour hold. Well, to be honest, the thought had briefly crossed my mind, and, on a normal day, I might have done just that. But then, well, the last two days have been kind of weird, with a capital "W." I should probably cut him some slack. He's the only guy I ever met who knows anything about how an infernal machine works. Besides, I sneaked a look at his blue eyes again, and, what the heh, I think I'll just run with it for now.

Chapter 9

The Inventory

<u>Refrigerator:</u>

15 pieces of American cheese

4 containers of Yoplait yogurt

Turkey breast (8 oz.) *

8 Protein Drinks (Boost) - 2 open

12 oz. cottage cheese *

9 containers of applesauce (1 open)

2 sticks of butter

½ gal. 1% milk

½ gal. skim milk *

½ gal. orange juice

½ gal. 2% milk *

Mayonnaise

1 bottle Chardonnay

<u>Freezer:</u>

2 pints Edy's frozen yogurt (black cherry and vanilla)

2 single-serving Byerly's french onion soup

3 single-serving Byerly's chicken noodle soup

<u>On Counter:</u>

Instant coffee

2 bagels

Cheerios

Keebler striped cookies

3 jars of peanut butter

4# sugar

2 bottles of Chardonnay

NOTE: All items marked with an * are past their expiration date.

Well, that was fun, I thought. No worries. My client had plenty of food! In fact, she actually had more food in her refrigerator than I do (except that I have beer instead of wine). The obvious problem was, however, as Rhonda the Rich kept exclaiming in a voice where the volume control was broken, almost every perishable item in the refrigerator was past its expiration date. And some of the other stuff didn't smell too good either. Nothing like trying to explain to an Italian Judge who eats homemade pasta with marinara sauce at least three times a week that my client was more than satisfied with her diet of food-like substances and three types of milk (with varying fat content) all past their expiration dates. Um. Hungry.

"Quinn?"

"Yes, Gracie."

"Are you hungry? It's past noon, and I have to eat something soon or I won't make it to Duluth. What about you?"

"Sure. Hungry. I am. I've got some sandwiches in the back seat. Why don't I take you home to pack and we can eat lunch there and then head up north?" Quinn said.

I glanced quickly at him. "Sounds good, but don't you need to pack some clothes, too? Get your toothbrush? I asked, wondering what kind of sandwiches he had made.

"Believe it or not, I'm ready to go, all prepared."

"I'll just bet you are." I replied a little sarcastically. "Is this preparedness part of the infernal machine stuff too?"

He gave me a look that I could have poured on a waffle. "Like it or not, well, we've got to get this sorted out. Come on Gracie, how about it? Tuna sandwiches at your place and then head up north?"

Speechless (how did he know that tuna fish is my favorite?) and still trying to describe the exact expression on his face, I replied. "Sure. You betcha. Let's do it."

Well, Quinn had peanut butter and I had tuna fish. He actually doesn't like tuna fish, but somehow he'd figured out it was my favorite. I have no problem with peanut butter, but I mostly like it in the morning, and we were edging close to 1:30 p.m. by the time we sat down to eat at the little round table in my kitchen nook. I cleared the table covered with my current reading list: <u>The Magic in Foods,</u> <u>The Secret Life of Plants,</u> and <u>2013 Foreclosures in Minnesota: A Report Based on County Sheriff's Sale Data.</u> We had a couple of dark beers, I grabbed Anna's Cub bag of goodies, and we hit the road. Quinn gave me a funny look when I loaded Anna's bag into the back seat of the cab, but he didn't say anything. In fact, we didn't talk much at all until we got to Forest Lake, about twenty-five miles north of the Twin Cities.

I just needed to sort things out. My world had been turned upside down. Just twenty-four hours ago, I led a somewhat normal life. True, I was an untypical lawyer. I was constantly pondering life's meaning and experiences, often wondering if I ever really helped anyone at all. I ached for feedback from the universe, hoping that my existence had more meaning than what showed on the surface. I continually wondered if I was connected to anything or anyone. I also wondered where all the aliens were. Quinn had said that I was the - person - or event - that his machine (the synchrotron?) was fixated on. What did that mean? So. Reality check. Once again, here I am, in this cab with the blue leather seats. I am headed to Duluth, with this very attractive, compelling man. An old woman died in my office last night. And, I was supposed to have written her Will. I know what the rules are, but I don't have a clue as to what's going on right now. I need the full picture. Quinn said he thought I could help him. Maybe he can help me. Can I trust him? He didn't like tuna fish, but he had an honest face, a sincere attitude, and he had no problem driving me to North Jesus. As an after-thought, it occurred to me that if I judged the character of a man by whether he liked tuna fish or not, I was in big trouble!

"Quinn," I asked. "Is your meter running?"

He glanced, startled, at me. "Gracie?" (At least he didn't make THAT face again.)

"Are you charging me for this trip to Duluth?" I asked.

"Well, not exactly," he said. "I stopped the meter in Saint Paul. This is personal, between us."

"OK," I breathed a sigh of relief. $10.57 was a pretty accurate number for the balance in my checking account. "So, Quinn, will you take it slow, and tell me, to the best of your ability, about your research? It might help if we start at the beginning."

"All right. Makes sense." He must have been contemplating how to begin since the expressions on his face kept changing. I waited patiently. Finally, having organized his thoughts, he began speaking in his 'professorial' voice: "It all started about fifteen years ago, while I was working on my Ph.D. I became fascinated with The Theory of Everything. Physicists usually call this 'TOE'."

"You're kidding, right?" I managed to suppress a grin. His profile seemed serious enough.

"No, TOE is real, and its implications are becoming more important every day."

"Quinn," I said, "I admit that I am out of touch with current events from time to time - well maybe most of the time. But, seriously, how come I never heard of TOE before today? And, how can something I have never heard about before happen to be increasingly more important every day? It's not like some end-of-the world thing that scientists are hiding from everyone just to avoid mass hysteria is it?"

"No, Gracie, nothing like that. You've heard of Albert Einstein haven't you?"

"Of course. I'm a lawyer, not a moron. I know he was a famous physicist and that he and I have a lot in common."

"You and Einstein have a lot in common?"

"Yes, indeed. He and I share the same philosophy with respect to beer. He said, and I quote, 'Beer is proof that God loves us and wants us to be happy'."

"No, Gracie, that was Ben Franklin, not Albert Einstein."

"Oh. Well, you could be right, I suppose. I have never been too great at remembering famous quotes or telling good jokes."

"I'll keep that in mind. Now, back to Einstein. So, it all starts off with Einstein's theory of relativity and quantum mechanics. It's really about how the two theories are connected to describe our universe. In other words, the connection between the very, very tiny and the very, very big.

"You mean, like, quantum theory?" Quinn raised his eyebrows. I replied tartly, "It's not like I've never heard the word 'quantum' before. I'll have you know, I've watched every episode of Star Trek, The Next Generation at least twice!"

Raising his eyebrows just a little more Quinn tactfully replied, "OK then, you certainly are qualified to discuss TOE." He cleared his throat and continued. I got the impression he had given this particular lecture before. "Yes. That's part of it. Quantum basically starts with the very, very tiny... the crazy, probabilistic wave particle duality nonlinear multiple historical nature of the universe - the smallest bits, the atomic particle bits." He scratched his chin.

Is this guy for real? I thought. Quinn is even farther out in the ether than I am.

"See, TOE strives to show how all the small bits relate to all the big stuff. Like how you and me and elephants - and planets and stars - are related to one another. The really interesting part is that there are paradoxes. Crazy, nonsensical stuff going on in the smallest scales of the universe, and crazy, nonsensical happenings going on with the big stuff too."

I must have looked confused. So, Quinn continued his explanation.

"Let me put it a different way. Some things that happen at the quantum level don't make normal, logical sense. And some things that happen in the presence of huge stars - like a black hole or traveling near the speed of light - don't make sense to our logical mind either. So, TOE, the Theory of Everything, attempts to resolve those crazy paradoxes and reconcile the existence and properties of protons AND black holes. It goes all the way from one to the other."

"You mean, from the micro to the macro?"

"Yes, Gracie, exactly."

"You mean the physics you're involved in could begin to explain crazy things that don't make sense in my world?" A small glimmer of excitement began to build up in my belly. Could Quinn have real answers to my questions? Could he be the ONE, just like Keano Reeves in The Matrix?

"Hopefully. We are looking at the relationship between quantum teleportation, and black holes, and worm holes, and faster-than-light travel, and communication, and... BLAH, BLAH, BLAH, BLAH, BLAH, BLAH, BLAH..." After a few minutes, he gave me a concerned glance, knowing he was losing me. So, rapidly accelerating his delivery, with a deep breath, he concluded. "So, I asked myself, if they can build a large super-conducting hadron collider at Cern in Switzerland - then why couldn't I build a small super-conducting synchrotron in my basement lab? So I did."

Then he stopped speaking. I knew he wanted me to say something. Actually, thinking about it, he might just have been praying that I wouldn't start screaming and jump out of the moving cab.

My turn.

"So what were you actually trying to accomplish with this, ah, mega - thinggee?"

He seemed relieved. "I was trying to build a device to reproduce conditions at the time of the Big Bang."

"The Big Bang? Why is that important?"

"Because, at that point, it appears that everything in the universe was essentially the same, and in balance. You could say that everything was UNIFIED. In my lab, I think what happened was that we contained so much energy in such a small spot, that it opened up a worm hole in space∞time. Somehow we made a closed loop in space∞time actually - looping back into the what we perceive as the past."

"So is that how you met Anna?"

"Anna?" He had a baffled look on his face.

"Anna Strong. The woman who died in my office last night?"

"A woman died in your office last night?" Now he was the one who looked confused and a little panicked.

"Yes. We both know you witnessed a Will yesterday afternoon about 3:00 p.m. The person who signed the Will was an old woman named 'Anna Strong'. You had to have known her. Well, Anna died in my office last night about 6:00 p.m."

Quinn gave me a horrified look. His face had turned a weird shade of green, and it looked like he was about to throw-up. He swallowed, "You said the woman who died in your office was named Anna, Anna Strong?"

"Yes. That's exactly what I said. So, how did you know Anna? Did you step through your black hole into Harvey's office to witness her Will yesterday afternoon?"

"Apparently. Or maybe I haven't done it yet!" Quinn signaled and moved over to the right lane to take the Hinckley exit. "You drive. I need a drink."

Chapter 10

Harvey II/Connections

As I accelerated down the ramp back onto Highway 35 continuing North to Duluth, I set the cruise on Quinn's cab and reached for the lemon bismarck I had purchased at Tobies. First things first.

Quinn still looked a little sick, but it was obvious that the coffee had helped. And, from the sounds coming from the passenger side of the cab, I was quite sure that the carmel roll Quinn was shoveling into his mouth was helping too. "Yum, good. Really good. Can I try some of that lemon stuff?" He reached across the front seat trying to stick a finger into my lemon filing. I almost swerved off the road.

"No. Mine, all mine." When he looked sheepishly at me I told him, "I might be willing to share a small portion of this delicious, extraordinarily tasty lemon filling if, and only if, you give me some details about how you knew Anna. Take your time. Start from the beginning. We've still got about seventy-five miles till we hit Duluth."

"Man, you're tough. Here I am, a single guy trying to score just a tiny taste of lemon..."

Wow, was Quinn coming onto me? My face flamed just a little. His statement felt like, well, pure innuendo, and I hadn't had any innuendo in a long, long time. A little breathless, I replied, "OK. Deal. You talk, I give lemon."

Again, those raised eyebrows. "Well, its a long story. It might almost take the rest of the trip," he started.

I nodded for him to proceed.

"OK. Here goes. Like I said, it really begins in my lab. Things were progressing satisfactorily with the synchrotron experiments. We were beginning to get a whole lot of promising data; some of it quite unexpected. Hey! Don't eat all that lemon stuff!"

"Mmm," I said, rolling my eyes. "This is absolutely the most luscious lemon filling I've ever had." I took a few deep breaths and gave Quinn the most suggestive look I could muster. "So, what went wrong?"

He licked his lips. "We had a real emergency. About three weeks ago, when I strolled into the lab - without my lemon bismarck," he wiggled his eyebrows like Groucho Marx, "it was a madhouse. Apparently, Dirk's computer had just crashed, and all the systems were down. Dirk is one of my post-grads, brilliant actually. The synchrotron had been acting erratically, spewing out some unbelievable data, and he had rebooted his computer several times, trying to get the synchrotron back on-line. Students were rushing around in a panic. So, jokingly, I asked if we were having a core meltdown or what? Although we are doing cutting edge stuff, Gracie, my staff is usually pretty laid-back. So, it was, well, a little unnerving when everyone turned to face me and I saw no humor there, only stark fear and uncertainty. All of a sudden, my joke was real. Apparently, I had verbalized their worst fears. It didn't help. Words are powerful things. I need to remember that. I knew then we were in deep kimshee."

"Wait. Wait a minute. Kimshee? Kimshee! How do you know about kimshee?" I exploded.

Quinn gave me another one of those looks.

"OK. Duh. Of course you know about kimshee. Never mind, go on."

"Well, I rushed over to Dirk's console and, indeed, things did look pretty bad. No matter what algorithm I tried, I had no luck re-booting Dirk's computer either. The readings from the synchrotron were spiking and dipping in a vibrational cycle that I have never seen before. I knew it would only be a matter of a few more minutes before..."

"Wait. When you said 'meltdown', did you mean, like, a 'meltdown'? A real nuclear disaster... a 3 Mile Island, Chernobyl, or Fukushima meltdown?"

"Not exactly, Gracie." Quinn paused, considering his words," Let's just say that if we didn't get the synchrotron under control within, oh, say about ten minutes on the outside, the worst-case scenario was that we would have sent half of Minneapolis back in time, or generated a very small black hole - in theory, of course."

Now it was my turn to raise my eyebrows. "Half of Minneapolis? Does the Dean know about this?"

Shaking his head, Quinn continued. "As I said, in theory, of course. More probably, the EMP would have wiped out all of the electronics in a seven state area. You know, cell phones, computers, the cloud? Probably would have wiped the NSA's data storage facility in Idaho too."

"That's the best-case scenario?"

"Yep."

"Boy, the NSA would have been pissed. What's an EMP, anyway?" I asked.

"An electromagnetic pulse, of course. I guess you never tuned into Eureka huh?"[8] Noticing my blank look, Quinn said, "I'll explain it later," and continued with his story. "Well, all of a sudden this old guy rushes in. He's wearing white pants, just like in the '60s. He's got a big, red scotch nose, white hair, and he stalks over to Dirk's computer console like he owns the place, keys in a new algorithm, and just re-boots everything. No explanation whatsoever. It was spooky. He knew exactly what to do, and I had never seen him before. I want to tell you Gracie, there aren't too

_____

[8] I missed that reference altogether. Besides, I did too, watch Eureka, eventually, on Netflix. I even cried when the series was over. I must have missed the EMP episode though.

many men in the world who understand the work we're doing in my lab… and I don't know how he…"

Not too many women either, I'm thinking. And, certainly not the Dean.

"…and, it was kind of weird too, in a good sort of way, because this guy had the biggest grin on his face. Like he was really happy. He seemed unconcerned with the chaos. So, after he did his magic, I asked the guy to step into my office to discuss the shutdown protocol he used." We talked for awhile - I won't bore you with details, but he abruptly cut our meeting short. He said he had some kind of transference… no, maybe he said 'convergence'… to attend to immediately, and he couldn't stay. Then he gave me his address and invited me to his office later that evening. His office is actually on the 6th Floor of your building…"

"You said the guy had white hair and a scotch nose, like God?" I sputtered.

"Yeah." Quinn had a funny look on his face now. "I suppose you could draw that analogy, in a somewhat weird or obscure way."

"Let me guess. The guy's name is Harvey Waterston, right?"

"How did you know?" Quinn replied. "You know Harvey?"

"Oh, yeah. Only my whole life. Harvey's the reason we're heading to Duluth right now. Funny, I had no idea he was into…"

"We're on our way to Duluth to see Harvey?"

"You betcha. And, Harvey's going to pay. He's got one hell of a lot of explaining to do."

"OK, I can get alongside that."

"Please continue. What happened later, at Harvey's office?" I actually felt like I was taking pretty good testimony by this time. Asking only the "who, what, when, how" questions, just like a good litigator is supposed to do. You know, this may be the first time I get it right!

"Well, when I got there, Harvey gave me a tall scotch and we sat down on the sofa in his office. He told me he was a lawyer, among other things. We started discussing the set-up in my lab, and then I noticed that he had series of books containing unpublished lectures of Richard Feynman on his bookshelf. This was amazing."

"Amazing? Why? What's so amazing about books written by Richard Feynman? I bet there are many people who write books that are never published." Even me. "Why, someday even I might decide to write a book that nobody wants to read and that is never published!" But, I digress.

"Feynman was different from everyone else. For one thing, he was the resident genius at Cal Tech. One of the physicists who worked on the Manhattan Project - the hydrogen bomb?"

"Sure. Of course, that Feynman. I knew that."

"So, anyway, what the hell were unpublished lectures of a genius physicist doing on a lawyer's bookcase anyway, I wondered? When I asked Harvey that exact question, he told me that he had studied physics in Scotland a long time ago. He said he met Feynman there and they became close friends after awhile. He said Feynman's unpublished work directly relates to the problems we were facing in my lab."

"You mean the time-loopy thing that is somehow 'personal' to me? I didn't even know that Harvey ever went to Scotland - or that he had any interest in physics at all! And, I've known Harvey pretty much my whole life."

"Frankly, I haven't known Harvey all that long, but I think he is pretty private or tight-lipped, you might say. In fact, in my experience, he keeps his lips shut pretty tight unless he is swallowing some damn-fine scotch." Quinn delivered the pun in a sheepish, kind of apologetic way, as if he wasn't sure I would get the joke. I could only shake my head in wonderment. As a rule, I don't get jokes, but I do get puns - most of the time.

"You know, I didn't even know Harvey liked scotch." But I should have figured. God would like scotch, too, I'm sure. I gave Quinn my best "syrupy" look and asked him to continue.

"Well, we kept drinking his scotch, and every time I tried to pin Harvey down about how he'd managed to avert the disaster in my lab, he would change the subject. He just kept saying that I'd find all the answers in Feynman's work.

He invited me to read Feynman's lectures at any reasonable time, but he told me that I had to keep the books in his office since they were so rare and irreplaceable. So, for the last three weeks, I've spent just about every spare moment pouring over Feynman's lost lectures in Harvey's office. They are amazing, Gracie. It's like Feynman knew my own mind."

"So, where does Anna fit into the picture?" I asked. Did she just step through your black hole into Harvey's office?" We both looked at each other. I felt my skin prickle a little. A twiggle.

"I actually don't know much about Anna. What I do know is that she dropped by quite a few times while I was reading the Feynman lectures. She would bring in tea and these little chocolate chip cookies. Sometimes we would talk."

"Talk about what?"

"Well, theoretical physics mostly. She seemed interested in the multi-dimensional possibilities of my work. She actually suggested a few changes in the mapping software. I liked her. She was a little quirky, but her chocolate chip cookies were really outstanding. I think she was related to Harvey, somehow. Maybe his sister. He would glance at her, and touch her hand from time to time, like he was reassuring her about something. He would never talk about her when I asked. He wouldn't even tell me where Anna had received her physics training. He always found a way to change the subject. Just like he never talked about how he acquired Feynman's unpublished works."

"So, after awhile, you just stopped questioning Harvey, but kept pouring through Feynman's unpublished lectures while drinking Harvey's scotch?"

"Precisely."

"That sums up Harvey's perfect and predictable strategy. He keeps evading until you're just too worn out to continue questioning him. Actually, come to think of it, Harvey's strategy has advanced to Level 2: If you won't stop asking questions or if he doesn't want to answer, he'll just disappear, leaving a note for you to show up in Duluth, at a designated time and place. That is exactly what he did when I tried to ask him about Anna. That is why Harvey must die."

With his blue eyes widening just a bit, Quinn replied with a big goofy grin on his face, "Oh, I get it now. We're going to Duluth to kill a harmless old man with a scotch nose because he was protective of a slightly eccentric old woman who baked outstanding chocolate chip cookies. I suggest a firing squad. We should make him suffer. Wait. I forgot. I don't believe in the death penalty. I guess we'll have to find some other way to kill him dead without actually having him die."

"Shit, Quinn," I said, trying to suppress laughter and feeling a little bit of the tightness in my stomach loosen. "You do tend to the ridiculous."

He looked hurt. "Me?" He said. "Only the ridiculous; not the dramatic?"

That was the moment when I knew, despite any misgivings I had about Quinn before, that he was OK. Actually, he was more than OK. He had a sense of humor and he was trying to make me feel better. I was beginning to understand the type of man he was, underneath the mad scientist/cool cabbie facade. Also, I thought gladly, he's certainly not gay... another BIG plus. Taking a deep breath, I knew that my situation still remained amazingly obscure; however, with Quinn close by, all this bizarre stuff seemed somewhat more manageable. Was this the beginning of trust, I wondered, or merely lust? Or... possibly, was this more of the feedback I was demanding from the universe? I needed to ponder that one for awhile. Better be sooner than later, I resolved - once I get a break from the universe throwing wild balls at me. Oh. Again. Bad choice of words. Subliminal?

I fanned myself a little, and cleared my throat. "Let's try to get back on track. So, about Anna..." No response.

"You know, Anna, the old lady who died, actually died, in my office last night? And, how did you come to be a witness to the signing of her Will? AND, she baked you chocolate chip cookies?"

But when I glanced over, Quinn wasn't listening to me. We were at the top of Thompson Hill, and Quinn was gazing down at the city lights. Twinkling lights in a clear night sky. Just like stars. Just like hope.

Chapter 11

Hillside Cottage

"I guess we'll have to table our discussion about Anna until we find a place to stay." I knew how hard it was to find an available hotel room on a Friday night in Duluth. And, with all the startling events of the day, I hadn't had a chance to make any calls before we left the Twin Cities. It could take us all night to find a couple of rooms. And, the rooms would be expensive, even in November. Great. I was really hoping that I wouldn't have to shack up with a longshoreman for the night, or sleep on the boardwalk.

"Actually, Gracie, I have a small, um, partial confession to make." Quinn said.

Oh shit. "A 'partial' confession?" I squeaked. To be honest, I hate full disclosures anyway. "Oh?" I said as I chewed my lip, just a little worried at what Quinn had to say. Was he gay after all? Was he an ax-murderer? I wasn't sure that I could handle any more convoluted twists on this particular day. Let's just say, being ordered to inventory a client's refrigerator stood high on the list of unexpected events for sure, not to mention Anna's Will, and Harvey's disappearance. Just one more (even small) event could simply push me over the edge. Then again, looking at the broader picture, I'm sure the nice people at St. Mary's Hospital might be willing to offer me a cozy room in the Psych Ward tonight, along with a great view of the lake (at no extra charge).

"While you were packing, I made a few calls about this place in Duluth, in Little Italy - on Observation Hill actually, where I've stayed before, and they've got it ready for us. Of course, if you'd rather stay at Canal Park, we can see if there are any rooms available. Otherwise, this little cottage actually has four nice bedrooms to choose from. Pretty good view too. Want to give it a try?"

My pondering took only a second or two. Gee, let me think - no rooms at Canal Park - I don't know any longshoremen - and I would die of exposure on the boardwalk. A cottage usually has a kitchen, a bathtub, and a toilet, all of which would come in handy right about now. Also four bedrooms. No pressure.

"I call dibs on the bedroom?"

"Sure. You pick."

"Is there food there?"

"Probably, but if not we can go out or order a pizza."

"Does it cost a lot?

"Don't worry, I've got it covered, Babe."

I winced. Oh no. He called me Babe. This is a problem.

"Separate bedrooms?"

"Of course."

"Deal."

I'm not very good at negotiations. That's why I'm a probate lawyer. For me, probate is easy, because it's statutory. In other words, the rules are all written down in plain language in the statute, and, like the good Catholic girl I used to be, I follow the rules. So, for example, when somebody dies, the statute tells us who gets what. I follow the rules. When somebody leaves a Will, the statute tells us how the Will works. I follow the rules. I'm good at probate because it is systematic and straightforward: Step 1, Step 2, Step 3, and so forth. This is a major handicap in the real world, however. For example, every time I have tried to buy a car, I offer the full ticket price. I don't even know how to bargain someone down at a garage sale.

Inexplicably, I also believe what people say. So I believed Quinn about his "partial confession." I didn't even follow-up. This makes me a very naïve lawyer. My clients can lie to me, and I just don't get it. No matter what they say, I believe them. Of course, when a client tells me that the Mayor of North Saint Paul has hired a hit-man to kill her, I do wonder. If a client tells me that she has been impregnated by aliens, I do wonder. But I don't wonder if they are telling me the truth. Of course they are. They are telling me the truth because that is exactly what they believe. At that time. In that moment. What I believe is that they are mentally ill. I win.

Of course, I know that clients who are completely sane don't always tell the truth, don't always follow the rules, and try to manipulate me, usually with respect to fees. And usually with great success. I'm fair game. Before I went to law school, I always thought that the law was fair, and that the concept of truth formed the foundation of our legal system. Imagine my disenchantment when I found out that our legal system is based on advocacy! The idea that it doesn't matter what the truth is, only that the "process" is fair. The British Legal System is based on the concept of getting all the facts out so that the truth can be known. I actually seriously considered emigrating to the UK at one time because of this. In the United States, everyone's truth is subjective. Circumstantial. Almost as changeable as the weather in Duluth.

It follows that I'm not very good at bending the rules or manipulation either. To compensate, I'm very blunt.

"Quinn. Tell me the truth. I'll believe you no matter what you say, anyway. I can't help it. Are you setting me up for a night of illicit sex, as in 'sexual predator', or are you simply an ax-murderer?"

"Are we back to that, again, Gracie? Are there any other choices?" He made some kind of face again. I couldn't tell if it signified incredulity or exasperation. I'm going to have to figure out what his various expressions may mean - later.

"The simple, truthful, and full answer is 'No'. I'm not a sexual predator or an ax-murderer, and I don't bend spoons with my mind either - although I know people who can. I'm just a guy who happens to be a physicist and a cab driver concurrently. I need a place to stay tonight. I've somehow become mixed up with this very unexpectedly interesting lawyer lady who I met for the first time this morning, very early this morning. I've just had a long ride to Duluth and I'm hungry. Can't we just go to the Cottage for tonight, please Gracie? We'll decide about the sex part later, OK?"

"OK. Works for me."

A kitchen with marble countertops, a carved rosewood fireplace, a gothic window to the east overlooking the lake. An almost-full moon reflecting off the water. Wow. This "little" cottage was quite a place. And, what's more, there was whimsy everywhere. The gatekeeper to the "Escher" stairway and the lofted second floor was a bronzed statute of a monkey reading Darwin under a palm tree. What was I thinking? Of course there would have to be a monkey reading a book under a palm tree at any place that Quinn stayed. No surprise there. I should have figured.

Barn doors opened onto a gigantic soaking tub with stained glass above. A tub obviously big enough for two persons to share. Um. A spiral staircase going even farther up - up to where? This cottage felt like pure and unadulterated... I have no words to describe it. It felt magic. Like a good red wine, warm and romantic with undertones of sexy and dangerous. I bet people danced here. How had Quinn found this place? He said he had stayed here before - was this his love nest? Yikes. Maybe he was married! Was being married the other part of his "partial" confession? But - no ring on his finger. No shadow of a missing ring either. (Girls really do notice this, you know.) Another mystery - something else to discover - but not until tomorrow. I was too tired to ask any more questions tonight. I could only appreciate the unexpected peaceful splendor of this welcoming place. It was a true gift. And, there was food! After scrambled eggs with peppers and chorizo, I hit the hay, alone. In the east bedroom, underneath the silvery moon shining over the water.

... *I was in a warm, comfortable, loving place. It was night, and the air felt soft and warm on my skin. I was standing on cobblestones, at the corner of a wide street, a boulevard actually. As I stepped onto the pavement, two bicycles went whizzing past, so close to me that I could have touched them. As they passed, I looked up at the full moon shining above and at the tall palatial buildings on the other side of the street. I knew this place; I liked it here. There was no noise, only the soothing murmurings of the night along with a beautiful almost-recognizable melody gently playing somewhere nearby. I noticed a very small candlelit table located directly in the center of the boulevard, where the cars should have been. As I approached, a shadowed figure spoke to me. "Sit down, my dear one, have some tea."*

"Where am I?" I asked as I sat at the table.

"Why Andrássy Avenue, of course. In Budapest," the voice answered. "It's one of your favorite places, and I thought you'd like to meet here."

"But I've never been in Budapest." I said.

"Oh you will be; many, many times." I knew that voice. It was Anna's voice. The voice of Anna Strong, my dead client.

"How…" I began to say,

"Here," she said quickly, "take this." I looked down. Anna had placed a tiny snow-white flower in the center of my palm. "It will help you to find this place again." She said. Then Anna turned and pointed at two people, bathed in moonlight, who were holding one another and dancing. Why, it was me - and Quinn! Wow. We looked so happy. My hair was reddish, long and flowing; my gown was a shimmery blue. Quinn was twirling me as if I were a precious gift, moving me gently closer and closer to him…

Then Anna was speaking to me in a clear and soothing voice, "Remember to treasure every day. Treasure… every moment. Every moment is unique, a spark of the life that is within you, an experience in time. Each moment resonates into the past, present and future, creating new lifetimes full of possibilities. Probable futures. Never-

ending, forever new and... happy. It's your choice. Now. Your lifetime... many, many lifetimes, all happening now, shared with the ones you don't even know you love - yet. Read the journal. Learn and understand!"

Blue, green, golden colors. Orgasmic waves of warmth and understanding floating me gently toward awake. This was important. This was even better than Harrison! I needed to remember this feeling of being totally filled up and wrapped in love. To remember all the possibilities. I tried a mental suggestion, almost a prayer, "I want to remember; I want to remember this place, this dream! Please let me remember, let me remember. I want to..."

My cell rang. The loud jarring sound startled me to full irritated consciousness. "What? What? Hello, hello? Yes, yes, its Gracie, who else? Yes. Quinn's here with me. What do you mean, good? Where? OK. Yeah. Ten o'clock. If you take off this time, Harvey, I'm really going to kill you." Then he had the gall to hang up! And, the dream... what was I dreaming about? Something I should remember, but... it's lost now.

I opened the rose-colored door and streaked into the hallway, calling for Quinn. And, there he was, solid as a boulder in the middle of the hall. Looking at me, in my T-shirt and panties, looking at him.

He had no shirt on; his thick blonde hair was tangled; and his jeans were only partially zipped. My mouth went dry all of a sudden. I looked down and noticed that my nipples were hard. I looked up and noticed that Quinn had noticed that my nipples were hard too. He had a sort of fixated look on his face. Time to get dressed. I stammered, "We'd better get going. Harvey just called. He wanted us to meet him - at 10:00 o'clock." Quinn's blue eyes settled on my face, then returned to survey my other parts again. He took a step toward me and reached for my hand. A tiny snow-white flower floated to the floor. As he bent to retrieve the fallen object, I gave another little squeak and retreated to the bedroom. The sun was rising over the lake. Foggy. I glanced at the clock, only 6:00 a.m. Really? Here we go again.

I quickly dressed in my favorite blue sweater and old, soft jeans. Ah. No heels today. Just shit-kicking boots. As I glanced out the window, I was mesmerized by the fog rising from the lake. The fact is, you could almost see the lake, except for the intermittent sheets of sleet. Oh no. Fog and sleet at the same time. Resigned to a day of unpredictable weather (normal for Duluth), I did the best I could to manage my unruly hair, added a little mascara and some loopy earrings. Sort of on vacation, aren't I? Well, don't need to wear a suit to kick some ass, I ruminated. I quickly made my bed, compulsively, and headed down to the kitchen.

Quinn was still shirtless, although he was totally zipped up, and pouring coffee. Thank God. He was obviously in control of the kitchen, which was all right with me. "Here,

Gracie," he said. "Coffee will help, a little. It's not Starbucks, but it's not too bad either."

I gratefully took the cup he offered me in a bright orange cup with a giant mosquito on it. The cup had the words, "Minnesota State Bird," printed its side. True, oh so true. I noticed that Quinn's coffee mug said "Brandeis Travel Service." Brandeis? But, wait! That was my... I'll think about that connection later. Admittedly, the coffee was good. The view was good. The service was good. I shook my head as I finally jolted awake.

"Good morning, Quinn," I said. "Sorry about that bit in the hallway. I usually don't have to worry about meeting large men - or men of any stature actually - in my hallway. I was caught a little off guard."

He grinned disarmingly. "Well, that's something at least. I was afraid that I had demon breath, or that I had morphed into dungeon man the way you took off back there."

"Oh no, nothing like that. Harvey called."

"Yes. I heard the phone ring, and I was on my way to answer it when you arrived in my... in the hallway in quite a state."

I definitely wanted to change the subject so I chatted on, "where'd you find this place anyway? It's amazing. I slept so good, and I don't usually sleep well when I'm away from home. I had this incredible dream, but I can't seem to remember much of it." I picked up the tiny snow-white flower Quinn had placed on the kitchen counter and twirled it in my fingers. "Um. Curious." Without knowing why, I slipped the tiny snow-white flower into my pocket.

"Do you remember any part of your dream?" Quinn asked.

"Not too much." I said. "I think it had something to do with Anna, or bicycling to the moon."

"Lake Superior has an interesting effect on some people. It gives them vivid dreams. The first time I stayed here, my dreams were so real that I had a hard time realizing they were just dreams. I've read some research upon the effect of large bodies of water on dream states for some people. Dreams and other senses are enhanced somehow. Like taking hallucinogens without the side effects. I plan to study the phenomenon someday. That's one of the reasons why I…" His words trailed off.

"Why you what? I asked.

"Oh, that's why I was… just wondering what you wanted for breakfast…?"[9]

"Huh?"

"I'll tell you what, let's get some breakfast at Sara's Table and we'll pick up our conversation where we left off last night. Gracie, are you sure about Anna? You know, that Anna's really…"

---

[9] NOTE TO READER: At this point I did not understand that I had been redirected. A master job, too.

"Dead as a doorknob. I saw it for myself." I replied.

Quinn paled again, making me feel a little guilty. I guess I will have to be more delicate when I talk about dead people around Quinn. He'd probably be more comfortable if I talked about Anna "passing away" rather than "dead as a doorknob." Some people are funny that way. Occupational hazard, I guess.

"I mean, I'm sure Anna has passed." I rephrased. "There was some kind of odd energy surge when she touched me - when we were meeting in my office on Thursday night - and I actually passed out. When I woke up, Anna was lying on the floor dead - I mean, I couldn't find her pulse. We called the EMTs and they took her body away. Quinn, it was just about the weirdest thing that's ever happened to me. And, just for the record, I need to warn you that weird things do happen to me or around me with some regularity. You would be wise to be prepared for it. I just can't figure it out. It's like I'm a vortex or something. Maybe I just emanate insanity?"

"What do you mean 'weird' things happen around you? Give me one example."

"As if having a potential client zap you and then die - I mean - pass away in my office isn't weird enough? Not to mention a Judge ordering me to inventory my client's refrigerator? That's all within twenty-four hours, by the way."

"No big. Two events hardly make you a target for weirdness."

"OK, Professor. How about this one?" I took a deep breath. "Well, here goes. A few years ago while I was at the Saint Paul library, a person left this crazy poem on my windshield. If I read it a certain way, some of the lines of the poem seemed to refer to a place of sanctuary, a hidden place, outside of time. It also had a weird recipe for some kind of bridge through time and space. Wacko interpretation, right?"

"Sure. If you think so." Quinn replied.

"Well, I did think so, at the beginning. But then parts of the poem would come back to me at odd times. Then, I got this phone call from a realtor who wanted to sell me a timeshare up north. I thought it was a scam, so I played along at first. But, something she said made me think of one of the lines from the poem. All of a sudden, the poem started to make sense. So, I took the realtor up on her offer - a free weekend at the timeshare up north. When I got lost on the way, I followed the directions in the poem instead. The poem turned out to be a map! No surprise, I never got to the timeshare. Instead, I found this small cabin on Leech Lake. The realtor made arrangements for me to rent the cabin that first summer. I've been renting that same cabin every summer for five years now, and Quinn, honest to God, nothing ever changes up there. And there's this little round window in the door of the closet..." Looking at the perplexed expression on Quinn's face, I knew I had to stop.

"So, Gracie, you were inspired by a poem to find a special place; and nothing ever changes in this cabin up north? Sounds like most cabins. Maybe you're just making too much of this."

"Quinn, when I say 'nothing ever changes,' I really mean 'nothing ever changes!' For example, two years ago, I left a paperclip in a small cup at the back of the second shelf in the kitchen. Just as a test. The paper clip - it was still there when I got back to the cabin last July!"

"Wow, a paper clip in a cup on a shelf. That would never happen in a rental cabin up north, would it?" Quinn had a sunny smile on his face now.

I gave Quinn's shoulder a small shove. Again, he didn't budge. It was clear that Quinn wasn't ready for any of my weird stories yet. Maybe he never would be. There was certainly no way I could tell him about Whistle Binkies now! And, it was also clear that Quinn was as solid as a rock, and I would never be able to budge him unless he wanted to be budged. "Well," I coughed. "Anyway. I need food."

"You got it. I think you'll like Sara's Table. I promise I'll tell you whatever else I can about Anna, and you can finish telling me about how a cabin up north, where nothing ever changes, is a weird experience for a girl," he winced at my expression, "I mean, a young woman from

Minnesota?" He grinned. I shook my head to be sure the bats were truly gone. Quinn and I loaded ourselves into his cab, and left for breakfast.

The sky over the lake was now red, the sleeting had stopped. There were little bits of sun and fog all mixed together, with sun dogs casting their icy reflections in the sky. Crisp and cold. The fog horn blew loudly. The air smelled fresh. For the first time in a long time, everything felt good. Hope, optimism, coffee, and fog horns. Just what a Minnesota girl needs for her soul, usually. I was a difficult case, though. I knew I was a Minnesota girl, but I also knew that I was a wild child, with a gypsy soul. I knew I needed just a little something extra. The lawyer part of me was always evaluating and analyzing. So, I finally admitted to myself, maybe I did need something extra; but I also fully understood that I was looking for something more. Glancing over at Quinn, he winked at me. I didn't fall over this time. In fact, I winked back. It was all good...

Chapter 12

Breakfast at Tiffany's
(Well, Maybe Not Exactly)

We strolled into the airlock at Sara's Table (the Chester Creek Cafe) a few minutes later. The airlock hummed with energy, stuffed full of people (and fringe personalities of all persuasions) waiting to enter the main restaurant. Predictably, every person who had some sort of cause to trumpet had placed a business card or brochure on the billboard facing the front doors. There were announcements ranging from "new" yoga interpretations, to free birth control pills at publicly-funded clinics, to reminders to claim your earned income credit "because you earned it," to used hydroponic gardening setups for sale.[10]

---

[10] Not to mention "the highest quality urine cleaning kits available, just call 722-3249."

Duluth's politics (and thus its public bulletin boards) come as no surprise to anyone who understands human nature. At least human nature in the cold nort-land. The simple and undeniable fact is that Duluth attracts people at the extreme ends of the bell curve. They are the outliers, quite predictably, since Duluth is the last semi-civilized outpost at the end of the world. Basically, every lonesome soul attracted to Duluth has to find some way to cope with their searching spirits and that coping typically involves trying to convince others to join their cause.

I would be willing to bet there are more social workers and pilot social programs in Duluth than in any other place in the United States, not to mention all the artists and writers. I am not sure why they all end up in Duluth, with any certainty, but my theory is that it is the influence of the enormous inland sea. It draws to itself needy people, for myriad reasons. The most obvious reason is the reality check directly linked to the outlandish weather. You just can't ignore freezing your ass off, even if you are in the throes of a seemingly insurmountable philosophical debate. So, it's a physicality thing. It's also the art. Neither the most introverted intellectual nor the most troubled personality can ignore the outrageous weather or the breath-taking beauty here. Even the clouds are not normal in Duluth.

A sun-filled space, Sara's Table is blatant and unapologetic in its upscale hippie design. The fact is, if you aren't ultra left-wing or PC at a minimum, you might feel like you've gone over to the dark side.[11] Respecting the "nort-land's" egalitarian and previously communist roots however, Sara's Table welcomes all. Consequently, liberal or conservative, Sara's Table patrons feast on the best and most interesting breakfast menu in town.

Stepping through the airlock, we were greeted by a blond pony-tailed waitress, named Sara of course, who led us to the back room paneled with books shelved on solid pine hand-hewn bookcases. Real books. Everywhere. For sale, even. Not your Barnes & Noble kind of books, but new and used books on many subjects, all interesting or at least unusual. Quinn immediately began scanning a book from the Politics and Political Philosophy section. I pulled down a book entitled, "Atlantis in Wisconsin." When I realized the author was serious, I replaced the book on the shelf and began surveying the tin ceilings and the authentic Macintosh fixtures, pondering. After the waitress took our

---

[11] To be fair though, the Duluth News Tribune did endorse Mitt Romney in the last presidential election. Duluth News Tribune article published October 24, 2012, 12:00 a.m.: "Endorsement: Vote Romney, his promise of a way forward." One blog read, "Duluth - District home to the 1st communist Mayor. Lake Superior doesn't freeze over, but hell just did."

order, my gaze finally locked on Quinn, who had put his book aside.

"Well?" I said.

"Well?" He said.

"Let's talk about Anna," I said. "I want to know how you came to be a witness to her Will."

"As I said, I don't know all that much about Anna."

"C'mon," I said, "I need more than that. You promised. Gimme something!"

"Oh, all right. She was an enigma really." He shrugged.

I frowned and he continued, "I met her a few times at Harvey's office and I got to know her a little. Like I said, she would bring in tea and these little cookies sometimes, and we would sit and talk."

"What exactly did you talk about?" I tried disambiguation.

"Oh, this and that."

It wasn't working. I made a face at him. "Specifically?"

Quinn's lips quirked. He was playing me. "You know, physics, time, the stock market, consciousness, orange candy."

"Huh? Orange candy?" I said, with raised eyebrows. Trying to get back on track, I pressed, "When..."

"She liked those little orange candies. You know, the citrus kind wrapped in orange paper. She was always offering them to me, but I'm not an orange candy kind of guy. As you know, I'm a lemon filling kind of guy." He winked at me again.

I gulped. Oh-oh. Time out. "Need more coffee, Quinn?" I asked. Before he could answer, I grabbed his cup and my own and nervously strode to the coffee pumps at the end of the dining room. Yikes, I thought. Here we go again. Rubbing the goose bumps on my arms, I filled our cups and walked back to our table. Cold in here, I thought. Standing up to take the full cups from my hands, Quinn placed the cups on the table as I slid into the booth opposite him.

"Your hands are cold, Gracie. Here." Before I could answer, he had captured my hands in his, and, with a lop-sided grin he said, "Don't worry, we'll figure this all out."

"We will?" I managed to squeak.

"Yeah. We will, I guarantee it. I have a feeling that... everything will be better and be really good... great, in fact. Don't despair... don't give up." Quinn's eyes were intense, bluer than before; now a stormy blue.

"What did you say?" I murmured, mesmerized.

Quinn shook his head, as if clearing out some fragmented memory. His eyes returned to their normal blue hue. "I was saying that I met Anna a few weeks ago at Harvey's office. You know, when I was going through Feynman's works. She was great. A little quirky, funny at times, and I liked her. She was really tuned into Feynman's mathematical models. She never did tell me where she got her mathematics degree though. And she had a surprisingly good grasp of the physics behind time paradoxes..."

"What do you mean time paradoxes?" I asked.

"Well, I guess the term 'time paradox' isn't precisely accurate. It would be better to characterize our discussions in terms of her ideas about 'white holes.' Dimensional communication involving 'white holes,' to be exact. She was fixated on the idea that we live inside a white hole. And that 'clock' time exists only while we are inside the white hole." He paused.

"Seriously, Quinn. I don't understand any part of what you just said." I was so befuddled that I was afraid I would begin to twitch shortly. And, to make things worse, I could tell that he was about to give me "that" look again!

He must have reconsidered, giving me the benefit of the doubt, because he paused and then simply continued, "To put it another way, Anna argued that consciousness existed outside of the white hole we live in, and that we should be able to communicate with other dimensions."

"Other dimensions? You mean like ghosts and stuff?" I asked.

"No. More like energy dimensions; non-physical dimensions where consciousness exists; where psychic experiences and intuition come from."

"Oh?" I was really confused now. I didn't know what to say.

"Anyway, Thursday afternoon, Harvey asked me to witness Anna's Will. I had never witnessed a Will before, but he said it was simple, and it was." He paused for a moment. "That was the last time I saw Anna. You know, it was kind of funny actually."

"What do you mean, 'funny'?" I asked. "Do you mean 'ha-ha' funny or 'weird' funny?"

He considered. "Well, for one thing, she had dyed her hair bright orange. It was a little startling. When I walked into the room, she winked at me several times, so I thought she was fishing for a compliment."

"So?"

"Well, I told her that her hair looked nice." Quinn looked chagrined. He shrugged his shoulders. "What else could I say? She was a nice old woman and I didn't want to hurt her feelings. Besides, if she wanted to dye her hair orange, that was her business, and I respected her. Anyway, Harvey took me into his conference room, and I watched Anna sign her Will. Then I signed it. Then Harvey signed it." He stopped speaking.

"Anything else?" I prodded.

"There was another woman there - I don't know her name - I think she was from the other office down the hall - and she put her notary seal on the Will. That's all."

"OK." I said, trying a different track. "Did anything else important or significant happen after that?"

"Well, about that time we all had a shot of whiskey and Anna left. Then I went back to my lab to check in." Quinn paused again, considering his words. His eyes seemed to darken again as he looked at me.

I couldn't look away.

"Oh yeah." He continued. "Harvey called me later that night. He said it was important that I be at a certain place in Oakdale at 7:30 a.m. the next morning. I asked him why. He just said that there was a good chance that I might meet someone who could help me with the synchrotron if I showed up at that exact place at that exact time. He wouldn't explain any further. I didn't know who or what to expect. I was intrigued; curious. It felt right. So, I agreed. He gave me your address, and I picked you up. Now that I have you, I honestly don't know what to do with you. He never told me that you would..." and Quinn's voice trailed off.

"That I... would what?" I stammered.

"That you would be so... tasty. Like a lemon bismarck."

INTERMISSION

Chapter 13

There was a girl from Saint Paul
Who wore a newspaper dress to the ball
The dress caught on fire
and burned up her entire...
front page, sporting section and all.

OR

There was a girl from OAK DALE
Whose world view could land her in jail.
Her demands of the 'verse
kept getting worser and worse
Until she learned to exhale.

Her fortune cookie read, "Be prepared to receive something special with no strings attached."

*** HEY, UNIVERSE!

...Here I am, still waiting.***

Gracie's God

The God of Gracie is a curly-haired God.
She starts her day with sky colors and
turns them into black and
white lines on a page.

Her dreams are of houses and magic -
of cool summers with warm humid winds.
Filled with hope for places far away,
and croissants under the Tower.

The God of Gracie asks too many questions -
Why? How? When? Where?
A confused muddle of media and
mind-worms grappling for juxtaposition.

The God of Gracie
Lives
In a Changing World.

cautionary Statement: For those Readers who are firmly
entrenched in the Physical; who have never watched or did not
like the films: Joe Versus the Volcano or Hudson Hawk; or for any
Reader who believes that lawyers are rational human beings at all
times, it would be wise to stop reading this book now - or at the
very least - skip to chapter 30.

Chapter 14

The Carnegie Building

"We'd better get going. We're late. Do you know how to get to 101 West 2nd Street?" I asked Quinn.

"Sure. I can find anything. I never get lost." Quinn replied.

Oh no! "Don't say that." I mumble. "Off the record."

"What? Why not? What do you mean, 'off the record?' What record?" Quinn glanced over at me with a quizzical look in his eyes.

I am in a panic. I'm not quite sure how to explain. I plunge ahead bravely anyway. "Well, I NEVER challenge the universe in that way." Oops. I shook my head. "What I mean to say is that I have discovered that absolute statements, like the one you just uttered, are one sure way to get you into trouble. Big trouble. It's like spitting in the wind; pissing up a rope; challenging the ALL to an arm-wrestling contest. You know… tempting fate. So, I hurriedly say, 'off the record'."

"Huh?"

"Oh, just a little foible of mine." I managed a fake little giggle. I noticed that Quinn's eyebrows were beginning to meet in the middle, so I hurried on, trying to explain. "Let me restate. When I say things - accidentally - that would… seem like hubris, I simply cancel my unfortunate statement by saying, 'off the record.' I try not to say, for example, 'I will never do this thing or that thing.' This is the main way I avert disaster in my life. You know, Quinn, protection."

Flabbergasted, Quinn replied, "Gracie, I had no clue that lawyers were so superstitious. Especially you… a highly educated woman of the new millennia! And, what's that bit about challenging fate by pissing 'up' wind? Or spitting on a… rope? I mean…" His face was getting red now. "Do you create chaos everywhere you go, or are chaotic events just attracted to you?"

Heavens, he didn't take that too well, did he? Quinn continued his small tantrum by asking, "How many years of post high school education do you have anyway? Do you throw salt over your shoulder for good luck too?"

Now it was my turn to look frankly astonished. I tried to make "that face" at him. "Quinn, I'm sure you're just teasing me now, not actually trying to make me mad. But, you're getting perilously close. You just can't kid about this kind of thing. My world view is very organized and precise.

For future reference, as you already know, words are powerful things, so be careful what you say. I may not always be around to protect you."

"Well. Um." Quinn cleared his throat and apparently managed to get control of himself because he just shrugged his shoulders and raised his eyebrows[12] again. He wanted to change the subject, that was clear enough. "So, why are we meeting Harvey at that particular address anyway?" He asked.

"A reasonable question. I have no clue. We'll soon find out." I said.

We stepped out of Sara's Table and started toward the cab. Quinn and I moved to the passenger side of the cab almost simultaneously. My hand had just touched the door handle when Quinn's hand covered mine, just for a second. His hand was warm, strong, and very real. I looked up into his eyes and... swallowed. I like him, but... Wow! Everything was moving so fast. It was a good thing I was in Duluth; I needed a reality check. I stepped back and Quinn opened the door. I climbed into the front seat and he fastened my seat belt. Another touch. He circled the cab and got into the driver's seat. Saying nothing, he started the ignition and headed down the hill, toward the lake.

------

[12] I'm actually concerned that Quinn's eyebrows might get permanently stuck in the "up" position at some point. I wonder if he will still be as cute then?

I wondered what he was thinking of, just then. I, of course, was thinking that it had been so long since anyone had opened a door for me, or had even taken care to be sure I was secure and comfortable that I simply didn't know how to react. I remembered my first trial at the Government Center in Minneapolis. Opposing counsel had rushed into the Courtroom as soon as the case was called, all but slamming the door in my face. This was so different, except for the 'my heart pounding in my ears' part. That was exactly the same. Not wanting to face up to what I might feel about Quinn touching me again, I tried to distract myself by pondering if there was some kind of correlation between slamming doors and fog horns? You know, perhaps there was a magical sort of tonal hypnosis involved in the combination of slamming doors and fog horns that resulted in people being nicer to each other? Like a gigantic "ohm." It made sense, in a weird kind of way, since there were no fog horns in Hennepin County but there were plenty of slamming doors, I'd wager. So, it followed, of course, that people had an excuse for not being nice to each other. The magic was simply missing. I had managed to work myself half-way back to reality when I noticed that the cab seemed to be making a lot of turns, both up and down the hill.

To put it bluntly, for a guy who never gets lost, it seemed like Quinn had an awful hard time finding 101 West 2nd Street. Eventually he started mumbling things like, "The streets seem to run perpendicular to the hill, with the lowest numbered streets closer to the lake, but the numbered avenues apparently go up and down the hill. Um. Who would have known?" And then, "Aha! Finally, West First Street! No. Wait. It's East First Street!" And then, "Lake Avenue must be the 'zero' Avenue." Or, "What! A one-way, again!" Finally, I had to laugh right out loud when he exclaimed, "There are no cardinal points in Duluth! All the streets here are whompus!" Duh. Pretty disconcerting to a boy who grew up on the plains, huh? But, tactfully, I just smirked as I unhooked my seat belt, thirty minutes after we left Sara's Table. Hubris. Gets you into trouble every time. If my mental map of Duluth was correct, I could have walked to 101 West 2nd Street faster than Quinn managed to drive us there. But, of course, Quinn never gets lost; and he had no trouble finding 101 West 2nd Street at all, did he? Hubris, pure and simple. My point.

Quinn finally pulled up in front of a five-story stone edifice with a large rotunda centered above the roof and very impressive pillars at the front. My guess is that it was built more than a century ago. Quinn straightened up as he got out of the cab, and walked around to open my door. I quickly jumped out before Quinn could assist me and cause me to have another mini meltdown. As we both gaped at the magnificent building, he reached for my hand. One of us moved first, leading the other toward the entrance. The steps were very broad and weathered; stone steps converging at the very, very tall front doors. Quinn pulled on the enormous crafted brass door handles and we stepped together into the wide mosaic foyer, which showcased a timeless Greek keystone design underfoot.

We entered the inner sanctuary simultaneously, staring in amazement at the interior dome thirty feet above our heads. Circling the dome were pillars again, obviously marble this time. I had a visceral response though when I gazed down at the floor, carpeted in red.

"Quinn," I said, "this is so odd. I'm sure I've never been here before, but it feels like I know this place."

"Well, Babe..." On no, he called me 'Babe' again! "...maybe you came here as a child?"

"No, nothing like that. I've been to Duluth many times before, but never to this old library."

"It's a library? Where are all the books?"

I'm not sure, but some time in the late '60s or early '70s, I think - before I was born - the City built a new library on Superior Street. It's supposed to look like a Great Lakes freighter - well, maybe in somebody's dreams but..."

"How could they have abandoned this incredible structure?" Quinn asked.

"Well, they probably argued that it was too small and over-crowded, or they needed something more modern. Maybe they had some federal money they wanted to spend.

You've read about the '60s and '70s haven't you? It was all about free love and urban renewal. I think they initially sold the building to some investors from the Twin Cities. The investors probably had a vision about the fortune they'd make on a pay parking lot close to downtown - but don't get me started."

"You've got to be kidding, right? A parking lot?"

"Could be. Of course, being the left-wingers they are, some influential Duluthians blocked the destruction of the building - thank God - and here it still stands today. It's probably on the Historic Register. That's all I know. Except, I think Carnegie built it. "

"Carnegie built it?"

"Yeah. You know, that Scottish guy who built all those libraries all over the United States."

"The Carnegie that Harvey was always talking about?"

"Sure, I guess. There was really only one Carnegie. Funny. I didn't know Harvey was interested in Andrew Carnegie. How strange."

"Boy is that an understatement. You know, Gracie, when I was going through Feynman's books, Harvey said that he and Feynman used to give Carnegie a hard time about the enormous sums of money he was spending on all those public libraries he was endowing. They said he was trying to buy his way into heaven. Feynman wanted Carnegie to spend more of his money building night clubs (i.e. strip joints), so that he could 'expand his horizons'."

Now it was my turn for my eyebrows to get stuck in the "up" position.

Quinn misunderstood my surprise and continued, "Apparently Feynman enjoyed being around smart people, but he felt that most people were not observant or logical enough and they certainly didn't ask the right questions. So, he took the earthy position that basically most people would appreciate an architecturally significant strip joint rather than a library, and that Carnegie was just wasting his money - that he was going to go to hell for sure anyway."

Fully astonished now, I started to interrupt. "But…"

"Now, don't get me wrong, Feynman *is* a genius, but he had a hard time after his wife died. He got kind of wild, or so they said. Harvey said that they'd continually argue about Carnegie's spending habits, then cobble up some supper, toss down another shot and continue their discussions of space∞time. Carnegie kept building libraries; Feynman kept doing physics with a few visits to strip joints as recreation; and Harvey just well, actually, I don't know what Harvey continued to do."

By this time, I was so astonished by Quinn's diatribe that I was struck speechless, which was highly unusual for me. Quinn obviously thought I was engrossed in his story and kept going, "At first I thought it was impossible for Carnegie, Harvey and Feynman to ever have had the conversations Harvey described to me. You know, because of the age differences, of course. Carnegie died in the 1930s, - an old man. Feynman had just finished his master's work in physics before he signed on for the Manhattan Project - in the '40s. So Carnegie, Feynman, and Harvey couldn't possibly have been in the same room - as adults anyway. Harvey might be old enough to have been friends with both guys, but Feynman would have been a little kid at the time. And most kids typically don't even understand the differences between the sexes at age seven, not to mention having an opinion about strip joints! I finally concluded that Harvey was just blowing smoke; that it was all a fantasy, you know, early Alzheimer's. But since he was giving me access to Feynman's secret library, I didn't want to rock the boat by challenging him on his fantasies. Besides, being a little quirky isn't altogether bad is it? Harvey's story didn't check out until I met Feynman myself."

He winked at me, then. Or, at least I think he winked at me. Geez, what is it about guys with big eyebrows winking at women anyway? Are guys with big eyebrows required to take a class on 'How to Wink And Disarm the Opposite Sex?' Just like women with big boobs have to take a class on... oh, well, never mind.

I felt myself sliding into panic mode. I glanced up. Quinn had stopped talking abruptly, and had this strange look on his face. For the record, I usually only have to worry about my own sanity and, occasionally, the sanity of my clients. Now, however unfortunate it was, I was beginning to worry about Quinn's sanity. No possible way that Harvey could have personally known Carnegie and Feynman. Quinn got that right. So, either Quinn was lying to me about what Harvey said to him, Quinn was delusional, or Harvey himself was delusional. Using logic: Quinn and Harvey are men. One or both of them are lying or insane. Maybe all men are liars. Maybe all men are insane. Actually, that would explain quite a lot. However, this syllogism obviously leads to madness. My instinct told me that Quinn was honest. My instinct told me that Harvey could be devious and he had a lot of explaining to do, but he wasn't a liar either. And, I was the only one verging on insanity. Therefore, having faith in the honesty of most men, I reasoned that I had heard Quinn wrong.

"Quinn, I know that you don't know me well – yet – and I'm a bit touchy about people lying to me. As you know, I believe in everything, but only to a point. At this particular point, I am wondering if you misunderstood what Harvey told you about having a relationship with both Feynman and Carnegie? You know this isn't physically possible. So, are you either: 1) making fun of me? 2) think I'm an idiot? 3) trying to gauge my ability to discern fact from fiction? or..."

"Gracie..." Quinn started to reply. Then his words faded away abruptly, and we stood in silence.

Quinn looked down at Gracie, whose face was flushed with anger, or was it concern - for him? Or was it something else altogether? He wondered. He realized that she'd had quite a few unsettling experiences in the last few days but, amazingly, she wasn't freaking out. She wasn't running away from it or him; she was trying to take it all in; trying to understand. She was brave. A strong, remarkable, brave woman. Wow. And, besides, the light from the stained glass window high above them was making her face glow just like one of Mucha's fantasy beauties. He couldn't stop himself. He wanted to touch her.

"Quinn, are you all right?" I finally asked, nervously.

"I'm not sure, Gracie. At this particular moment all I really want to do is..." He stepped forward, tilted my chin up, and, with me staring helplessly into his now darkened blue and stormy eyes, he kissed me.

And it took my breath away.

This is extremely unwise, I thought. And I kissed him back.

Then I stepped back.

I looked up at him, trying to think of something to say. Something that would still the pounding of my heart. Something that would seem, well... sophisticated. Like I did this sort of thing every day. Like it wasn't that important to me. Ha! "Well, now that we got that over with..." I said in a panic. Oh, God! Why did I say that? But, I had to say something, didn't I? And then, even before I could finish one more incoherent statement, Quinn grabbed me, pulled me toward him, and kissed me again - hard.

Then he stepped back.

"Whoa," we both said simultaneously.

Then we stepped together again. After a few minutes of intense exploration, Quinn murmured, "Well that was certainly interesting and definitely worth another…"

From behind one of the columns surrounding the rotunda, I heard Harvey clear his throat. Oh shit. Good timing, Harvey, I thought, turning toward the column. Harvey stepped forward. Or, at least a muscular middle–aged guy stepped forward. He had black curly hair (not bald at all) and he had Harvey's characteristic cough, but it definitely wasn't Harvey's body. The guy was wearing white pants it is true, but he looked like… well, he looked vaguely like the man I had briefly spoken to in the elevator yesterday. That's what was so familiar about the guy in the elevator, I reasoned - he had Harvey's voice! And, watching carefully as he stepped further into the rotunda, he even walked like Harvey. So, he talks like Harvey; he walks like Harvey; well… "Harvey?" I asked. He nodded. "You sure are looking well today." I managed to gulp. "About thirty years weller, actually. More well, better, younger. Whatever." Words had finally failed me. "Harvey," I pleaded, "What the hell is going on?"

"Glad to see Quinn found you, Gracie. Perhaps we should sit down and chat. There's someone I want you to meet in the conference room downstairs."

"Harvey?" Quinn questioned.

I glanced at Quinn. He looked as dazed as I felt. I was hoping that his dazed look reflected the fervor of our now forgotten kisses, but I had the distinct impression that Quinn was as astonished and/or confused at Harvey's youthful appearance as I was. Quinn reached for my hand and we hypnotically followed Harvey to a grand staircase leading down to the lower level of the building.

Constantly moving, Harvey prattled on about the original mosaic floors; how a generous and forward–thinking family in Duluth, the Johnson's, had been restoring the building for years; all the original colors and cost of construction; the current use of the building, etc. Finally, as my incredulity diminished, I asked, "Harvey, did you have a body transplant or something?"

"Well, Gracie, that's not exactly too far off. Actually, you could say that Quinn here... glancing over at Quinn and at his hand in mine... is something of a magician of time. He knows just the right 'spells' to bridge time and space. So, it's actually Quinn's doing that I am looking (and feeling by the way) so much better today." I turned to look at my hand still clasped in Quinn's hand, and Quinn exclaimed: "Harvey, what the hell - a time magician? You've got to be kidding me. Can't you and Feynman come up with some better label than 'time magician'? I have no credibility whatsoever with a label like that."

"Well, what about 'temporal mechanic' then? It has a nice new-age ring to it." Harvey replied with a crooked grin.

By this time I was getting a little perturbed with both Harvey and with Quinn. If this was a joke, I wasn't getting it. Harvey must have sensed the tension, and he turned to me saying, "Don't worry, Gracie, it will all be revealed shortly." He finally stepped into the conference room, followed closely by both Quinn and I. There in front of the fireplace, pouring tea and setting out chocolate chip cookies was a stunningly beautiful woman with flowing red hair. She appeared to be just a little older than me, maybe in her middle 30s, and her clothing reflected Harvey's apparent taste, sort of 1960ish. You know, a tie-dyed sundress and platform strappy shoes. As we entered the room, she glanced up and moved to the door. She grasped my hand and drew me close. "Gracie, my dear child!" She embraced me warmly, and as I glanced up I noticed there were tears in her eyes.[13] After a moment, I looked over her shoulder at Harvey who had the most peculiar look on his face.

---

[13] I don't usually elicit that kind of reaction in people when I meet them for the first time; they usually wait until after they get my first bill to cry.

"Harvey? Who..."

He said, "Gracie, this is your mother, and my wife. Her name is also Grace. Grace Swan Waterston. I felt my skin tingle and my ears began to ring. Oh no! Not twice in the same week! I must have a brain tumor, I thought, as my knees began to buckle. Harvey moved quickly but Quinn reached my side first. Sensory overload, I remember thinking. For a moment I felt as if I was enclosed in a luminous circle, a dancing circle of white light. And then all the lights went out. Again.

Chapter 15

A Leap of Faith – or – Jumpin' Jack Flash

The old Stones' tune, "Jumpin' Jack Flash" was playing in my head when I awoke and found myself stretched out on a blue-velvet sofa near the fireplace. I felt a little fuzzy, warm, and Quinn's concerned gaze warmed me too. Wow, this is what it must feel like when... I looked down. His giant paw still held my smaller one. I said, "Quinn, you won't believe my dream. I thought that Harvey was here and he was thirty years younger. He said he was my dad and introduced me to this beautiful woman who he said was my mother! Unbelievable! I must have been hallucinating. Wait. Did you put something in my tuna fish sandwich yesterday? Maybe it was the coffee this morning? I want you to know that I do not, as a rule, lose consciousness twice in the same week, no matter what the provocation." Quinn said nothing. I finally stopped babbling.

"It wasn't a dream, was it?" In answer, Quinn unfolded his large body and stepped aside. And there they were, Harvey and the beautiful red-haired woman (my mother??)

He nodded and began… "Gracie, remember when I said that I thought you could help me in my work?"

"Sure, but I thought it was just a come-on line, Quinn. Cute, but a come on."

"No, Gracie, it was true, although I didn't know you then, or even…" he rushed on, "…or even how connected we seem to have become. I didn't know that Harvey was your dad, or that Anna had died in your office. And now…"

I saw Harvey glance over at the beautiful redhead and nod, a curious look in his eyes; then he spoke directly to me. "It may be a little hard, at first, for you to believe what I have to tell you now - in light of your training as a lawyer. But try and keep up."

I gave him a snotty look. "Well?" I said. "Get to it. You've got a lot of explaining to do!"

As the "old" Harvey used to do, he scratched his head, not bald now, and continued, "What I mean… I encouraged you to go into the law because I thought it would help stretch your imagination and insight, so that you would have the capacity to understand different perspectives and realities. You got that part good, Gracie. But, I had no idea…" Harvey started to explain, but apparently decided to start over. I looked down as I felt him take my hand in his. "Oh hell. I didn't anticipate how out of sync and alone you would feel at times. For that, I'm sorry. I did the best I could." Harvey's, now handsome face seemed sad - or, maybe it was compassion I was reading on his face? Whoa! I thought. What's going on here? Do I have cancer; did I grow a second nose, or what?

He glanced over at my so-called "mother," the beautiful redheaded lady, again. There was a long pause as some silent communication passed between them.

This was just too weird. Seriously considering taking another short but profound nap, I replied in a panic, "but how can you be my father – my parents were killed in a car accident before I was a year old. You know - Edith raised me. You were my next-door neighbor, weren't you? Not my dad! And where did she…" gesturing at the beautiful red-haired lady, "come from?" I continued, "Besides, you're too young to be my father. He would be almost seventy years old today."

"Gracie, remember? I was almost seventy years old just yesterday!" My lower lip began to quiver and my face paled again. Quinn quickly jumped to my side and took hold of my hand, pushing Harvey's hand aside.

Harvey elbowed Quinn aside and kneeled next to me. "It's all true, Gracie. You know it is. I know you. I taught you. You're open to just about everything. You always strive to understand the meaning behind all events, even the weirdest stuff. You're empathetic to a fault. You don't pass

151

judgment, even if your clients are far different than you. Actually, Gracie, most of the time you don't even 'see' your clients. You just 'feel' them."

"Harvey, that's just not true!" I shouted.

"Gracie, you didn't even realize that President Obama was black until I told you!"

"Well," Gracie hesitated, "he just didn't seem black to me."

"Sure. Like I said, you tend to 'feel' people, not 'see' them. In fact, Gracie, over the years, I've noticed that your clients tend to be among the most outlandish of all people. It's almost as if you had a neon sign flashing outside your office door. Admit it! The most bizarre cases and personalities seem to gravitate toward you. Remember the lady who was afraid of clocks? The fellow who could only speak in analogies? Or the lady who said that the mayor of North Saint Paul had hired an assassin to kill her? You remember, the one who told you she had been impregnated by aliens?" Harvey continued to frown at me. "You know what I mean, Gracie. Don't try to deny it!"

"Okay, Harvey," the redhead interrupted. "I think Gracie gets your point, but maybe some kind of explanation is in order." I felt the beautiful red-haired woman take hold of my other hand, pushing away Harvey's hand. (I almost felt sorry for Harvey, with no hand to hold.) Her grasp was warm, tentative at first, then stronger, comforting. I could not pull my hand away. There was some kind of connection here. It was a little like a small electric current running from her hand to mine. A little comfort, somehow. My heart raced and I looked directly at her. "You tell me."

"Gracie, do you remember the time you stood gazing out of the window at the lake, wondering whether there was anything worth living for? Whether life itself was worth the continuing struggle? Asking all the profound questions of life, when you were only a little girl. About fourteen or fifteen years old, weren't you?"

I nodded.

"Do you remember what happened?"

"Well," I gulped. "How do you know about that time?" I asked, wondering. I had never told anyone about the despair and hopelessness that I had been feeling at that time in my life. How could she know?

She ignored my question. "Tell me what happened, Gracie." She commanded.

"Well, I know this is strange, but I heard a voice or something that seemed like a voice in my head saying that it was all going to be OK - that I should hang in there - that things would be better and be really good... great, in fact. Not to despair... not to give up." WAIT. Isn't that what Quinn said to me at Sara's Table just a few minutes ago? How could he...? Everyone was staring at me now, waiting for an answer.

"And?" The redhead gently prodded, with an unreadable smile on her face.

I shook my head, trying to re-focus. "Well, everything turned out OK, just like the voice said. It felt like, somehow, that I was getting an answer from myself. An answer from the future."

"And?"

"And, I guess I hung in there, and everything turned out OK. But, now I'm here, looking at you and Harvey, and still not understanding. And, furthermore, I'm in a shitload of trouble with the Lawyer's Board."

"And?"

"This 'And' stuff is getting kind of old, Grace. Or, Mom? Oh... whatever!"

"So, tell me what's really going on - tell me the good stuff."

"The good stuff?"

"Yes."

I considered a moment and then just spouted off. "Well, there's Quinn, there's you, and there's Harvey - crazy as an old - well young - well some kind of coot, but he's OK too. Not harmed anyway, even if he's crazy."

"So, you have your answer."

"What do you mean, 'I have my answer?' I have no answers!"

"I mean that when you felt all alone, wondering whether to go on, you were able to make the connection. The connection to yourself in the future; to me; to all of the love that surrounds you, past, present and future. To nature, to God."

"Are you God?"

There was a loud hoot, and we all looked over at Harvey who was rolling his eyes. "You went a little overboard with all that stuff didn't you, darling? Better simplify it for Gracie, in her terms, so she doesn't get the idea that we are members of the Greek pantheon, or come from Valhalla, or something like that."

The redhead... my mother... the beautiful lady... whatever.... glared at Harvey (appropriately so, in my opinion), and then she continued, looking back at me: "We were connected then, you see, as we are connected now. I found you when you reached out - looking for some kind of connection, some understanding. Your response, from yourself, was that everything would be OK. I know this sounds absurd, but it's all true."

At my blank look, she continued, "The easiest way to understand it is that all of creation is sacred and alive. When I say 'all,' I mean it; every part. Each part is connected to each other part."

"So?" My ears were beginning to ring again.

"So, because of this connectedness, each of us has the potential ability to communicate with each other, and with our own selves, into the past, present and future. This is because the smallest parts of you, and the biggest parts of you, are equally involved."

"You mean, like Quinn's micro and macro universe being quantum?" I wondered out loud. "There's really a connection there?"

The beautiful lady continued. "Yes. Yes indeed." Her face was radiant now. "These ideas form the foundation for wondrous creativity and establish the basis for all communication. You really didn't think that the so-called computer on top of your head - your brain - is the place where consciousness begins, did you?"

"Well, I guess not," I said hesitantly.

At my perplexed expression, Harvey jumped in. "Listen up, my girl. Backward and forward in time, it makes no difference. Time makes no difference. It's all about connections."

"Connections?"

"Geez," Harvey grumbled, looking over at his wife, the beautiful red-haired lady, "with about ten years of post-high school education, you'd think she wouldn't be so dense. It's not as if she hasn't had all these psychic experiences all along. Rumbles from all of the other goddamn dimensions - so to speak," Harvey interrupted. But with one glare from his wife, Harvey shut up - again.

The redhead continued, "I am your mother. I am connected to you. And, even though I was not present – in the sense of standing next to you - in your dimensional space – I knew that you needed me then. So I reached out to help you make a connection with your future self."

"So, so... go on," I stammered. At this point, things were so strange and unsettling, that it didn't make any sense for me to do anything other than listen. And, by God, the Goddess, the Force, the Universe, the good... or... whatever... I wanted to know what the hell was going on. I vowed to listen all day and all night if it was necessary. I wouldn't let anyone stop talking until I could put it all together in some fashion. I would have to decide whether to call the cops and have everyone transported to the Psych Ward sooner or later, but not quite yet.

"Well, Gracie, when you heard your own voice from the future tell you that things were going to be good - really great actually - it piqued your curiosity. Your unrelenting curiosity. You viscerally understood and accepted the truth of that statement. It had to be true. You needed that contact because it generated both faith and curiosity. Enough for you to continue. You recognized - every single part of your whole being recognized the truth of our connectedness. Every single cell, every single atom, knew with certitude that all would be well."

Wow! Heaven help me, looking at the concern and sincerity in the beautiful redhead's eyes (my mother?), this whole thing was beginning to make some sort of weird sense. If we all were connected, then it would explain how I knew things, sometimes, that I shouldn't be able to know. Were my feelings, my instincts about a situation or client right on the mark, most of the time, because I could make this sort of connection? Glancing over at Quinn, I said, "Does any of this make sense to you? Do you understand what she's talking about, I mean? About what's happening here? Why Harvey is thirty years younger? Or how I can talk to myself from the future, I mean the past, I mean...?" I stopped for air. "How are you and I involved in all of this? Are we really connected to each other?" I was forced to stop, gasping for air.

Startled by my outburst, Quinn gulped and blinked. He glanced over at Harvey who grinned, nodded, and gave Quinn a thumbs-up sign and a little shove. "The best explanation that I can give you, right now, before we can get back to my lab, is that it's all about consciousness. All forms of energy being conscious - containing consciousness. You see, my research was uncovering - revealing you could say - some very improbable connections. Like the time..." As if being forced to make a confession, Quinn rubbed his forehead with two fingers, rotated his neck from side to side, squared his shoulders, stroked his chin, and continued, "...like at the beginning, the day Harvey stormed into my office, I mean. Remember, I told you about that?" I nodded.

"When Harvey showed up, my machine was going through a series of oscillations and started giving idiosyncratic readings, but Harvey just kept getting happier and happier. Like some weirded-out Looney Tune character. Needless to say, I had some trouble under-standing why Harvey was so goddamn happy. He started humming some old song, in fact. When none of the readings seemed to make any sense, when my whole staff was ready to run for the bomb shelter, Harvey was grinning like a mindless idiot."

With a sheepish look on his face, Quinn glanced over at Harvey, "Sorry, Harvey," he said, and then turned, looking back at me.

"Wait," I said, "you have a bomb shelter at the U?"

"Of course. Then when Feynman got involved, he also kept getting more and more excited and his calculations..."

"Wait, Quinn, you mean you really met Feynman? I thought you said he worked on the Manhattan project, you know, during WWII? Wouldn't he be about 150 years old by now - dead for certain? How could you have met Feynman?"

"Well, that's the thing, Gracie, I did meet Feynman, and he was able to help me work out some details about..."

I broke into a cold sweat, began to shake, and reached for my cell phone to call "9-1-1." The beautiful but certainly weird lady came over and sat on the chaise next to me, putting her arm around my shoulder. Giving Quinn and Harvey a commanding look, she said, "We need to take this down a notch, and start at the beginning." Her eyes were so compelling and kind. OK, I thought, a little more enlightenment, a little more information would probably assist the psych doctors anyway. I tentatively put my cell phone down, hoping for some clarity. She nodded, took a shaky breath, and continued, "Dear One. Darling daughter. Yes, is true. It's all true. I will summarize as best I can. Your father - Harvey - and Quinn can fill in the details later. They've been around here much longer than I have been; they know the rules of this dimension so much better."

I was beginning to truly hyperventilate now. Monitoring my increasing anxiety, Harvey said to his wife, "Yes, you go for it, darling. I'm quite sure your last few statements will inspire confidence in us and help Gracie understand our predicament."

"Sorry." The beautiful redhead said, squeezing Harvey's hand. Glancing back at me, she took a deep breath and began again, "My name is Grace Swan - you are named after me; you are a part of me. You have always wondered about who you are, the good of what you do, your connection with the universe. That is because you are more. You may not want to believe it - not just yet - but you do not fit in for a very real reason. You are a multi-dimensional person living in a 3D universe."

"No kidding. Her? Fit in this box-world? Gracie couldn't fit herself inside this self-constructed box-world if she wanted to." Harvey interrupted. "In my opinion, she doesn't even know there is a box, or even a world for that matter, most of the time."

"Harvey, let me handle this," the beautiful redhead said, frowning at Harvey. "Dear one, one could say that you are psychically charged, attracting certain events and people into your life because of the nature of who you are."

Dumbfounded and enthralled, I couldn't utter a word.

The beautiful redhead continued as if what she was saying made perfect sense. "Keep in mind, the fundamental rule is that we are all connected to each other. That is the most important part. Where should I begin?" She asked herself, then answered her own question. "Ah, at the very beginning?"

I nodded for her to continue.

"The simplest way to describe it, is that Harvey and I were deeply in love with each other. Glancing at Harvey for a brief moment, her eyes became darker and more luminous. I believed her, but said nothing. Then she continued. "There are deep and intimate connections in each kind of existence, you know. I don't have to explain that to you, do I, Gracie?" She looked up for confirmation from me, then glanced at Quinn, and continued without stopping. "Harvey and I belong in what you would classify as a kind of... energy dimension. Before you were born, Harvey was involved in the study of multi-dimensional physics, similar to what Quinn is presently working on in his lab. I was more of what you might refer to as a social scientist. I was studying the human personality - the ever changing physically-charged individualized energies of certain types of consciousness. The way some personalities possess a special perceptive freedom. How some personalities can at times reach outside of their own dimensional space to connect with other types of consciousness. These special people can somehow sidestep 'clock time' and move into 'psychological time'."

"What do you mean 'psychological time?'" I finally managed to make my voice work.

"Psychological time is... a place... a state of being where time has no relevance. A place outside of time. A place where decades of "clock time" can pass in just moments of psychological time. In your terms, you might think of it as a light trance state - with benefits. Using psychological time, some individual personalities are able to free themselves from the constraints of dimensionality. They are explorers of the new age..." The redhead elaborated.

"Geez, Louise, Grace," you're making it sound like we're ghosts or something," Harvey complained. "We're just as solid as Gracie is. We have the same challenges; we just don't usually have to..."

"Wait, let me get this straight. You're an inter-dimensional social worker?" I said, aghast. My worst fears were realized. Wow. Social workers existed in all universes! So, realtors probably did too! Great! I'm now truly entering the Twilight Zone.

The redhead answered. "Well, not exactly. But that's another story. Anyway, Harvey and I got mixed up in some kind of inter-dimensional tangle, you could say, just minutes after you were born. One of Harvey's experiments."

"Wait a minute, Grace, you know it wasn't just me. Carnegie and I had verified all of the data before the incident..." Harvey began.

"We'll discuss that later," the redhead turned to Harvey, giving him a stern look that shut him up again. Then, she returned her gaze to me and continued. "Obviously, I don't understand it all exactly. I think it had something to do with the physical act of giving birth - my labor. Something no man could 'verify.' Something went seriously wrong, and I sort of 'blinked out.' I guess I was thrown back to our initiation point - alone. I thought Harvey was lost forever. After awhile it all seemed like a dream. I'm not sure why, but I had almost convinced myself that my pregnancy was just a dream - all the morning sickness, the enormous belly, and so on. It felt like none of my experiences in your dimension had been real at all. I should have recognized the truth all along. That every bit of it was real, but that I had simply lost the connection."

"You couldn't have known, Grace." Harvey interrupted. "It was beyond your understanding at the time. Feynman and I didn't even know what had happened. We were even cut off from Carnegie for awhile." Harvey interjected.

The redhead continued. "Well, it turns out that Harvey was trapped here - in your universe of matter, but about thirty years forward in clock time - your time. That's one of the reasons I couldn't find him or you. I was looking in the wrong place. I should have trusted what I really know; that life never ends. After awhile I stopped searching because I didn't trust myself." Her eyes widened; she took in a breath. "That day, when you were a little girl, searching for meaning - I found you. Because we are connected. And, finding you, I located Harvey in your time and dimension. It was a miracle." Her smile was radiant. "Then, when Quinn's machine re-opened the portal, I had hope that I could actually bring Harvey and you back home." With this statement, she reached for Harvey's hand. "Gracie, you are a child of both dimensions. Somehow, you have become the foci, the focus point for this inter-dimensional tangle."

"Me? A focus point? Are you kidding?" Most of the time I try to hide from the limelight. "Why me? What does it mean to be a focus point, anyway? Harvey?" I could feel my blood pressure rising precipitously fast; definitely on the way to a full-blown panic attack.

"It's hard to put words to it, Gracie, it's so conceptual, although your mother has stated the basics well enough. Quinn understands the intricacies much better than I do in this dimension, but I'll give it a shot." He cleared his throat. "To put it simply though, it's similar to the physics concept of 'entanglement.' It appears that Quinn's machine created some kind of a dimensional time loop, focused on you and, strangely enough, Anna."

"Anna? Anna who?" I questioned. "Oh no! You can't mean that strange old lady who died in my office last Thursday night!"

"Well. Yeah. That Anna." Harvey verified. "If we are able to get Quinn's machine to work right by calibrating it correctly, then Quinn will be able to send your mother and I back to our own dimensional space. I've been here with you Gracie, for almost thirty years. I need to go home."

"You mean, like in the movie, ET? You're the funny looking alien?"[14]

"You could say that."

"And Quinn's machine 'phoned home' for you?

---

[14] Steven Spielberg's, "ET, The Extra Terrestrial."

"Pretty much, although a somewhat lame analogy." Harvey said. The redhead coughed, and gave him an inexplicable look. "Right enough," Harvey corrected.

"Harvey!" I exclaimed. Understanding just a little, "So, all these odd things that have been happening to me have been caused by the malfunctioning of Quinn's machine?"

"That's not exactly true, and you know it, Gracie. You've always been psychically charged. If anything odd is going to happen, it will certainly happen to you or around you." Harvey replied sheepishly.

Harvey and Quinn both nod in agreement.

"And, I'm not supposed to be here?" I asked with a quiver in my voice.

"Wait, no. I didn't say that." Harvey tried to reassure me.

The beautiful lady jumped in, "You are exactly where you are meant to be, doing exactly what you are meant to do, but you will need to make some very important choices soon. Gracie, remember always that you are a creature of light and energy, no matter what dimension you are in. There is no one quite like you. The type of transformation that occurred when you were born here, and not in your home dimension, was unique."

"You mean – like – I'm a freak? Or, some kind of Virgin Mary?" I squeaked.

"Well, I wouldn't put it that way. Not precisely." Harvey said with a lopsided grin, considering. "Hum. I actually never looked at it that way before."

"Darling!" the beautiful lady coughed tactfully.

"Wait a minute." I interjected. "What about Anna? Remember, Anna? Anna Strong, the old lady who died in my office?" I turned my gaze from the beautiful lady, perhaps my mother, back to Harvey.

Quinn and the beautiful lady turned to look at Harvey as well. "Yeah. How the hell does Anna fit into all of this?" Quinn voiced the question for everyone.

Harvey spoke directly to Quinn, "Well, as far as I can figure it out, at the time of the accident which sent my wife back to our home dimension, Anna materialized - somehow - and was dragged forward in time, trapped with Gracie and me. I think Anna was some sort of physical copy of my wife. Probably caused by the faulty transference in your dimension. A kind of 'fragment' or splinter soul, you might say, of my beautiful wife." Harvey nodded at the beautiful lady. "She had all of Grace's memories up until the energy burst - the inter-dimensional tangle - occurred. After that, her life was totally and completely separate. She had her own soul, her own memories, her own life experiences. She was a full and unique person altogether."

"A knock-off?" I said.

"Well, something like that. Yeah. I guess so. I've tried to figure this out over the years, without much success. Like I said, Anna's personality possessed some aspects very similar to your mother's, but there were some large differences as well. Anna was always a little off, you know. I think she somehow inherited the weirder traits."

"My weirder traits? What weirder traits?" The red-haired lady said sharply.

"Sorry." Harvey hastily apologized, but fearlessly continued, "Anna was able to manage fairly well on her own, and we kept in pretty close touch over the years. But she wasn't you. That was clear from the start.

Harvey turned back to Gracie and continued, "Anna's body aged faster than mine did, and she actually seemed to get battier as time went on. She eventually had a passion for anything that was orange–colored. She was also a psychic." He glanced over at the beautiful lady, and explained, "You remember, my Dear, 'a psychic' is a label used in this world for someone who has 'unusual' gifts - in their terms - extrasensory perception, precognition, clairvoyance, that kind of stuff. You know - any direct knowledge accessed outside of the rational-thinking paradigm - not able to be quantified by their 'science,' so to speak, so routinely ignored."

"She certainly rejected any of my theories about space and time, that's for sure." Quinn added. "But we had a great deal of fun debating the subject."

Harvey exhaled sharply before he continued. "Bluntly, Anna's psyche wasn't bounded by cause and effect theories. She rejected your world's ideas of time, and intuitively understood that all true concepts have their origins outside of this 3D box. She wasn't subtle about it either. That's one of the reasons she had such a hard time fitting in. However, as a result of these certain 'attributes' and her inherent shrewdness, Anna had a very interesting life and managed to accumulate a great deal of wealth."

"Quinn told me that her chocolate chip cookies were excellent too." I interjected. Harvey nodded, and turned back to the beautiful red-haired lady. "Actually, Anna's cookies were almost as good as yours are, Darling." Harvey said as he moved over to touch his wife's hand and to lovingly smooth her red curls. I thought I heard a small sigh escape his throat. The beautiful red-haired lady briefly rested her head on Harvey's chest.

Quinn had been steadily moving closer to me, as if he were standing guard - my own personal sentry. At this point, I had the urge to move into his arms to make all this weirdness disappear. If only it were that simple. It would have been nice to have someone - someone like Quinn rescue me. But, I knew it wasn't Quinn's job to rescue me. I had to rescue myself. I was used to rescuing myself anyhow. I had been doing it for quite awhile. Besides, if something was developing between Quinn and myself, I didn't want it to be based on a victim/hero kind of scenario. I looked up at Quinn. His eyes held a question. I knew what he was asking. I wasn't ready to answer. I looked away.

After a moment, Harvey went on, "Anna took a great interest in your life, Gracie. She fronted the money for your education. She kept a journal of her ideas which she felt would change your life and the world in general – but her personality was just too erratic, too unpredictable to fit into mainstream America."

"I see that happening more and more all the time. People becoming less and less able to cope. Sometimes they can't even manage the simple day to day stuff. In that sense, Anna and I are pretty similar, I guess. If I have to add one more app to my phone I'm going to explode." I said. No one commented.

"There were a couple of times that I had to intervene to keep her from being committed." He meaningfully paused. "I mean Anna, not Gracie." Then Harvey continued. "She was never a danger to herself or to anyone else, but she was definitely outlandish in her appearance and in her affect. Anna desperately wanted to meet you Gracie, and to talk to you, especially in the last few months. She was almost frantic about it. We discussed, over and over, that when the time was right, she would be able to meet you, give you her journal, and try to explain as much of all of this as she could. I had to be certain you were ready. And I had to be certain there wasn't some sort of energy event that would occur when you two finally did meet - just like when you were born. We didn't need another Anna too."

Yikes. I thought. Remembering the weird, old, orange-haired lady who had died in my office. How would the world cope with two Anna's? I couldn't even handle one.

"But, when the portal opened as a result of Quinn's experiments, Anna began to deteriorate rapidly, both physically and mentally, and she insisted on meeting you - immediately. She also wanted to be sure that she could pass along her wealth to you. Unfortunately, we had run out of time, so to speak."

Quinn said, "There must be a connection. Some kind of temporal problem with Anna and your wife existing simultaneously in the same dimension."

Harvey nodded, agreeing, "The trigger event was probably when Gracie's mother crossed over to find me."

"When was that?" Quinn asked.

"Last Wednesday." Harvey replied.

Harvey turned back to me. "There was no time left, Gracie, as it turned out. Anna insisted on meeting you the next day, on Thursday, at your office." He sighed, reaching for my hand. "I arranged for your mother and Anna to meet at my office Thursday morning. It was quite amazing really. Your mother had no clue that Anna even existed - as a sort of fragment of herself - and it was kind of funny. Well - when it wasn't awkward, of course. Anna told her about you, and showed her the journal she had been keeping for you. They actually talked for hours. Your mother ending up drafting Anna's Will. Anna sure couldn't do it right." He paused with a pained looked on his face. "You know the rest."

"Wait, so my mother," I glanced over at the beauty holding Harvey's hand, "drafted Anna's Will?" The logic circuits began working again in my brain! "My mother is Grace Swan 'Waterston', and she drafted Anna's Will? This means that I'm not in trouble, right, Harvey? The Will leaves everything to me, but since I didn't write the Will, it's OK under the ethical rules, right? I mean, someone else - my mother - wrote the Will! I'm off the hook."

Harvey raised his eyebrows. "Well, it turns out..." Harvey began.

I interrupted. "Oops - still a problem. My mother is not a lawyer. This means that she is practicing law without a license – a violation..."

"No, Gracie. When your father and I were working in your world - here, I mean - I was a lawyer, in your terms. Or at least I was registered as a lawyer in this jurisdiction. It was a good way for me to blend in while studying the interactions in your dimensional space - before the energy tangle which parted us." My mother answered.

Now that was really hard to believe. Yet it opened up a whole new world of possibilities! Were there other time-traveling interstellar social workers admitted to the Bar? But, as always, hope continued to emerge. All of the possibilities of exoneration were playing out in my head, so I continued babbling, "So, the ethical rules would allow you to write the Will. Right? But, wait, you still can't write Anna's Will and leave everything to someone in your own family - ME. I'm your daughter, so that's still a violation of the ethical rules." I stammered. Oh, so close! "Unless…"

Completing my train of thought, Harvey said, "It would be, if you weren't related to Anna."

"Huh? What do you mean?" I almost shouted, my heart beating fast with hope. I turned to Harvey who, once again, had this weird look on his face. "Harvey?" I queried.

"Well, I had to give Anna some credibility in this dimension since she didn't exactly exist - in your terms."

There was a stunned silence. "Harvey, what did you do?" We all said simultaneously.

In a sheepish tone, Harvey replied, "Actually, not that much. Some identification papers, of course. It was fairly simple." All eyes were on Harvey now.

"Well, I was already Harvey Waterston. My wife had disappeared - gone missing actually - but a missing person is still presumed to be alive under Minnesota law unless a Court makes a legal finding that she is dead. I refused to go that far. So, Anna Strong became my wife's sister, my sister-in-law. It made sense, since Anna was a part of Grace, albeit a weird part, but technically a part."

"So, if Anna is my mother's sister - legally - it means that…"

"Yep. It means that Anna Strong, the old lady who died in your office last Thursday night, was legally your aunt. So, no problem-o."

I gulped. What did I feel? Relief. Hope. Wonderment. And then, all is not lost, but what have I found?

"A friend helps you move. A real friend helps you move a body."

Chapter 16

New Friends and Lovers
(Make Plans to Save the World)

~Part I~

"So, what's the plan?" I ask as I look up at the three people staring down at me.

"The plan?" They repeat in unison.

"Well, we've got to do something about 'something', right? Even if I don't understand what that 'something' is. So, what's the plan of action?" I ask.

"Always thinking ahead aren't you? Just like your mother." Harvey grinned proudly. "Well, first things first. Your mother and I have to meet with a couple of colleagues this afternoon; then we'll know more." Harvey continued.

"You're meeting with Carnegie and Feynman this afternoon?" Quinn asked Harvey.

"Sush!" Harvey grimaced. "For heaven's sake, Quinn, Gracie needs to settle a bit. We need her to be up to speed and on board before Tuesday. Don't scare her anymore!" It looked like Harvey's hair was standing up.

"What do you mean, 'get Gracie on board'? On board for what?" I was beginning to get a little worried - again.

Finally getting the drift, Quinn said, "I tell you what, Gracie and I need some fresh air and some dinner. Then we'll go back to the Cottage for a good night's rest. Can we talk tomorrow? Remember, we have to be at the lab no later than Tuesday at 7:00 p.m."

Harvey nodded. "Right-o. That'll work." He glanced at his wife. "We'll make it work. Text me if it gets too complicated." Quinn nods at Harvey and his wife, takes my hand, and moves me to the door. He buttons me into my coat, and plops my hat on my head. "Got your gloves?" He says, just as if we had just concluded a nice social visit with two normal people, or as if we had been married 100 years.

"Quinn..." I start.

"Oh, and Quinn," Harvey interjected. "Better tell Gracie about the syzygy."

"OK." Quinn replied as he took my hand and reached for my arm to steady me.

"Syzygy?" Puzzled, I glared at Harvey. "What's a sy... thing ... zy?" Harvey didn't answer, but just winked at me.

For the record, I do most certainly wish that people would stop winking at me. My first really significant "winking" memory was of a criminal law professor labeling me as "the hanging judge." Every time he needed an example of frontier justice, he would wink at me, just before he called on me in class. Like we were the collaborators in some sort of private joke. Never and never! For a very shy and private person like me - I used to be shy - being forced to respond whenever a hanging judge's opinion was required was excruciating.

In other words, by using the Socratic method (along with the "winking" protocol"), Professor Trowbridge regularly set me up for a fall. Literally. Ah, but the Socratic method works so well, you say. It's nothing but role-playing, you say. No, it's torture, pure and simple. Let there be no doubt, the Socratic method in law school has one purpose and one purpose only. It is meant to transform a shy, contemplative, idealistic, and perhaps well-balanced personality, into an argumentative asshole. It works like this. A naive 1L (first year law student) will eagerly raise his or her hand in response to an innocent question, unwittingly aligning himself or herself with an esoteric point of law. In my case, Professor Trowbridge was attempting to explain the concept of "justifiable homicide." His scenario went something like this: You and your four buddies are climbing a mountain. A blizzard comes up. You have roped yourselves together for safety. You are the third guy down from the top of the rope. You look up and notice that the rope is fraying badly from the sharp rocks. The rope above you is only strong enough to hold one person, not three. If you do nothing, the rope will break within seconds, and you and your two buddies below you will plunge to your certain deaths. So, you deliberately take out your knife and cut the rope below you, consigning your two buddies straight to hell. Essentially, you have committed murder. But, only two lives are lost instead of three. Mitigating factor? That is, isn't murder justified under some extreme circumstances? At least you preserved the life of one person - YOU. Should you be prosecuted for homicide? Your act was intentional; there was no doubt that your buddies would die. Stupidly excited and taking the moral high ground, I opened my mouth and responded: "There is no such thing as justifiable homicide." Voilà! So, for the next forty-five minutes and periodically for the <u>entire rest of the semester</u>, I was the "hanging judge," forced to respond to every argument set out by Professor Trowbridge and other law students taking a contrary position. All in aid of argument. And, to top it all off, the old bugger was always winking at me. A traumatic experience to say the least. No wonder I shy away from criminal law. Whenever someone telephones me on any criminal law matter, I immediately hand the phone to the nearest available person, be it waitress or veterinarian. They surely know more about criminal law than I do. That is, unless they're hanging on a rope below me in a blizzard. Then I know exactly what to do.

I was jerked back to the present by Quinn's, "The way our universe operates is largely unknown..." Seeing the blank look on my face and misunderstanding my confusion, Quinn takes my mittened hand into his own stating, "Don't worry. We'll find the answers. Together." I notice that my heart rate accelerates slightly. Must be the influence of the frigid air, I surmise. Quinn opens the door to his cab and I slide into the passenger seat. I buckle the seat belt myself this time. Then he walks around to the driver's side and slides himself in, starts the engine, and turns the heat on full blast. Eventually the heater begins to put out some real heat, but just barely.

We ride around in silence for awhile. My heart rate returns to normal. Quinn points the cab down the hill toward the lake to Canal Park. He crosses the lift bridge and we ride all the way to the end of Park Point. Then he stops the car, leaves the engine running, and cracks his window open a bit.

He spoke, "Gracie," he said, "I think we should go back to the Cottage. We need to map out all of the connections to get a better understanding of what's going on. We have to try to fill in the gaps and calculate the flux points."

"What do you mean?" I asked.

"Well, I have a whiteboard set up in the workroom at the Cottage and we can try a visual mapping of the data points to begin with. I can use the internet connection to cross-reference the data with the computer in my lab and ..."

"You mean, like set up a victim blackboard in a forensic lab?" I was getting excited now. "Drawing lines to show all the connections between the victims?"

"That's the general idea, but no victims - yet. Come to think of it, that might be just the thing. If we can diagram all of the points of intersection it might help us understand the sequencing for the projection. We've only got about seventy-two hours."

Gulp. "What do you mean we only have 72 hours? Seventy-two hours before what?" I said, alarmed again. "Are we talking tragedy here, or a simple apocalypse?" At Quinn's blank look, I continued, "As in 'a tragedy of the Shakespearian type where all the main characters die at the end' or, as in 'a disclosure of knowledge, hidden from humanity in an era dominated by falsehood and mis-conception, i.e., a lifting of the veil or revelation?'"

"Huh?" Quinn responded.

"Wikipedia." I said, batting my eyes at him. "You're not the only person with resources, you know!"

"Oh. No. Actually I meant the next intersection of the universes, of course. The portal."

"What?"

"The connection between the universes, the exact time and place - so that Harvey and your mother can get back."

"Get back to where?"

Quinn had a surprised look on his face. "Back to their own dimensional universe, of course."

"Of course? You actually believe they are time traveling/dimensional/energy... physicist and social worker... people? Seriously?"

"Why not? There is no other logical explanation for everything that's happened in my lab, and for all the stuff that's happened to you lately - probably your whole life. You're the foci. The connection must be us. It must have something to do with the syzygy - the biological connection between us - you and me." Quinn said this with that totally "ah ha!" look on his face, as if his conclusion was crystal clear to everyone who understood anything at all.

Exasperated. I had finally reached the "end of my limits." I had an uncontrollable urge to do something. Something physical. Perhaps kick someone. I needed to take some kind of directed action, but my options were extremely limited. I could get out of the cab and hitchhike back to Saint Paul, 147 miles away - in a blizzard - or... Essentially, the problem was that all I could do was to keep gibbering. Typical of my type of panic attacks. It was clear that things were devolving out of my control. I went through the litany: I can't control the weather. I can't control my clients. I can't control Harvey; my so-called mother; Tom; or the Lawyer's Board. I couldn't control Anna. And I've never had a hope of controlling Natalie. I was a sieve, with all my power and self-determination being usurped by some amorphous universe. I felt like the water in the Mississippi River flowing down to New Orleans, getting cloudier and muddier all the time. Soon, I would have no power left. I needed to take control of this situation with Quinn while I still had some power over the outcome, or at the very least, grasp the concept of what I was trying to control. I knew how to control boy/girl things, didn't I? The problem was, I just couldn't shut up.

"Slow down. Wait one minute." I blundered on. "You know, Quinn, I really like you, and this relationship might even be going somewhere - maybe. The gap between 'might' and 'maybe' is getting bigger all the time, by the way. But, as far as I remember, and my memory is fairly good, there is no biological connection between us! I slept alone last night, in this great big bed at that nice cottage you found. And, as I recall, you weren't in my bed at any time today either! Furthermore, remember, you promised that you weren't a sexual predator, right?"

"I don't mean that kind of biological connection, Gracie!" Quinn's face had reddened. "A syzygy."

"What other kind of biological connection is there, then? And what the hell is a syzygy anyway?" Am I going mad? I thought, asking myself the same question for at least the tenth time that day.

Using his professorial voice again, Quinn answered, "In astronomical terms, a syzygy is usually a type of conjunction, two planets in opposition. In today's common usage, a syzygy is simply a pair of connected or corresponding things. The term is typically applied in a biological setting. Hum. Maybe my choice of words was a little misleading." He muttered to himself, "subliminal, perhaps?" He shook his head to change mental gears - finally getting it. "Oh… It doesn't actually have to be based on a biological connection. Not that I have anything against biological connections..." Then he stopped. It was his turn to gulp. His face reddened slightly.

"Let's go back to the Cottage," I said. Quinn looked relieved as he turned the cab around to start back up the hill.

~Part II~

Harvey moved toward his mate, tenderly embracing her. Then, arm in arm, they followed Gracie and Quinn up the stairs into the red-carpeted rotunda area of the Carnegie Building. They watched as Quinn opened the door for Gracie, using his body as a shield against the wind, sweeping her into the whiteness outside. The door closed and they stood together, alone. Then they turned to each other. Harvey spoke first, with a small hitch in his voice, "She's a fine woman, Grace. A fine woman, indeed. Very much like you."

"Thank you, Harvey, for taking care of her in all those lost years." She kisses him gently. "Because of you, she wasn't all alone. I'm very grateful for that." Eyes tearing up, Grace became quiet again.

"And, now she has Quinn. He's a great guy. In fact, as far as I can tell, he's just about the only person in the universe who has half a chance of keeping up with our Gracie."

"He is? How can you be so sure?" Grace asked.

Harvey considered his answer carefully. "Let me put it this way. We both know there are always choices to be made. But, despite the fact that we may wander from our chosen path from time to time, our paths are fluid, an ever-changing and miraculous dance of light in the universe."

Grace nodded. "Yes, of course. Go on."

"So, the reason that I know that Quinn is right for Gracie is because not only is he a fine scientist, but he is a seeker of truth just like we are. Just like Gracie is. He looks deeply at things, at the dilemma between consciousness and objective knowledge, for example, and he's not afraid to challenge his perceptions or acknowledge his emotions. He is a man of the new age." Then mumbling, he finished under his breath, "I only hope that he and Gracie are smart enough to realize how similar and compatible they are. She's always been a little dense when it comes to relationships."

"What did you say? That last little bit?"

"Oh nothing." Knowing that his mate was a little overwhelmed just now by the meeting with their daughter and by the immediate challenges awaiting them, Harvey continued reassuringly, "They'll make it. I know they will. And, Grace," he stroked her hair, "They'll be happy together."

"How can you be so certain?" Grace asks hesitantly.

"Remember what it was like for us, at the beginning? Grace nods, remembering. "We knew so little about each other then, and so little about our own world, not to mention this crazy world. Yet, we found the answers, together, and somehow, miraculously, we managed to make her too."

"You're right, of course. And she won't be lonely either, will she? Now that she has Quinn, I mean." Grace reasons, looking at Harvey. There is a clear question in her eyes, and Harvey answers.

"No, she won't be coming back with us. It's her choice, of course, but we both know that she belongs here. She'll choose this place. She's a part of this dimension, even as she's a part of us."

"I thought I had lost you. Now I am losing her too." Grace stammers.

"Yes, we lost each other - for awhile. But love is never lost, is it? Remember our connectedness. Life is never lost either. It simply transforms itself. We both know this, don't we Grace?"

"Yes, of course. You're right again. I'm just being sentimental. There is so much feeling here - so much emotion in this dimension, isn't there?" Harvey nods in agreement. Grace shrugs her shoulders and takes a deep breath. "Well, at least I'll be able to get to know Anna! It's one thing to have a twin, but it's an entirely different matter to have another - self! It'll be very interesting, even if she's a little bent."

"Now, be kind, Grace. Anna isn't actually 'bent' she's just a little 'off'." Harvey replies.

"In any case, it will be very interesting to learn about myself from myself, so to speak."

"Well," Harvey continues, "she's not exactly you, of course. She is totally and distinctly a separate person. She just sort of... branched off from you when Gracie was born. Naturally, some of your earliest memories will be shared. Theoretically, you would have started out with essentially the same character, but that's about it. Since Gracie's birth both of you have been individual entities; two separate and distinct personalities."

"Like separated Siamese twins, I guess you could say. Well, it is what it is."

"Wow. Did you ever meet Tracy Luther?" Harvey asks.

"No. Not to my knowledge. Who is Tracy Luther?" Grace questions.

"You know, the auctioneer in North Saint Paul." Harvey replies. Grace looks up, completely baffled.

"It is what it is?" Harvey repeats.

Grace gives Harvey a blank look.

"Oh, never mind. It's not important." Harvey responds.

"You think she's OK without us, Harvey?" Grace questions.

"You mean Anna, or Gracie?"

"Anna, I guess."

"Sure, Anna's OK. We'll be home soon anyway. Now we just have to make sure that the fool Carnegie doesn't screw things up again. If Carnegie hadn't tampered with the dimensional shift just before Gracie was born, initiating the time sequence prematurely, you, I, and Gracie would have spent a few years in this dimension and then we could all have returned home - together." Harvey declared.

"I think Carnegie was worried about me, and the labor and delivery thing. He wanted to be sure that I was able to survive the birth experience. None of us really understood it very well at the time, as you know."

"I think he timed things deliberately to separate us."

"What do you mean?

"I think he wanted you for himself. He always had a thing for you."

"Harvey!"

"Well, what have you been doing for the last thirty years?"

"For one thing, it hasn't been thirty years for me; only for you. For another thing, Carnegie may have had a 'thing' for me, but I had a 'thing' for you."

"So, answer my question, woman! Have you been fooling around with Carnegie in my absence?

"With that guy? Not a chance!"

"OK, then. With some other guy, maybe?"

"Of course not. You know I never could abide the philosophy, "if you can't be with the one you love, honey, love the one you're with. Some crazy song of the '60s, I think."

"Yes, I do remember that song used to tick you off, a bit."

"You got that right."

"So?"

"So, you're the one for me; you always have been; and you always will be."

Some time later.

"You know, Harvey, sex was always really good in this dimension."

"I won't argue that with you, Grace."

"Do you think we can manage to come back here for a quickie every now and then?" Grace asked.

"I'll do my best." Harvey replied with eyebrows raised.

"So, when do we meet with Carnegie and Feynman?"

"In about forty-five minutes."

"Where?"

"In the reception room upstairs."

"Good... oh. That means we might have just enough time to...?" Grace inquires.

"Yes. I think we might be able to... manage... again." Harvey replies as he turns back to Grace, his eyes twinkling. "It may have been a long time, Grace, but everything seems to be in perfect working order."

Grace glances down at Harvey. "That's quite a big... understatement, I'd say," Grace meets Harvey's gaze a moment later. "Clock time has some advantages after all," she acknowledges, with a big smile on her face. A very big smile indeed.

Chapter 17

Exuberance, Color & Light

As he was heading West on Superior Street, Quinn noticed that the wind was picking up.

By the time he reached Mesaba Avenue, the guy on K-UMD Radio was reporting white-out conditions.

By the time Quinn was spinning his tires, skidding diagonally up the hill toward 3rd Street, snow plows were out in full force, salting and sanding all of the major routes. The neon-lighted bulletin board on Thompson Hill announced: "Danger. Slippery Conditions on Pavement." Too late. There was already a six car pile-up on the downhill side of 5th Avenue West, just below the Radisson.

By the time Quinn got to 11th Avenue West and 3rd Street, he was praying that the brakes would actually slow the cab's descent long enough to turn up 2nd Street alley. His goal was simple: to safely maneuver the cab up the 35 degree grade onto the parking slab behind the Cottage without hitting the retaining wall.

Piece of cake.

Gracie had been silent since Park Point. Multi-tasking, Quinn wondered if he should tell Gracie the truth. The second part of the "partial confession" he had made last night. The truth about the Cottage. That he owned the Cottage. The only thing he had decided for sure, however, was that his next purchase would be a four-wheel drive Jeep with a hemi.

The gods were kind, or at the very least, inattentive. Quinn slid into the parking area without hitting the retaining wall behind the Cottage he had purchased six months ago. The blizzard had not yet reached its full force when he yanked open Gracie's door and pulled her out, sheltering her from the howling wind with his own body. He continued to shield her body from the full force of the wind while he keyed in the combination to the back door, opened it, and ushered her inside. Into the warm safety of the Cottage. He held onto the door latch firmly so that the hinges had no chance to pull out of the door frame as he slammed the door shut and locked it securely. Sanctuary.

He knew with certainty that this was turning into a true blizzard. He felt it in his bones. Huge snowflakes were already obliterating the meager winter sunlight. Soon the temperature would plummet. As the false darkness descended in the middle of the afternoon, Quinn also knew there was no way that he or Gracie could safely leave the Cottage tonight. And there wouldn't be any pizza delivery either. Gracie looked a little dazed. Her curls were wet from the snow. He switched on some of the lights and moved to ignite the gas fireplace. He wondered if Harvey and his wife would be able to come up with some answers before Tuesday. He hoped so. Then, he wondered how long the blizzard would last. He had to be back at the lab by Monday night - no later.

Quinn considered their immediate situation. Gracie was probably hungry; a hell of a day for her. He was hungry too. After a quick check of the pantry and refrigerator, he was thankful that there was enough food to last a small army a week or so, compliments of his caretaker. He tried to remember if he owned a shovel.

The howling of the wind grew louder. The windows rattled. Quinn glanced out of the long windows facing the lake - his windows - and watched the icy sheets of snow racing from one side of the street to the other, and then back again. The energy and the power of the storm was palpable. His first real blizzard. In his own home. In Duluth. And, glancing over at Gracie, he realized there was something more. Yes, something more, indeed. It wasn't just her wildly curly hair - whatever color it was. It wasn't just her attitude either. There was something about her. He knew she was brave. It took guts and intelligence to go through what she had at the Carnegie Library and not flip out. She had listened, had tried to understand - to take it all in, even though most of the concepts were far, far out of her field of experience and expertise. Or were they? Um.

So, she had a curious mind. OK. And, she was interesting, despite the fact that she was a lawyer. Let's face it. She was a weird kind of lawyer. But, she seemed to get by. And, she liked beer. Not your run-of-the-mill easy come, easy go girl for sure. And, he had to admit it, there was some connection here, between them; he had no doubt about it; something intangible. He wondered if she'd ever built a tree fort.

So, not only was he here, now, in this exactly right place, but he was here, right now, with this woman. Possibly the exactly right woman. The revelation shocked him! Why, he was actually looking forward to being stuck here with Gracie! Come to think of it, Gracie was the only woman that he had ever been happy to be stuck with! But how had that happened? He had not even known she existed until yesterday. Yet, it seemed like he had known her... before. Maybe forever. There was no use denying it. They were entangled. And he wanted her. Desperately. For his own. From her tiny little waist to her slender legs to her gypsy attitude. She even smelled right. Better and better.

"So, Quinn," Gracie said a little nervously, glancing up. Quinn's face held an intensity she had not seen before. Must be the blizzard. "You said the owners of the Cottage have a whiteboard here?"

"The owners? Oh, right. It's in the lower level. Come on, I'll show you." Quinn replied, heading for the stairs to the lower level. Then he turned around to face her. "Wait,

Gracie. It's about the second part of the partial confession."

"Oh, yes. The partial confession." Gracie looked up at him. "Let's recap. The first part of the partial confession was...?"

"Was that I had made arrangements for us to stay here last night." Quinn blurted.

"Right. A very good idea. You told me that before. So what's the second part?"

"The second part is pretty simple. I didn't have to make arrangements for us to stay here. I own this Cottage. I bought it about six months ago. Kind of on a whim."

"On a whim? How could you buy a place like this on a whim?"

"It just sang to me, you could say."

Gracie gave him a questioning, disbelieving look, so he tried to explain. "I was at UMD for a meeting, about four miles from here. I decided to skip the freeway and ended up in this old part of Duluth on my way out of town. The natives call it 'Little Italy.' A whim, as I said. I saw this house, jutting out from the hill. It moved me. Something about this place seemed just right. The steeply-pitched roof; the bargeboard. There were even lilac bushes blooming in the yard at the time. I noticed a realtor's sign on the lawn out front. So, I called about it; I walked through it; and I bought it."

"This place must have cost a fortune! I thought you were a poor physicist/cab driver, clamoring for grant money." Gracie replied, astonished.

"Well, that's not entirely true. I am a physicist/cab driver, clamoring for grant money. But, objectively speaking, I guess you'd have to say that I'm not technically poor. That was your assumption. I had some luck with option trading a few years ago. So, I'm flush. And, well, there's also some income from the perpetual trust my grandparents set up for me in Alaska."

Gracie raised her eyebrows this time. "So, why do you work at all, Mr. Option Trading/Trust Fund Boy? And, for heaven's sake, why do you drive a cab?"

"Wow, Gracie, I had no idea you were such a snob. Rich people have rights too. I drive my cab because it pleases me, and it gives me a mental break - some time for contemplation. I pay 55% of what I earn in federal income taxes each year. And, I live in Minnesota, remember? So I pay another 23% in state income taxes besides. Then, let's see." He raised his fingers and counted off: "There's sales tax, property tax, use tax, restaurant tax, button tax, shoe lace tax, comb tax, cat tax, boomerang tax, and stray voltage tax. By my calculations, I'll soon have to apply for public benefits so I can buy my weekly bowl of Pho. I estimate that our government generously lets me keep about 7-8% of what I earn each year, so far. Pretty soon I'll be paying 105% of my income each year in taxes.[15] At least I managed to be able to buy this place."

He has a point there. Gracie thought. Then, he has a comb? And a cat? But, stray voltage?

"The good part about being flush is that I can do the work that I am interested in - what I consider to be important and worth my time and energy. I can work and think, not just work to survive. So, I drive a cab when I want to, and I don't have to survive by selling vacuum cleaners. Remember Thomas Jefferson? He had a trust fund too. He didn't have to sell vacuum cleaners to live either, and so he managed to do some rather amazing stuff didn't he? I'm positive that he wouldn't have been able to do half as much amazing stuff if he had to ask, 'Do you want fries with that?' And, one more benefit which I will discuss with you later." He raised his eyebrows. "So, lawyer-lady Gracie, is my being rich a problem for you?" He wanted to touch her. Badly.

"Well. Actually. No."

"Good. I didn't think so. Besides, as owner of this wildly extravagant cottage, I granted you the privilege of sleeping in the master bedroom last night."

"Oh?"

---

[15] Must be using Sweden as a model.

"It's my favorite room in the Cottage. Did you notice the windows? The prior owners told me that the large gothic window was salvaged from the old UMD, long gone.

"Yes. It's pretty amazing. I saw the moon last night." Gracie replied.

"Oh yeah. It's too bad the moon will be obliterated by the snow tonight. When the moon is full, its refection is like a million tiny energy pulses shattered across the water. All light, color and energy. Every particle shimmers and seems to be moving, sparkling; separate and individual, yet joined together somehow." Just like a syzygy, he understood in amazement. "It's like nothing you've ever seen before. I was hoping to share it with..." Quinn's voice fell silent.

"With?"

"With someone special, some day. Heh, Gracie. How do you feel about tree forts?"

"Tree forts? You mean, like... a treehouse?"

Quinn nods. "But not just a house in a tree. A fortress in a tree, with battlements!"

"In the middle of a blizzard, you ask me about tree forts... tree houses with... whatever?"

"Yeah, sure. I always plan ahead. I've been considering building a gigantic tree fort for a couple of months now. I can hardly wait to get started. A little down the slope. With some kind of tower structure so we could climb above the tree line for an unobstructed view of the lake. It would be a great place to have a beer in the summertime, wouldn't it? Maybe with a kind of bridge-thing attached."

"Oh." Gulp. She hesitated. What now? Gracie wondered. "There was a whiteboard here you said?" In desperation, she tried to change the subject.

"Sure. Downstairs. In the map room. Follow me."

Well, redirection seemed to work. This time, at least. Breathing a sigh of relief, she wondered what she had gotten herself into. Sure he was cute and interesting, but - slow it down, she cautioned herself. Was she really ready for this? There was some kind of connection here, her inner senses were telling her. In fact, it felt like a potentially intimate and life-changing connection. Or was she just imagining it all? Hopelessly befuddled, she wondered if anyone was ever really ready when amazing, startling moments occur in their lives? She considered all of this as she followed Quinn downstairs.

In the lower level, the howling wind was buffered by the earth and thick concrete walls. The floor was warm. Quinn led Gracie to a room at the back of the Cottage, half buried in the hillside. He switched on the lights. There were floor to ceiling whiteboards on two of the four walls; a long work table in the middle of the room, with two computers - one MAC and one PC - at each end. Quickly erasing what looked like gibberish or pagan symbols from one of the whiteboards, Gracie watched Quinn begin rapidly filling the boards again with a crude schematic. It must be a diagram of his malfunctioning machine, Gracie thought. When Quinn finished the diagram, he stepped back, considering. Then, he added a few more squiggles here and there. And he turned back to Gracie who was still standing at the entrance to the room.

"I was always fascinated with the idea of time travel, you know. After that, it was inter-dimensional travel." Quinn reached over and took Gracie's hand. Then he pulled her closer. "After awhile, I understood that these concepts were synonymous, reflections of each other. Just like the moon on the lake. Each idea was independently provable, but linked, if you used applied math at a high level. The key was how to make it work in the real world, not just on paper."

... Quinn's hand was warm, surprisingly calloused. His fingers were short and stout, more like a farmer's or a carpenter's, not a scientist/cabbie/rich guy. He actually had thumbs. Thumbs that had started stroking my palms ...

With a faraway look, Quinn continued. "So, I studied Einstein. But Einstein got stuck in his grand unification theory, which was really close to what we call TOE today. Remember, Gracie? We talked about TOE before - in the cab yesterday - the 'Theory of Everything?' When I nodded, he continued. "Well, Feynman's work came closer to what I was looking for. I had real hope, but I still couldn't quite get it all. I realized something important was missing; something vital, foundational. After a crazy dream one night, it finally dawned on me. The essential problem was with the scientific method and consciousness. I realized that certainty has a way of defeating both science and truth."

"What do you mean?" Gracie asked.

"Scientists have never really tried to study or map consciousness. Mostly because it's too hard to measure with our normal senses. So, the most important part of life, the part that makes us human, for the most part, is simply ignored."

"Because it's unseen and unprovable, right?" Gracie asked.

... I liked Quinn's hand, so I decided to try out his shoulder by placing my head on it. Mmm. Not too bad. He smelled good too. A kind of dried sweater/Tide-blizzard-man sort of fragrance. Oh my. Quinn was still explaining and I forced myself to pay attention to his words ...

"You see, science has decided that if you can't quantify something - in other words - recreate it objectively in a lab - then it doesn't exist. But, science can't begin to logically explain inspiration, vitality, creativity, or even love, for that matter."

...Ah. Inspiration, vitality, creativity, love, I repeated the mantra in my mind. Wow, there's a mouthful. Powerful words; an exceedingly harmonious combination of words, actually. But, the 'love' part was problematic. Falling in love always seemed to happen at the most inconvenient times. Probably even in the middle of a blizzard, for that matter. Ouch. I gave myself a mental pinch - don't even go there, I told myself sternly...

"So," Quinn continued. "Religion was assigned to deal with unquantifiable questions about life and human emotions, because science couldn't...

"...couldn't understand or explain the spiritual connection." Gracie finished Quinn's sentence, then shrugged.

"Right. The idea was that some things had to be taken on 'faith'."

"Sure. I get it. Religion was supposed to be the missing link; the link between consciousness and science - to tie it all together." Gracie said.

"Right again. Unfortunately though, religions have traditionally tried to control human behavior in some really unhealthy ways. You know, inventing angels, devils, heavens and hells, and becoming enmeshed in politics, for starters."

"So, you believe in all that stuff - angels, devils, zombies?"

"No, absolutely not."

"Why? Because you have no physical evidence they exist?"

"No. Don't put words into my mouth. Because angels, devils, and the whole plethora of gods and goddesses were adopted from other religions and folk legends, all constructs designed to control people and behavior."

"Ah ha. I'm following you now. So, if we don't follow the rules or the required behaviors, then we're sinners, right?" Gracie paused. "Then, after awhile we wind up with the 'sinful self' concept, don't we? And all the guilt that goes with it, too."

... I knew this concept well ...

"You got it. But what a crock. Guilt can control behavior for a short time. But, after awhile, it fails..."

"Or makes people psychotic. Or turns them into zombies." Gracie interjected.

... He was looking at me funny again...

"because people basically get tired of..."

"...tired of feeling bad. Right?"

"Sure. Mostly because guilt denies basic good intention." Quinn finally managed to finish his thought despite Gracie's interruptions.

In total agreement, Gracie nodded. "It always amazes me that we can believe that animals are inherently good, but not people. You know, dogs and cats, cows and parrots - automatically good. We even believe that nature and the environment are automatically good. But why can't we believe that humans are essentially good too? I mean, you've never heard anyone declare that a parrot was evil to the core or that it had maliciously stalked its mate, have you?"

Quinn still had that unreadable expression on his face as Gracie continued, "Even hurricanes and volcanoes are considered good - or at least excusable - because they're 'natural events.' Except for when President Bush used his connections to assure that Hurricane Katrina would wipe out New Orleans to benefit his oil cronies, of course. Or was that the invasion of Iraq? Anyway, then there's climate change. Some people really go off the deep end on that issue for sure. You know, all of us ugly and evil Americans creating climate change?"

Quinn smirked. "You said you went to law school? Where?"

"At the U," Gracie replied. "Except... well... with a name like mine, I suppose they only let me in because they thought I was some New Age minority student from Asia. I'm sure they got a big surprise when I showed up for class the first day - with my unusual world view and curly hair to boot!"

"No doubt about that!" Quinn muttered under his breath.

... Glancing over at me, I could see that he was anxious to continue his diatribe...

"Well, I never said I was a normal lawyer, you know. It was the parrot thing, wasn't it? Or maybe the zombie comment?"

Quinn raised his eyebrows again, grinning.

Gracie launched back in for him. "So. It's all about consciousness. And intention, you say? Intention is a key element in any crime you know. It's the legal concept of 'mens rea'. In other words, if you intentionally do something wrong, the law exacts a stiffer punishment than if the perpetrator accidentally fucks up but had no evil intent. In other words, if you do something with purpose - and intention - it's better. Hum. It is more lasting anyway - even if it's killing someone dead. I suppose it's the same with good intention?"

... Quinn had this faraway look on his face, gazing out the window at nothing but darkness and swirling white. Fascinating. The inner man emerges. I could almost visualize the wheels turning.

"You're right, it's all about intention. The bottom line is that neither religion nor science acknowledge the inherent power of human personality."

Quinn finally touched down and thankfully ignored my last few comments ...

He continued, "And, if you don't buy into the human-being-as-inherently-evil concept, things change. If you accept the idea that we are all connected to each other and have enormous power to change our lives and our universe - not just conceptually, but literally - it becomes easy!"

"Easy? You mean, you can literally change the universe we live in?" Gracie asked.

Quinn nodded. "Ultimately, I was so desperate to make the connection - the leap - and I was so frustrated, that I was forced to trust my intuition and instinct."

"Go on," Gracie said.

"I had to abandon the 'human being as a machine' concept. You know, the machine gets broken and requires a little "tune up" every now and then. That whole concept became popular when people began to lose faith in religion to help them understand the universe. That's when psychology took over, trying to put a scientific spin on consciousness without admitting the spiritual connection either. Then psychology introduced more 'scientific' strategies to control behavior."

"That's for sure." Gracie said. "Psychologists have even worked out a classification system for dysfunction. Then they pass out little pills to alter behavior. In the long run, pushing pills doesn't really work, although it's extremely cost-effective for insurance companies. Human-to-human talk therapy takes longer and works so much better, but it costs more."

"Obama Care via insurance companies is the quick fix these days; only the bottom line counts, not the human beings involved." Quinn said.

"Yeah. That's how we wind up with a culture of zombies, all drugged; all unconnected."

... It's the Borg Continuum turned on its head. So, how do we explain 'sparkly vampires?' I wondered. Something else to think about, later ...

"The end result is that no one needs to have a personal or intimate connection with anyone else." Quinn added.

... Um. Personal or intimate connections, eh? Wouldn't it be great if there was a pill for love? I considered that concept. It'd have to be similar to a birth control pill. You could begin taking the 'love' pill when you were ready to fall in love. And, when you got tired of someone or if things changed, you could simply stop taking the 'love' pill. No harm, no foul, just a simple good-bye. Of course, it would have to be a uni-sex pill. Probably administered on Saturday nights. I

bet the pharmaceutical industry is already working on a prototype! It's probably in Phase III clinical trials already.

"Yep. As long as they're compliant with meds or on Face Book, they're OK, right? Kind of like the ultimate Privacy Act." Gracie said.[16]

Yawning, feeling toasty warm, comfortable and safe, I thought it might be nice to get even closer to Quinn. So I perched on his lap, and pressed my check to his chest... Quinn didn't even notice. He was really on a roll...

He continued. "But we are connected! There is so much untapped human potential that we haven't even explored yet! Science just doesn't have the tools to measure rare or unusual human abilities. Clairvoyance and precognition are real. There are many anecdotal stories from reliable sources and even some convincing data that these inner senses do exist, yet the scientific method just doesn't work in those situations. Ignoring our connections or drugging our conscious minds won't work either. Our connections can't be denied or repressed forever! Even

---

[16] Yeah. But only so long as the NSA, DOJ or the FBI can manage to find a 'back door' to access your personal information. Heck, what am I saying? They could simply get it from the IRS anyway, couldn't they?

zombies can be reanimated and saved according to the latest popular culture."

...There you go. Sparkly vampires, I thought. I almost blurted it out, really giving myself a scare...

Quinn noticed my startled expression and responded. "No, Gracie, as it happens, my work is not based on clairvoyance or any other kind of psychic phenomenon. Its more like a convergence of experimental and spontaneous data - connections." He cleared his throat and continued, "Anyway, we know from quantum physics that the observer affects the outcome of any experiment. So, every time we try to quantify a person's psychic experience or precognitive dream, we change it. The results are skewed. We simply haven't developed the tools to measure consciousness and connectedness yet." He finally glanced down at Gracie, sitting on his lap.

"So, I threw it all out." He growled. "Science, religion, psychology, everything. No boundaries. I started from scratch. Tabula rasa."[17]

...Wow, he even knows Latin, I thought. Could he possibly get any hotter?

---

[17] Latin for "a blank slate" or to start from the beginning, with no preconceptions or assumptions.

"Once I made the decision to abandon the scientific method and decided to question everything, and I mean literally everything, it all came together. The light shone through. No, actually, the light blasted through."

"What do you mean?" Gracie asked. "What did you do?"

"The first thing I did was to pay attention to coincidences. I sensed there was something out there, unquantifiable, maybe another dimension - a higher dimension - which bled through every now and then, but only if I was paying attention. I also started looking for a different kind of order; an unseen pattern which might represent an intersection point between this other dimension that I sensed, somehow, and our physical one. I looked at physics and mathematics in a different way. Some of my ideas kind of scared me. They were exuberant, sometimes outrageous. I surprised myself at every new idea. But I just couldn't shut up or shut it off. It felt like I was being given permission to explore the most idiosyncratic paths, encouraged the whole way, safely exploring what I had been hoping to explore for a long, long time. In a way, it was a miracle."

... He had begun stroking my arms. It felt so good I almost purred...

"I think the guys in my lab thought I had morphed into bi-polar man - at least the manic phase. I measured what I could measure, and I recorded everything I could record, but I also followed my hunches, no matter how weird. Eventually I realized that time travel or inter-dimensional travel was more of a problem in consciousness, reconfiguring our awareness and perceptions. I gave up the idea that everything had to be logical, make sense, and be reproducible. I wrote the program. I built the machine. I met Harvey. Then, I read Feynman's unpublished work."

"Too bad he wasn't able to publish his work before he died, but maybe he wasn't meant to. You said he died in 1988?" Gracie asked.

Quinn continued without a beat. "Yeah. That's what he told me when I met him, a couple of weeks ago."

"What do you mean you met Feynman a couple of weeks ago? After he died? In 1988? How could you ..?"

... My head began spinning. It was 2014, November of 2014 ...

"No way, Quinn. I don't believe it. It's not possible." Gracie slid off Quinn's lap. He stood up.

"Believe it, Gracie. My machine works. Call it a time machine, an inter-dimensional transference device or a toaster. I don't care. It's really all about consciousness, as I said. And Tuesday, you'll meet Feynman too, and he won't be a zombie. That is, if it ever stops snowing." He glanced down in sympathy at the appalled look on Gracie's face, his warm lap now empty. He reached for her again. "How about a drink, Gracie? You look like you could use one just about now."

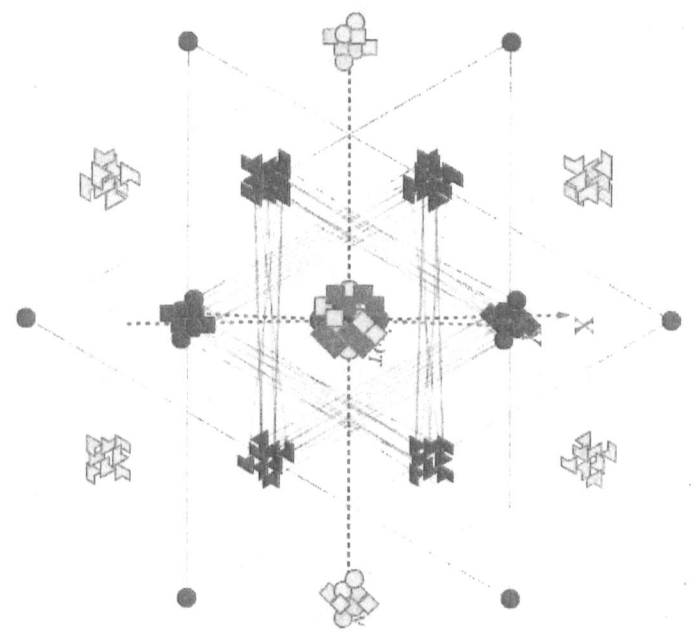

Lisis E-8 Set
<TOE>

Chapter 18

Hunt for the Not-So-Obvious

Carnegie and Feynman were drinking scotch and seemed to be engaged in a heated discussion as Harvey and Grace entered the reception room at precisely 6:00 p.m., clock time.

Carnegie noticed them first, and said, in his Scottish brogue, "Harvey, old man, you sure are looking better today than when Grace and I arrived a few days ago."

Feeling smug and more than a little satisfied, Harvey felt unusually generous and replied quite civilly, "Been funding any new libraries lately, Carnegie?"

"Not too much." Carnegie replied.

Harvey nodded at Feynman who chimed in. "Almost got him convinced to buy a nice little nightclub in Minneapolis. People sure could use a little incentive to get out of their caves in the cold, dark winters here. It's unnatural, watching sports on television all the time." Feynman said as he winked at Grace.

On cue, Grace interjected, "Just like you tried to convince him to purchase the Dingleberry Dance Palace in Maplewood back in the 1930s?"

"Absolutely. He should have listened to me. If the proprietor had lovely ladies on display rather than wrestling bears in an attempt to titillate his customers, the joint would have been packed. Then, 3M would never have been able to buy him out." Feynman retorted.

"The Dingleberry Dance Palace? Never heard of it before." Harvey said. "And the proprietor wrestled bears? No way. I don't believe it. Too barbaric for Minnesota, even back then. Animal rights, you know." Harvey sputtered, somewhat incredulously.

"Oh yeah, he did. Believe it. On Saturday nights." Feynman answered.

"For his patrons?" Harvey asked.

"Sure, did. Wrestled them in a cage. The bears, I mean. So if Carnegie had only listened to me, the Dingleberry Dance Palace would still be in existence today and 3M would never have had the chance to take over the whole east side of Saint Paul, ultimately forming the first 'corpocracy' in United States. And you know where that leads, don't you?" Feynman continued.

"All downhill since then, I suppose?" Harvey sniggered.

"That's right. It's all relative, as you know." Feynman replied with a wisecracker's grin on his face. "Would you rather have scotch tape, post-its, and screwed up water supplies or real excitement?"

"So, it's a question of 'bear' butts or 'bare' butts, I suppose?" Harvey quipped.

"More's the pity, I'd say, you morons!" Carnegie sniped. "Not you, of course, Grace. Just those two idiots over there."

Grace coughed for attention. "Gentlemen. Let's move on. We need to figure out if Quinn's machine, as it is currently configured, is capable of sending us all safely back on Tuesday or not."

"Another 'relative' question, as it turns out." Feynman said with a smirk.

"For cryin' out loud, guys! Stop it with the puns! Answer my simple question will you! What kind of progress have you two made?" Grace was losing patience, it was clear to all.

"Right." Feynman straightened up and replied. "It comes down to the modalities. There are four of us this time. Intersection points can usually only manage 1 to 2 persons, maximum, at a time." He turned and spoke directly to Carnegie and Harvey. "That was the problem when Grace ended up back home last time - alone. The energy in the system couldn't handle three transferences. So, Harvey and the baby, Gracie, were left behind." He paused. "And, then there was Anna. I'm not quite sure how the hell that happened at all, even now, after studying the incident for some time. We don't want that happening again."

"What do you mean?" Carnegie asked. "Who is Anna?"

"Oh, yes. I forgot. Carnegie doesn't know about Anna, does he?" Feynman shrugged his shoulders.

Harvey turned to Feynman, "You explain the physics. I'll fill in with the personality parts."

Feynman nodded and began to explain about Anna's peculiar existence. "Well, Carnegie, if you didn't spend so much time making money and then giving it away, you would have remembered the glitch in the system we discussed awhile ago."

"The so-called 'glitch we discussed' concerned repeating events, as I recall. What's that got to do with a woman named Anna?" Carnegie asked in a reasonable tone of voice, ignoring Feynman's intended barb.

"Do you remember that there was a chance - a small probability we thought then - that our machine would have a hiccup? Kind of like pushing a 'reset' button or tripping an electrical breaker?"

"Sure. There was an unknown variable in the calculations. We thought it was a constant, but it turned out it wasn't." Carnegie replied.

"You got it. Harmless - at least we thought so at the time." Carnegie still had a blank look on his face, so Feynman elaborated. "When Harvey and Grace first came to this dimension, we were in the process of working out the physics to make transferences totally safe, and commonplace, primarily as a means to study multi-dimensional existences and connections. Of course, I was doing research on an unconscious level, and you had already passed over, physically, I mean. In other words, you were dead. You were reviewing all the connections from your side of the veil - the energy dimension, I'll call it. I was still pretty firmly rooted in the physical then - doing the math in my sleep, you could say. In any event, we were engaged in a great deal of brainstorming about dimensional transferences."

"So?" Carnegie asked.

"Well, to simplify, the 'glitch' turned out to be Anna - Grace's double." Harvey interjected.

"Grace's double? There are two of Grace? Carnegie exploded. "How can that be? You mean Grace's daughter, Gracie, don't you? I know about her."

"No, another person altogether. Just like the Grace sitting next to you now." The three guys turned to look at the beautiful red-headed woman sitting next to Carnegie. All were thinking the same thing: Maybe it would be a wonderful idea if each of them had their own beautiful red-headed goddess. How could there be a downside to that? Reading their minds, Grace began to shake her head "No!" very vigorously. She commanded, "Tell him the whole story; tell him the weird part. Tell him about the orange candies!"

Sighing, Harvey continued, "Well, at least she started out as our beautiful Grace. Now we've got Anna."

Still reading total confusion on Carnegie's face, Feynman jumped in, "Somehow, at the time of the 'glitch' Anna split off from Grace. I guess you could say she 'emerged'. At least that's one way to look at it."

"She became a totally separate individual. As in two separate people; two gorgeous red-haired women, with two separate, completely independent bodies." Harvey explained. They all glanced over at Grace again. She just shook her head in resignation.

Harvey continued where Feynman left off, "However, from that point on, her personality diverged from Grace's in quite significant ways. Her body in this dimension began to age rapidly. Her mind was sharp and agile enough though. Except that she was fixated on orange candies. Oh, by the way, she passed over - you know, died last Thursday night in Gracie's office." Harvey said matter-of-factly, and then continued. "Anna was very unique."

"You don't say," Carnegie smirked.

Harvey ignored him and continued to explain, "She had an amazing grasp of the financial markets, and contributed in no small way to Taleb's[18] black swan theory. I think they had an email relationship going. She also baked outstanding chocolate chip cookies."

"What?" Carnegie exclaimed, making choking noises. Grace slapped him on the back, hoping to help. "Chocolate chip cookies, you say?" Carnegie had a strange expression on his face now. He looked a little flummoxed.

Harvey said, "Are you alright, Carnegie? Is there something wrong?"

Carnegie just shook his head and responded, "It's just that, you know, I'm very fond of chocolate chip cookies, and…"

Feynman cut him off, picking up the thread of his narrative, "Although I never had a chance to meet her in person, Anna apparently had an intuitive grasp of theoretical physics. I understand she was even working on her own theory concerning emotional energy, perception, and psychological time. Quinn was helping her with it."

"What do you mean?" Grace and Carnegie asked at the same time.

"They were trying to establish the existence of electromagnetic particles that basically carry perception units. The invisible 'breath of consciousness' Quinn told

---

[18] See Nassim Nicholas Taleb's, The Black Swan: The Impact of the Highly Improbable, released on April 17, 2007, by Random House.

me she liked to call it. She insisted that these invisible particles would be orange-colored if they were actually visible. That might be the reason why she surrounded herself with anything that was orange, apparently the brighter the better."

"That's quite a story! So, anyway," Grace coughed nervously, "you're worried about... making more copies of me?"

"Or of anyone else who would be involved in the transference." Feynman said.

Grace stood up.

Carnegie still looked dazed.

Before things got totally out of hand, Feynman rushed in again, "We can reasonably surmise that the same thing could happen again, if we don't figure out what caused the glitch the first time. It just means that we need to get the energy right this time. It must be stabilized."

"So, the question that remains is: how do we get all 4 of us safely back, without making four... carbon copies of some or all of us?" Harvey asked.

"Four of us?" Still shaking his head, Carnegie inquired.

"Yes." Harvey replied. "Grace and I, you and Feynman. Anna's already there, waiting for us, I'm sure."

"Wait. Isn't Gracie coming back too?" Feynman asked.

"No, I don't think so. Although it's Gracie's choice, of course. She'll have to decide." Harvey paused, noticing the concerned look on Grace's face. "So, it's really four, maybe five at the most. Have you worked out the energy signature yet?" Harvey asked Feynman.

"Quinn and I have been working on it pretty steadily. We're close. His machine is more powerful than what we were working with thirty years ago - in clock time. The energy sources are much more stable now. But we won't be able to manage any more than four persons - max. I'm sure of it. But, if Gracie stays here, it'll be OK. Actually, I have a feeling that Gracie and someone else - maybe Quinn - are the key. Their energy, together. It's some kind of hybrid syzygy. At first I thought it was only Gracie's energy. But the math calls for something more, another type of connection. I'll have to check with Quinn tomorrow to see what he's come up with." Feynman replied.

"Listen. Could you guys just take one small moment to explain to a non-scientist what you are blabbering about?" Carnegie sputtered.

Grace nodded. "Yes. Time out, boys. Carnegie and I just don't have the science background you two have. Could you simplify?"

Feynman started, "It's actually about electro-magnetic particles…"

"In simpler terms," Harvey interrupted, "it's about intertwining realities…"

Grace and Carnegie were shaking their heads in protest. "Come on, you fellows," Carnegie began to complain.

Feynman nodded at Harvey to take the lead.

"...and connections that cannot be denied." Harvey paused. "OK. Let's start over. Do you remember, Carnegie, what you felt like after your physical body died? After you passed-over, I mean?"

"Sure. Of course. Actually, I was quite surprised at how good I felt. I felt young - like a heavy weight had been lifted. I experienced a certain clarity, a wholeness." Carnegie replied.

"Understandable. OK. Now, do you recall what it was like just before you died though?" Harvey elaborated. "Weren't you worried about all that 'life after death' stuff? The possibility of eternal damnation? Wondering if you knew the correct code-word to get through the pearly gates? Or, were you one of those persons who thought your existence would simply end at death; the eternal void - nothingness?"

"Well, since I was raised Catholic, I believed in heaven and hell, of course. And, certainly I was nervous about dying." Carnegie replied.

"So, like everyone else, you weren't consciously aware during your lifetime - in this dimension - that you were so much more, were you? You didn't know - for sure - that your individual personality, your consciousness, wouldn't end at death, did you? But that your consciousness would be expanded instead?" Harvey asked.

"Sure, no doubt about that. That was part of my apprehension about dying. I had a feeling everything would be all right, of course. That I would go to heaven after my death, since I had made my peace with everything at this end, but I couldn't know for sure. Nobody could know for sure." Carnegie said.

"You mean, you knew 'they'd' let you into heaven because you endowed all those libraries with your ill-gotten gains, heh?" Harvey couldn't resist the barb.

"No, you scoundrel!" Carnegie began to rise. Grace pushed him back into his seat.

"Calm down boys!" Grace said with a severe expression on her face.

"Sorry, dear. Couldn't stop myself." Harvey shrugged. "So, follow me now. It makes sense that when someone is born into this 3-dimensional space∞time, their perceptions have to be focused here. Only here. In other words, all of the possibilities of existence would have to be limited, restricted, in a sense, to fit. Otherwise, they would go mad, right?" Harvey continued to explain.

"Gracie's problem arose because she actually came into physical existence here - in this 3-dimensional time and space, even though she was Harvey and Grace's child. And, to make it worse, it all happened during the transference event. In other words, as a result of our dimensional fuck-up, Gracie ended up with a certain kind of energy and more awareness than is normal. Her filters were in the 'off mode' you could say." Feynman added.

"You're telling me!" Harvey said. "I could tell you stories..."

Feynman tactfully coughed. "She hasn't been able to restrict her 'inputs' so to speak." He paused. "Some people would conclude that she has a kind of ESP; others would say she is schizophrenic or mentally ill and try to medicate her. She sure doesn't fit. However, the more she trusts her own inner awareness, the more she uses it to guide her actions, the more she will become a bridge between dimensions."

"How can she be a bridge between dimensions?" Grace questioned, with a worried look on her face.

"It's difficult to put some concepts in words. Math is so much more elegant and expressive." Seeing Grace frown, however, Feynman cleared his throat and continued, "But I'll attempt it - without using the math. You see, Gracie's energy is an essential component of what we need to do on Tuesday. Gracie is the initiation point."

"What do you mean? Isn't Quinn's lab the initiation point? That's where everything started after all." Grace asked.

"Not exactly. It's true that the lab is the physical location where the transference will occur, if it does, mainly because that's where Quinn's machine is located. But the initiation point? No, that's Gracie. Gracie's the one, and probably the only one, who can provide the unique, individual, and specific emotional energy to form the electromagnetic units that we need for the transference. The units become the entryway into physical matter."

"Huh?" Grace, Carnegie and Harvey all said simultaneously.

"Try and follow. None of you are slow."

"OK. Just make it a little clearer than mud," Harvey growled with Carnegie and Grace nodding in agreement.

"Think of a triangle. The initiation point is in the center. Think of the initiation point pulsating with energy, forming the three sides of the triangle around itself. Now, think of Gracie, pulsating with emotional energy, attracting all kinds of weird stuff to herself. Remember, Gracie was a glitch at the time she was born. Her energy signature is unique and unusual, somewhat sporadic. Clear so far?"

They all nodded.

"Sure."

"Right-O."

"Got it."

"Now think of emotional energy as tiny explosions, causing the triangle to spin, a little, and to change its shape."

"All right, so the triangle turns into what, a circle?" Carnegie asked.

"Carnegie, old man, you catch on fast." Feynman responded.

Carnegie smiled smugly. "One of my smaller achievements."

"Go on," Harvey prodded, making a face at Carnegie.

"Imagine that the triangle, now a circle, generates something like friction, as the three sides change position." Feynman glanced at his three friends, who all seemed to be following, so he continued, "Imagine further, that the energy point, the initiation point - Gracie's energy - constantly changes its shape and form and, as it does so, the emotional energy is intensified.

"My daughter is going to change into a triangle and then into a circle?" Grace asked, horrified.

"No, of course not," Feynman said. "This is not a physical form. Think of the emotional energy particles as if they were molecules, only infinitely smaller, constantly changing polarities, and attracting other units of emotional energy. Can you do that?"

"Sure."

"Right-O."

"Got it."

"OK. Eventually, all the units of emotional energy become compressed, into solid matter. Our bridge." Feynman sighed. "There's just one problem though."

"Just one?" Harvey asked.

"Is it a big problem?" Carnegie asked.

"What do you mean?" Grace asked.

"The emotional energy inside the units is very powerful. It would create a very intense magnetic field, a very strong motivator. If something goes wrong, and Gracie freaks out, the whole thing could shatter."

"What 'thing' are you talking about?" Harvey asked, apprehensively.

"Well, as in every 'thing' here in this 3-dimensional space could... um..."

"Go kaboom?" Carnegie supplied.

"Worst case scenario. We know that emotional energy, if sufficient, can shatter a physical object. We also know that if there is a field collapse near a superconducting magnet, it sucks all the energy out of the area. Like an MRI truck turning into an ice cube. It's not likely to happen, but I'd strongly suggest we get the energy right this time."

"Well, I did manage to create an empire out of nothing, and then sell it all to Rockefeller." Carnegie smirked.

"Still bragging about that are you?" Harvey quipped.

"The critical question is, how does Quinn fit into it all? Is he the transformer or is he the black hole?" Harvey muttered.

"Let's go back to the 'kaboom' part." Grace said.

"Who in the hell is this Quinn fellow anyway?" Carnegie exploded.

"He's the physicist who reactivated the transference device," Harvey said, "with my help, of course."

"Except," Feynman continued, "you also helped him to create a time loop centered on events that happened last Thursday. Just before he met Gracie while driving his cab."

"What the blazes are you all talking about?" Carnegie exploded again.

"Is Quinn really that important? Grace asked quietly, looking at the only two men in the room who knew the answer: Feynman and Harvey. Both men scholars, scientists, visionaries.

Suddenly, the room was silent, both men searching for an answer to the apparently simple question. Feynman raised his eyebrows. He had been waiting for this moment to come, knowing that someone would have to say the words out loud. Finally, he nodded sympathetically at Harvey, waiting. Harvey understood that it was his duty and privilege to respond to Grace's question.

How could he explain to his wife how Gracie and Quinn would be - or could be - together? How connected both of them were to their own world and to their own time? He considered. Sure, Quinn was as odd, offbeat, and funny as Gracie was. Yet, it was more than that. Much more. Quinn was important; not just to Gracie, but to this entire world - this dimension. He was one of the pioneers and Gracie was his partner. Their actions, together, were pivotal. Together, they had the potential to change everything. So he simply replied, with watery eyes, "Yes. Quinn is that important."

Confused, worried, and resigned to a long night of more physics, Carnegie finally admitted defeat. "Oh blast." He looked around at the startled faces of his best friends. "Sorry," he said. "Let's take this discussion downstairs, in front of the fire, shall we? Harvey, got any more scotch?"

Chapter 19

Stairway to... Heaven?

Quinn led Gracie up the stairs to the kitchen, and deposited her on the stool in front of the island. Gracie was cold again, trembling. "You know, Quinn. This stuff is getting really old. Just when I think you're normal, and nice, then you say something really, quite extraordinarily weird."

"Sorry, Gracie. At times it's even hard for me to believe it all. Depends on which hat I'm wearing at what time, actually. But it's true. All true. You just have to have faith."

"Faith?" She questioned, looking at Quinn blankly.

He continued, "Yes. Faith. But not blind faith. You need to have the kind of faith that kids have.

"I'm not a kid." Gracie replied.

Quinn ignored her comment. "Kids have a kind of 'faith-with-knowledge.' They simply trust their bodies to grow up, and don't think about it at all. Like getting pimples, breasts, or erections. It's all good." He paused, considering. "They don't have the religious kind of go-to-church faith either. That's learned behavior."

Despite her mood, Gracie's curiosity was piqued. So, she said, "What do you mean?"

"Kids trust their feelings and perceptions. They usually don't second-guess themselves or wonder if they're on the right path. They just know that everything will turn out OK, no matter what." Quinn glanced over at Gracie. "Somehow, I have a feeling you already do that on a pretty regular basis."

"How... why do you say that?" Gracie asked, horrified.

"I just know. Listen, every time I think things are getting just too weird - too bizarre - I run a diagnostic. On myself. You know, sort of like the diagnostics that IT guys run on computers? I check out everything. If I judge I'm not insane or bordering on schizophrenia - no voices in my head except my own - then I presume that I'm fine; that my assumptions are good; and then I just run with it. My expectations align with my belief that everything will turn out OK, and it does."

"Really? It's as easy as that?"

"Gracie, seriously. You know it is."

"Hum. Well, I've always had these ideas, unprovable ideas actually, usually concerning my clients. Sometimes I just pick things up. There are times when I know what someone is going to say before they say it. It can get pretty intense. It really irritates people, mostly judges actually, when I finish their sentences for them. I typically chalk it up to a kind of empathy, a sharing. You know, like Counselor Troy on Star Trek, The Next Generation. Every now and then I just get too weirded out, though. And when I do - and it happens more frequently than I like to admit - I dance." She paused. "Come to think of it, I've been dancing quite a lot lately."

"Dance?" Quinn's face went blank.

"Sure. Moving your body around in rhythmic patterns inspired by music?" At Quinn's dumbfounded look, Gracie sarcastically continued, "Maybe you should try it some time. It never really looks that great when I do it, but it always makes me feel better. I think it has something to do with raising energy."

"Mmm. Raising energy? Dance, you say? Rhythmic - repeating patterns?"

Quinn was gazing off into the distance. He seemed to be stuck ... on something.

"Yes. It works for me. Calms me down. Sometimes I just stomp my feet on the ground and jiggle my butt for awhile, kind of like a tribal belly dancer - just letting it all go, you know - and pretend that I'm an earth goddess. Other times I raise my arms to the sky and try to draw in all the sunlight and energy that I can hold. Storing it all up in my body, as if I were a giant battery."

... Oops. Better shut up now, Gracie, I sternly advised myself, before you reveal all and scare the poor mad scientist away. He has blue eyes after all. Thankfully, Quinn still had a glazed look in his eyes - brain engaged elsewhere. So, I decided to give him a little pinch to wake him up ...

"Is there anything to eat here in your lovely Cottage?" Gracie asked as she glanced outside at the madly swirling snow rattling the windows, knowing there was no way they could manage to go out for dinner.

... I guess I didn't pinch him hard enough ...

He responded absently, "Oh. Food. Yes. I think... check the refrigerator. Look in the cupboards. There might be something there. I seem to remember the pantry is... well-stocked. Oh, by the way, I noticed a good bottle of red wine on the counter. I think there's also a nice white in the refrigerator. Would you care to imbibe, my lady?" He said with his Groucho Marx eyebrows wiggling up and down.

... Oh! Chivalry! He called me 'my lady.' I'm a sucker for chivalry ...

"As a matter of fact, yes." Gracie answered. "If you show me your pantry, I'll see what I can whip up for dinner. But, only if you pour the wine."

"The wine? Oh. Yes. The wine." Quinn replied, completely disconnected from the conversation.

...What did Gracie say? What if... rhythmic... patterns... affect energy levels? Tribal? Energy... storage batteries? Intersections? Ummm.

"Listen, Gracie, the pantry is... somewhere - I mean downstairs next to the map room. Just take a look around. Fix whatever you think might be good. I'm easy. I have to check something out. I'll be back in a few minutes." And then Quinn rushed down the stairs. Gracie blinked; bewildered as to what had just transpired. A second later Quinn's head popped back up from the stairwell, and, again, with a lopsided grin on his face, he said, "Oh. By the way, about that 'jiggly butt' thing - could you give me a demonstration of that later - you know - for science?"

...Thunderstruck, before I could answer, he was gone, rushing down the stairs to the map room, muttering as he went. I was glad he couldn't see the flush rising from my neck to the roots of my hair. After a moment, I followed him downstairs and found the pantry. It wasn't too hard since the etched glass door said "pantry." Duh. I selected wide noodles, beef broth, and catsup, and grabbed fresh

onions and garlic from the bin. Returning to the kitchen, I poured my own wine and inventoried the refrigerator (I was getting good at this). Ah, sirloin. Yes. In less than an hour, I had Hungarian goulash simmering on the stove. The force of the blizzard had not diminished at all, making me profoundly happy that we did not have to implore a poor pizza delivery guy to challenge the elements on a night like this. I simply couldn't handle the responsibility of that after a day like this! Quinn had been down in his map room for awhile, more than the 'few minutes' he'd asked for. I'd better check on him. Maybe he needs a little wine.

I notice that the wine bottle seems about half empty. Oh. Oh ...

Gracie poured a glass of wine for Quinn and headed below ground. She paused on the landing, considering. They were snowed in. Probably about ten inches so far, and it was a sure bet that it would snow even more before morning. By now, the whole City of Duluth was probably shut down. Amazingly, here she was, snug and warm in this tidy little Cottage in Duluth, feeling pretty good after at least two generous glasses of wine.

So, maybe there was a mad scientist on the premises, but the mad scientist was awfully cute, and the dungeon was painted white. Like calories and chocolate, maybe what you did when you were stranded in a blizzard on a night like this, after a day like this, in the middle of nowhere, didn't count. Or, maybe it really did count. Gracie considered just a little bit more ...

"Hey." Gracie said as she stepped softly into Quinn's 'map' room a/k/a dungeon. He looked up noticing the wine glass Gracie was holding. "Hi. Wow. I forgot about the wine, didn't I?"

"No worries. Here you go, Quinn." Gracie handed him the large balloon swirling with deeply-colored red liquid with very good legs. Quinn took a sip. "Are you hungry? Gracie asked. "Supper will be done shortly. Can you take a break?"

"Hungry? Yes. I guess I am," said the mad scientist. "Supper's almost ready? What time is it?" His blue eyes were lighter, more intense. When he learned the time, he winced.

"Sorry, to be down here so long. I just had this crazy idea. A 'brain storm', you could say. Yuk. Yuk."

... Is he laughing? ...

Quinn shrugged his shoulders when Gracie winced at his pun, and continued, attempting to explain his lapse. "Something you said about 'rhythmic patterns'. Inspired, actually. Still, there's a part of the pattern missing - something I just can't get... yet. But, it's close."

... He looked at me, a different kind of look this time, and I gulped.

Quinn continued, "It's just... hanging out there on the periphery. A vital detail that I just can't grasp."

"Maybe after you've had some dinner and some more of this delightful wine, it'll come to you." Gracie said, hopefully, reaching for his hand. "Let's go up."

"Works for me," Quinn replied. "I'm always ready to be inspired by the universe, or a pretty lawyer lady for that matter." Quinn's hand was warm, and we went back up to the kitchen for supper.

The Hungarian goulash was rich and spicy, complements of the 'secret ingredient' which I shall never reveal. We loaded up the fancy dishwasher together, and moved into the reading room with its long windows and fireplace, overlooking the twinkling lights of the city. It was still snowing, but the wind had lessened.

Quinn put his arm across my shoulder as we stared out the windows in silence for a few minutes. It felt... comfortable and companionable. It felt just right.

...Quinn gently raised my chin, looked into my eyes, and slowly and thoroughly kissed me. I began to melt, so I pulled away and said, "Quinn, I noticed the spiral staircase in the hallway upstairs. Is there a fourth level in your Cottage?"

"Actually, yes. I had the staircase installed in the hallway just outside the twins' room - you know the room with the twin beds - because I wanted to put a telescope in the attic. There's a window up there that overlooks the lift bridge. I had the interior attic wall removed so the space now serves as a loft. Now, if you look straight down, it feels like being inside of an Escher print. The staircase on the main level doubles back upon itself. Pretty neat. Want to see it?" He took my hand. "Can you manage to climb a very small, steep staircase up to the top of the house - to the roof almost?"

"Up the ladder to the roof, where we can be closer to heaven?"

"What?"

"Oh. What you just said reminded me of an old tune." I replied. "It's funny you should use those words. The song is an oldie, but one of my favorites."

"I always pay attention to coincidences in life. You should too, Gracie. You never know what it will lead to." Quinn replied.

So, considering again, I said, "Let's go see your loft."

We twirled round and round and up the ladder to the roof. It might not actually have been heaven, but it wasn't too far off. The ceiling was low, so we sat on the sheep skin rug on the floor. The only object in the room was a powerful telescope aimed at the night sky. No starry night sky tonight though. Soft music floated up from the kitchen far below. "When the sky is clear," he said, "it's easy to spend hours up here, just looking at the stars."

"It's a mighty big sky." I said. "I can visualize you up here, at the top of the world, studying your maps and the night sky, trying to understand everything. You must have been a sailor in a past life." Quinn gave me a curious look.

"Even with everything we've learned in the last few decades - even with our most advanced, cutting edge technology, our computers, our 3D printers, our supersonic colliders, we know so very little, actually." Quinn was waxing philosophical again.

"What's to know, really? You're here; I'm here. The clouds are here. The snow is here. The sky is here. Underneath the snow somewhere, the..."

"Gracie, you just keep going on and on, don't you? Quinn asked, moving closer.

"When I get nervous, I just can't shut up!"

"Are you nervous now, Gracie?"

"Definitely, yes. Maybe we should... go down now. It's getting late."

After a moment Quinn said, "That's a fine idea. We should probably get some sleep."

"Yup."

We headed down the steep circular stair, stopping in the hallway in just about the exact spot where we had bumped into each other earlier that very same morning. It seemed liked months before. It had been a very long, and most eventful day.

I asked, nervously, "Where should I sleep tonight?" Before Quinn could answer, I blundered on, "I mean, which bedroom? Since it's your house, you should probably sleep in your own bedroom - in the master bedroom, I mean. I can take the magic room - the one down the hall."

"No, Gracie. It's all right, you sleep in the master. It's more comfortable."

I paused and gulped, bravely deciding in one brief moment.

"Maybe we can... both...?" I started to say. There was a moment of silence. Then, simultaneously reaching out, our hands touched ever so gently. Upon impact, it was like the whole universe exploded in our fingertips.

... A surge of energy passed back and forth between us, and someone moaned. I think it was me. Quinn touched his lips to my lips, without releasing my outstretched arms, our fingertips still touching ...

Quinn said, "I knew it... I knew it would be... you," and the unspoken words were lost in the eternal melting and joining of willing spirits. It was as if light surrounded us, enfolding, enclosing and protecting. Heat and passion joined into an overwhelming feeling of lightness and joy.

I pulled away, uncertain. "Wait," I said, "What is this? Can this be real?"

"Please, Gracie, let's just be here, in this moment together, now. No more questions," he murmured. "We'll make sense of it all later. OK?"

My body afire, with no hope of turning back, I said, "Dance first; think later?"

"Yes," he said. "Yes. That's right. Let's dance."

Hand in hand, we turned, walked into the master bedroom together, and shut the door.

SYZYGY: A pair of connected or corresponding things; a concept used in philosophy to denote a 'close union;' a term used by Carl Jung to mean a 'union of opposites.' In biology, the pairing of chromosomes in meiosis.

Chapter 20

The Syzygy

"Gracie, Gracie, wake up!" Quinn almost shouted. "What if... what if the pattern represents us? You and me! The unexpected energy - our connections to each other! A real syzygy! The perfect biological connection! What if the equations are based on paired energy points?"

"Huh? Paired energy points? What in the world are you talking about?" In the peachy colored dawn, Quinn could see that Gracie was all tangled up in the sheets, rubbing her eyes, struggling to to sit up. One provocative, short, perfectly shaped leg emerged from under the covers, pink toenails revealed. He glanced at her toenails, mesmerized. Gracie followed his gaze to her toenails and, feeling slightly shy, she retracted her leg under the covers.

Shaking his head, Quinn continued, "The connections are there! It was in my dream - the pattern. The eight-pointed star, like a snowflake! Physical reality and psychic connections paired! That's the key!" Wild-eyed, he continued, "There are at least two definite connections: you and I; and Harvey and your mom. Real syzygies. But we need four more. Two more pairs."

"Pairs? Pairs of what? Are you talking about Noah's ark or something? Did you have a bad dream?" Gracie stuttered, pushing the hair out of her eyes and squinting at Quinn.

"No, Carnegie and Feynman." He replied.

"Carnegie and Feynman are pairs? What! They're gay?"

Quinn rolled his eyes. "No. Of course not. They're as straight as I am. But they're definitely involved in all of this. So, how do they fit into the pattern? Um. I wonder." Quinn continued muttering to himself while Gracie glanced out the window. She noted briefly that the fog was rising again from the lake, but no blowing snow.

"They don't share any sort of biological connection." Quinn continued. "And, if my theory is correct, we need an underlying syzygy. Um, I wonder. Could it be Anna?"

"Anna? What do you mean? Are you talking about my Anna, the dead Anna, the splinter soul, my DEAD aunt?" Gracie asked.

Quinn was still free-associating, thinking out loud. "You know, it makes a weird kind of sense. It has to be. Somehow I think Anna is part of the pattern, one of the pairs. Either paired with Carnegie or Feynman. But we're still missing one. Who?"

Gracie was looking at Quinn in bewilderment. Quinn's brain was working so fast, she couldn't keep up. Her pale eyes were concerned, he could tell. But, he rushed on, "Anna must fit with Carnegie. She wouldn't fit with Feynman. For one thing, they would continually argue about white holes and black holes. Their lives would be a kind of living hell. She gets really defensive when you challenge her white hole theory. Found that out the hard way one time. Lost $50. Anyway. Carnegie was always more of a pragmatist; he would just go with the flow." Quinn was disturbed and extremely distracted by Gracie's bare breast, where the sheet had fallen away, but he stalwartly forged on.

"Besides they both love making money. Anna used to talk about how much she had bagged in the market. Well, that's one commonality anyway. Except Carnegie was always making money and then giving it away. It was a game with him. Anna was just the opposite. She was always making money too, but she kept it stashed. Or at least she said so. Aha! Opposites. Oh, yeah, and Carnegie has a thing for chocolate chip cookies. And, as we know, Anna was always making chocolate chip cookies. The second commonality. Yep. Anna is definitely linked with Carnegie. A match made in heaven, so to speak. That just leaves Feynman."

"Quinn, have you forgotten," Gracie yawned sleepily, "Anna is dead, as in 'dead-as-a-doorknob'?"

"Well, that doesn't matter. Carnegie's dead too, in our terms. Gracie, death is just relative... you know, dimensional - a transformation of energy kind of thing. We all know Anna's not really dead." Quinn reached over and absently stroked Gracie's breast. Gracie sighed a little sigh and then, just as she began relaxing into his touch, Quinn gave her a big, warm, joyful kiss, and went bounding out of their still warm bed, stark naked.

"Wait! Anna's not really dead? What's going on? Why is Carnegie linked with... who? Anna! And there's chocolate chip cookies? Where? Where are you going?" Gracie wailed, finally startled fully awake as Quinn's very handsome butt suddenly departed from their room. Sighing, she looked out the window again at the snowscape beyond. Would any of this stuff ever begin to make sense? She wondered. Even the weather doesn't make sense. At least one thing was certain, the blizzard of last night was over. But, that didn't mean that today's potential afternoon blizzard was over, did it? Gracie reminded herself. It was Duluth after all. A little apprehensively and to reassure herself, Gracie noted that there was no wind right now at all, just smooth white snow piled up everywhere, sparkling in the sun like diamond dust amidst the wisps of fog.

Gracie quickly pulled on her rumpled jeans and her favorite sweater (hereafter to be designated her "good luck sweater,") lying in a pile on the floor at the foot of the bed and rushed out of the room after Quinn.

She found him easily, of course, in the map room. By the time she got there, Quinn had erased all of his scribbling from the night before, and had drawn a very large eight-pointed star in the middle of the whiteboard. He was still furiously scribbling. He looked up as Gracie flew in. He was in the process of labeling a horizontal line with "Q" at one end, and "G#2" at the other.

"Can you believe it?" He said. "It's amazing! I should have figured it out before now. It's easy and clearly apparent, when you think of it in the right way."

Gracie looked him over carefully, from head to toe, and liked what she saw. "Yes, indeed, Quinn." She said. "I believe it. I agree. It is amazing. I'd also like to add 'wonderful' and throw in 'great' for good measure. Easy? Well, that's yet to be determined. Clearly apparent? I'll say!" She wiggled her eyebrows for emphasis. She felt like every cell in her whole body was smiling.

It didn't take Quinn too long to catch her drift. "Well, I wasn't exactly referring to... uh... you know."

"Well, Quinn, until you get dressed, I won't be able to pay attention to one single word you have to say, that's for sure."

"OK. Give me a minute. I'll be right back." Gracie got more than a glimpse, this time, of his wonderful butt and broad shoulders as Quinn exited the map room with an exaggerated swagger. She took a deep breath and turned to study the diagram Quinn had sketched on the whiteboard. Familiar somehow. It looks like... something... Gracie moved to the whiteboard and began drawing.

Ten minutes later, Quinn arrived in the map room, with two steaming cups of coffee, and, unfortunately, fully clothed. By the time he arrived, Gracie had drawn a lacy pattern around the eight-pointed star, although she didn't know why. It felt just right.

"What's that?" He asked, as Gracie laid down the marker and he handed her the mosquito cup.

"I'm not sure, exactly, but your pattern reminded me of something. Something I've seen recently. I just can't seem to remember where, though. I just needed to fill in some of the details." Gracie replied.

Quinn silently stared at what Gracie had added to his drawing. He copied the diagram onto a blank piece of paper and stuffed it into the pocket of his jeans. He had a quizzical look on his face. "Um. I wonder." He said.

Here we go again. "Wonder what?" Gracie said.

"I'll tell you later. I need to let it roll around awhile." Quinn replied as he took Gracie's hand and lead her to a small sofa facing the whiteboard. They sat down. Gracie shook her head and took the first sip of her coffee. "Mmm.

Good," she said. Gesturing at the whiteboard, she said, "You dreamed this up last night? What does it all mean?"

"It's amazingly simple. The points of the star are electrical conduits. There." Quinn pointed. "Energy passes between the pairs in a straight line. 'Q' stands for me, Quinn, and 'G#2' stands for you, Gracie."

"Why am I labeled as G#2?" Gracie reasonably asked.

"I made your Mom, G#1. She came first after all. Anyway, that line represents the energy shared by the attractors, kind of like positive and negative diodes, anode and cathode posts. An energy conduit. Except, in this case, the circuits are human beings, not posts."

"Quinn, I never heard of an eight-pointed energy conduit before. Is this some new kind of science, again?"

"You could say that, I guess. Never forget, Gracie, there is no box for me. I threw the box away a long time ago. In fact, I have reached the conclusion that true concepts originate outside of the box, and continue beyond the box. I told you before how I finally began to look for coincidences, for overlaps. How I began to pay attention to odd things in my life?" Quinn began.

"Sure." Gracie replied. "The weird stuff. You said that you ignored the boundaries set up by the scientific method and tried to take a fresh new look at everything. Then, you used your own creativity and inspiration to create your time-loopy machine right? And that your students thought you had gone mental."

"In a nutshell, yes."

"So?"

"So, that's what I did last night in my dream."

"You went mental?"

"No. I was inspired by my dream. Did I tell you that I've been inspired by dreams before?"

"No, but that makes a weird kind of sense - in your case. I've read that some geniuses invent stuff in their dreams. So, that's what you did? You invented this star pattern in your sleep?"

"Well, not exactly. I've been playing around with this pattern for awhile. I've seen it somewhere. Before. But I can't remember - exactly - where." Quinn shook his head a bit, as if to dislodge an old memory, and then continued, "But you're essentially right about dreams. Many breakthroughs in science, math, music, and art have had their origins in dreams. Occasionally when the time is ripe for an idea, two different people will develop a dream concept simultaneously. Synchronicity. Like when Isaac Newton and Gottfried Leibniz independently developed The Calculus at the exact same time in history - when it was needed the most. They had no relationship with each other and they were separated by continents. It was a breakthrough that plunged all of Europe into a new scientific age. It's almost as if they unconsciously plugged into the same network to pick up the needed data - and printed it out at the same time."

"Very interesting." Gracie replied, hoping for more.

"Well, I've had this certain dream a few times before, but it usually ends up differently than last night."

"Go on." Gracie said.

"Well, it starts with me juggling, walking backwards, naked, into a swimming pool full of penguins."

"Quinn. Stop. A piece of advice. Don't ever tell anyone that your important dreams start off that way. You will lose all credibility within the first few seconds!" Gracie cautioned.

With a sheepish grin, Quinn continued, "Point taken. Well, last night, after we... fell asleep, I had one of my recurring dreams. It may have started out the same way... as I just mentioned..." Quinn glanced quickly over at Gracie and then cleared his throat, "and I've been in this place before, but you were never there before, obviously because I didn't know you before. Anyhow, we were a couple. We were moving to a new town, and there was this... I can only describe it as a strong 'pull' between us. You were standing next to me, and I could see a line, kind of like a golden rope linking us together. Then we looked up at the sky, together, and we saw the pattern, the eight-pointed star burning brightly. I looked around, and Harvey and your Mom were standing next to us. They were also linked by a golden rope. Then I knew. I knew it was the answer."

"The answer to what?" Gracie asked, totally mystified.

"The energy connections. It takes a biological connection to complete the circuit. You and me. Harvey and your Mom. Carnegie and Anna. Feynman and... I don't know who. We'll have to find out."

"What do you mean, we'll have to find out? Find out what?"

"Find out who Feynman has a syzygy with."

At Gracie's bewildered look, Quinn explained, "We need to find someone who Feynman has a symbiotic, perhaps biological connection with. By Tuesday night."

"And if we don't, then what happens?"

"Well, Harvey will be stuck here, with us, in this 3-dimensional universe. Once the gate closes, however, he'll probably look about seventy years old again. I honestly don't know what will happen to your Mom though. She's here now in this dimensional space, but I don't really know what could happen. As long as the machine keeps looping back to Thursday afternoon, she's probably OK. Once the connection is severed - who knows? She seems real enough here, in a biological sense, but strange stuff happened when you were born. Remember what they told us yesterday? I'll have to discuss the probabilities with Feynman. He's the expert."

"And when exactly are we scheduled for this - this... what do you call it? Inter... dimensional, transference thingy?"

"Tuesday night, at 7:00 o'clock p.m. in my lab in Minneapolis."

"OK then. Where's your shovel?" Gracie asked. At the completely blank look on Quinn's face, Gracie asked, astonished, "You do own a shovel, don't you?"

"I think so," Quinn said with a shrug of his shoulders. "It's probably outside. Somewhere. Buried in a snow bank. Should we try to find it?"

"I'm on board with that. Let's do it."

Chapter 21

Dimensional Dilemma

~Part I~

Jane Roberts[19] describes a "dimensional dilemma" as an experience where the psychic content of something is changing. It could be a belief, symbol, idea, or intention. Everything looks the same and seems normal on the surface, yet your inner perception tells you something else is happening. Nothing fits. Things feel different. Events seem "out of shape" somehow, squeezed into a space [or time] that is too small or cramped. This incongruity happens because you are receiving new data, on inner levels. The end result is that your reality is expanded and you experience a new, richer life. In an ideal situation, new

---

[19] Jane Roberts, the author of the Seth Books, was a prolific writer of numerous books of her own. The concept of a dimensional dilemma comes from her own book, <u>Adventures in consciousness</u>, originally published by Prentice-Hall in 1975.

creativity results. Your life is different, but newer and fuller. There is one caveat, however. The new ideas must be successfully integrated into your life. Otherwise, you begin to see UFOs.

The phone rings. Quinn rolls over onto his stomach, throwing his arm across Gracie's waist. Gracie struggles to sit up, switches on the Minnie Mouse lamp on her nightstand, and picks up the receiver.

"Hello?" Gracie hesitantly answers, oddly awake. Glancing at the clock, she notices that it's 4:12 a.m.

"Gracie? Finally! It's me, Natalie. Are you still in bed?"

"Well, Natalie, of course I'm still in bed. It's 4:12 in the morning! What's up? Wait. Are you in trouble?" Gracie asks, with some trepidation. "You're always in some sort of trouble when you call me this early!"

"Oh, I'm so NOT in trouble. But you... something's up with you again, right? I can tell. I can always tell. Hey, what's that funny noise I'm hearing? Sounds like snoring..."

"Never mind." Gracie says. "Why are you calling me to tell me I'm in trouble? I know this already."

"I just wanted... Wait! Where the hell have you been, anyway? You've been off the grid since Friday afternoon!"

"Well, after Judge Henderson sent me to inventory Linda Jorgensen's refrigerator, I went to Duluth. With the cab driver. Then there was the blizzard."

"You did what? Judge Henderson sent you to... Duluth? Why Duluth? Ah... longshoremen! But, with a cab driver?

Wait. Is he the one snoring next to you?" Natalie exclaimed all without taking a breath. "I knew it. You went on one of your adventures again, didn't you! Without me? I'm supposed to watch your back, remember? Ever since that time at Whistle Binkies..."

"How could I ever forget?" Gracie replied. "We managed to get out of that one, OK though, didn't we? But, it was kind of scary, I have to admit."

"We made a deal after Whistle Binkies, remember? I watch your back. You watch mine." Natalie rambled on. "How can I watch your back if you're off in Duluth with some longshoreman, anyway?"

"He's not a longshoreman. He's a physicist ... cab driver ... mad scientist ... rich guy ... sort of."

"I knew it! So, another one of your lunatics again! What is it with you, Gracie? How come you never hang out with normal people?"

"Give me a break, Natalie. He's really cute, anyway. And, I have first dibs."

"Sure. Well... OK. But, bad timing, Gracie. Especially if you wind up in jail! That guy from the Lawyer's Board, Stein... Frankenstein or Dracula or some other kind of monster-name anyway, was calling every hour on the hour on Friday. And, the police are going to show up at the office this morning at 9:00 a.m. and they want to interview you. They told me you had to be here - or else! What am I supposed to tell them? They want to talk to you about that old lady who died in the office Thursday night. What was her name again? You know, Anna... something?"

"Oh, yes. Of course. Anna. Anna Strong. My aunt, I guess." I reply with a yawn, my heart beat slowing down to normal. Everything seemed more normal now, with Natalie rambling on. Quinn pulled me toward him, and began to snuggle in closer. I sighed.

"Your aunt?" Natalie asked, astonished. "How could she ..."

I knew that Natalie would stop talking, eventually, if only to catch her breath. So, I could be patient. Especially at 4:12 a.m. I could simply go back to sleep; eat a doughnut; or, better yet, I could play around with Quinn. A person had to be quick to get a word in edge-wise when Natalie was on a roll. Finally, there was a pause. I jumped in while I had the chance.

"Yes. I just found out. In Duluth. She was my aunt. And, don't worry, everything's going to work out just fine."

"Oh. Sure thing. But, don't waste your breath on me. You'd better convince Tom of that first. He chewed through at least two pencils on Friday already, trying to work up a feasible defense for you."

Amazing, I thought. Instead of firing me, he's trying to help! Wow. "I'm fine, really, Natalie. Things are just changing for me. There's lots of new stuff going on. Tell Tom not to worry. I'll explain everything when I get in."

"Oh, that's such a relief." Natalie said sarcastically, and hung up.

OK. So, here I am. It's now 4:22 a.m. on Monday morning. And, as Natalie had just reminded me, I'm back. Back in my apartment. In Oakdale. Back in my old life. But nothing feels the same. As in NOT ONE THING. My brain almost hurts trying to understand it all; trying to fit all the pieces together. I close my eyes. Reflecting, I try to focus on the easily observable differences: Well, for one thing, there's a man in my bed! Wow. Always a big plus. But, besides that, I feel... somehow better. Bordering on amazing actually. It's almost as if someone snuck into my house and painted all the walls vibrant colors, bursting with energy. Everything is new. Everything is fresh. Maybe it's just the great sex. Doesn't really matter though does it? In any case, I have been rebooted!

Peeking down, I notice the tightly curled golden hairs on Quinn's arm; the arm that is holding me tight. Well, continuing to enumerate the obvious differences: last Thursday morning, I mused, there was no amazing lover in my life; no father; no mother; no Anna; no Cottage; no blizzard. A lot of "no"s. My rational self interjects, "but, there was no need for a pattern or a plan to save the world either was there, girly girl?" My head begins to spin. I really wanted to flip off my rational self. So I closed my eyes and considered. If everything that had happened since Thursday was a dream, then I realized that I didn't want to wake up. Except for Anna, of course, no matter how weird, strange, connected or disconnected she was, or whether or not she was actually related to me, I wished she hadn't died in my office. Especially if she had really been my aunt. It might have been nice to get to know her. An aunt... a real relative... MY AUNT, well, maybe. But, no matter. I can't change what happened. Despite how odd or even strange things were right now, I didn't want to go back to my world the way it was. So, I decided, let's just give this new reality a chance and see what happens.

Having attained a modicum of clarity at last, I opened my eyes slowly. My old life was just too small, I realized. And even scary, at times. I recalled the time I had ended up in a small locked room at the Anoka County Treatment Center. Not that I was the one committed, of course, but I was there as the legal representative of my court-appointed client: a schizophrenic, almost seven foot tall, enormously huge young guy with a home-boy hat on. Natalie told me later that he was also black. Seriously. How did I miss that?

Anyway, I remember he had been off his meds, mumbling incoherently the whole time. We were in his locked cell. It had all started for him about a month earlier when he had been picked up by the police and put on a seventy-two hour hold at the Hennepin County Medical Center. Among other things, he had been running naked down Hennepin Avenue, screaming at the top of his lungs that his mother was trying to poison him (mainly because her stove was an evil entity). Oh yeah. In self-defense, he had also been compelled to start her stove on fire. His own mother eventually called the cops to pick him up and restrain him. Damn straight.

After my client was committed to the Treatment Center, his mom had asked to be her son's legal guardian. So, the Court had appointed me, lucky me, to be his lawyer. Remembering more clearly now... on that particular day, as I tried to exit the Treatment Center, the Center's lockdown protocol was initiated. Somehow my "Visitor" badge had gone missing! Thankfully, the staff eventually realized that I wasn't a patient trying to escape. Although the status of my freedom was somewhat questionable during the entire interlude, I normally dress like a lawyer. So, because I looked like a lawyer, there was a reasonable belief on the part of *most* of the staff that I really was a lawyer[20] rather than a mental patient trying to escape. I was just lucky that they hadn't started me on neuroleptics before Natalie had arrived to rescue me. Even to this day, I still worry about being subjected to involuntary electroshock treatments whenever I visit a client at the Treatment Center. You know, payback for the extra trouble I had caused staff that day.[21]

---

[20] In spite of the fact that I have curly hair.

[21] And, I always wear my most expensive lawyer-suit when I show up at the Treatment center these days.

Still pondering the changes in my life, I realized that, except for a few friends, my path was quite solitary. Why? I wondered. Answering my silent question, I realized that I had made a habit of worrying about everything, care-taking my clients, and mostly choosing to be alone. But now, today, in this moment, I wanted more. I wanted to keep this feeling; this feeling of being connected; this new life. I wanted to keep Quinn. At that exact moment, I made a vow. I determined not to miss any part of the adventure of my life anymore. No matter what happened today or tomorrow, or how bizarre it might yet become. And, if last weekend was any indication, things could get very bizarre indeed!

Suddenly I felt brand new. Grace for Gracie? I silently approved of the newer, better, braver Gracie! Slightly apprehensive none-the-less, I glanced out the window. A whole lot of snow, but no UFOs. So far, so good.

My gaze floated back down to Quinn again. I had a vivid image in my mind of what might be accomplished in the next forty-five minutes or so, especially if I rolled Quinn over on his back and laid myself on top of him. Most interesting, indeed.

With renewed hope and contemplating upcoming events, I felt ecstatically happy that Quinn was not my client. Not that I generally sleep with clients, you must surely realize by now. The simple fact is that I have never, ever slept with even one client! Furthermore, I never intend to. However, it was still a great relief to realize that Quinn was not my client and that he never would be, for two very good reasons. The first reason involved my ethics professor, Professor Kroman. Not that I had ever slept with Professor Kroman either, but I simply didn't want him to be disappointed in me.

Why would I worry about whether or not a law professor was disappointed in me, you say? And, anyway, an ethics professor? They actually teach lawyers about ethics? Amazing! Before you go too far, dear reader, just for the record, all 3Ls[22] are required to take a grueling ten week course labeled "professional responsibility" or "lawyer ethics." But, that's only one itty-bitty step in the olympic process required to become a lawyer. Once we have successfully completed the classroom phase of the professional responsibility course, then we are required to pass an even-more rigorous Professional Responsibility Exam. If we can manage to pass the Professional Responsibility Exam then, and only then, are we permitted to sit for the Bar exam.

Even then, we must assure the law examiners that we do not have any underlying or undisclosed moral impediments. You know: too many parking tickets, a bankruptcy filing, suffer from depression or mental illness,

---

[22] A "3L" is a third year law student.

or have delinquent credit card debt.[23] So, naturally, if we can manage to surmount all of these obstacles, then "the powers that be" will somehow be assured that we have sufficient knowledge and judgment to act righteously, "twenty-four hours a day for the rest of our natural lives." Realistically, as in any closed club, if truth be told, the law examiners will then have some confidence that we are straight-laced, unsurprising assholes. Restated, if we can manage to get through three years of law school without jumping off a bridge, going broke, or losing all of our hair, then there is a pretty good chance that we have been sufficiently brain-washed so that we will not shame our profession by any moral turpitude. Theoretically. Simply a rite of passage. Similar to the requirements for entering a convent or the priesthood, I suppose. Of course, there may be times when a few aberrant individuals pass through the hallowed gates, and then all hell breaks loose in the legal profession for a short time. At least until the dust settles. Ah, well.

That's where the opinion and scholarship of Professor Kroman, my ethics professor, matters. Looking back, I realize that one of the first and most valuable things Professor Kroman taught us was that lawyers are "pianos" and "not buses." In other words, lawyers are not required

---

[23] I can't imagine the quandary if a 3L happened to have a carry permit!

to take every case. In fact, we can only ethically take a case if we can zealously represent the client. This is one sentiment that I can whole-heartedly embrace. It is an exceedingly important point as it turns out. It means that I don't have to represent the bad guys, so I try not to. It's always distressing when a client "goes over to the dark side."[24] But that's another whole chapter on its own. As a consequence of Professor Kroman's shared wisdom, I only represent the white hats. I like being a piano.

Another thing I liked about my ethics professor was that he didn't mince words. He got straight to the point. And, unlike most law professors, he certainly wasn't politically correct. He was a tough, and he wanted us to be toughs too. His goal was to force us to fully comprehend, in plain words, what we were getting ourselves into by becoming lawyers.

He was an adjunct professor, an elderly founder of one of the oldest and most prestigious law firms in the United States. Retired, short, skinny and balding, the rumor was that his wife was an Amazon, a blonde brazen beauty. And no one doubted it since Professor Kroman distinguished himself in many ways. For example, on the first day of our class, he explained that he had served our Country in World War II. Admirable. He elaborated by stating that he

---

[24] And it does happen from time to time. The ethical rules tell us how to "fire" a client if we need to.

was drafted actually, but apparently the Army didn't know what to do with such a little guy, too puny to carry a gun. And, worse yet, he already had a law degree so he was smarter than most generals, as the Professor told his story. So, naturally, the Army figured out the perfect job for him. They made Professor Kroman their "pecker checker." Yes. You heard me. He checked peckers.[25] Needless to say, I was traumatized by this story. In fact, I have tried to erase the vision of Professor Kroman checking peckers from my mind every year since I graduated from law school. Unsuccessfully as it turns out.

Consistent with his personality, Professor Kroman's pedagogy was explicit and direct. He was only bested one time, to my knowledge. And, amazingly, I was privileged to be present on that momentous day. In the presence of my entire section, about fifty 3Ls, Professor Kroman slipped up. He asked my married friend, a Danish beauty with an angelic face and the best legs in town - the most lusted-after beauty in the whole class in fact - a very simple question. He blandly asked, "Ms. Elsberg, "Is it a violation of the ethical rules to sleep with your client?" The whole class

---

[25] If you don't already know this, a "pecker" is slang for "penis." I am sure there are other slang words for "penis," but I haven't made an extensive study of this subject to date. Actually, I don't even know what the duties of a "pecker checker" might be. I have to wonder if rulers are involved.

waited with bated breath for my friend's answer. Glancing around the room, I noted that most of the male students appeared to be drooling, hoping that my friend's answer would give them some kind of an edge, personally or in the future, in their dreams of conquest. All the female students were giving silent thanks that they had not been put on the spot with a question like that. After a slight pause, my friend answered in a steady voice, "Well, Professor, I don't think it's a violation of professional ethics to sleep with your client... but I don't think you can charge for it either." After a stunned silence, the class just roared. Despite the Professor's stern attempts to restore order in the classroom, random giggles broke out every few minutes as he attempted to continue the lecture. It was useless. No one could pay attention anymore. Finally conceding defeat, Professor Kroman roared at the class, "Get out of here!" We all left in a hurry, still howling with glee. Touché and my best to you, Professor. You taught us well.

So, the second reason I'm glad that Quinn is not my client is that I'm hoping to charge him for my services, for the entire rest of his life. He's a keeper. So no ethical violations. Good.

~Part II~

As he locked the door of Gracie's apartment, Quinn's mind was furiously calculating probabilities: the probability of success; the probability of failure; the probability of a black swan[26]. On the surface, he realizes, he feels totally good. That is, really good.

Never one to shirk from confrontation, even with himself, Quinn admits that he feels really, extraordinary good! Loose even. He squares his shoulders, brushes his blonde hair back from his forehead, and looks to the sky. It barely registers that the dark bellies of clouds are massing over him, directly over him in fact. To a passerby, he looks like a wild man of power. Nervy energy and power just barely under control. A norse god minus his hammer. The wind picks up. The clouds swirl even more.

Not moving, Quinn's inner dialog continues. But... she's insane. And, she's a lawyer for God's sake. What the hell have I gotten myself into, with this... this... amazing... woman? Remembering the touch and feel of her, he smiles. Her alluring fragrance, gentle but oh so compelling. For Christ-sakes, I'm like a unicorn in heat he admits. Mindless, drawing closer and closer to the virgin. Well, I'm no unicorn, and she's no virgin, that's for sure. It still doesn't change the fact that I haven't felt like this in years. Wait. Let's face it, I've never felt like this before. But, I can't feel this good today! Not about this enigmatic woman. Where does she belong anyway?

---

[26] A "black swan" is an event that is totally unforeseen, entirely un-predictable, and it changes everything. See Taleb.

Gazing up at the sky again, Quinn grimly notices that the new morning light in the sky is swiftly fading. An unseen swirl of movement. A sense of weather emerging. He ignores it. Um. I have to concentrate. First things first. Feynman and I have to get the machine working and calibrated by Tuesday night. Tomorrow night. I'll show him the pattern. Yes. We can handle that - we're close. Today we'll figure out the machine. Tomorrow we'll open the portal and put things right. Then, I'll figure out what's going on between Gracie and me - if I can. If she's still here. Finding himself walking faster, continuing with his diatribe, Quinn speculates. I wonder if I'll ever be able to figure her out? Well, actually, maybe I don't want to. Maybe I shouldn't. What if...? He shrugged, and then slides the key into the cab door lock. If Gracie is an inter-dimensional child of some sort... I already know she's some kind of wild card, but will she even be able to stay after tomorrow tonight? Will they let her stay? And, who is 'they?' Harvey, her Mom, Feynman, Carnegie? And what the hell does Anna have to do with all of this? If Gracie decides to go, where in the hell will that be? Will she simply vanish into mid-air like she never existed at all? Then, what about us...? Does she want to stay here? Would she even want to stay here, with... me? Can I go with her if she decides to go? Does she have a choice? Do I want to go? Oh, Christ.

There's only one thing I know for sure, Quinn admits. She's at the center of it all. But, I knew that before. Even before I met her. But it's different now. What she decides will change everything for Gracie and me. Or worse, for everybody. With resolve, Quinn starts the engine and heads for his lab, finally consciously noticing the gathering storm clouds, sensing the changing weather patterns. The storm must be moving south from Duluth, he thinks. It'll snow by tonight. Great. Another blizzard. It figures.

Chapter 22

Secrets

There are some things that should never be revealed, not ever. Like the fact that during my high school years I routinely slept with a nylon stocking stretched over my "Dippity-do"-saturated curls to make my hair appear flat and straight like everyone else's. Or, more to the point, what exact kind of food was inside Linda Jorgensen's refrigerator.[27] Thankfully, I only have to reveal to Judge Henderson, promptly at 10:00 a.m., tomorrow morning, the exact contents of my client's refrigerator and not the "Dippity-do" incidents. I will still have to prove, by clear and convincing evidence, however, that edible food-like products are nutritious and healthy. If I can't persuade the Judge of this fact, there is a very good chance that my

---

[27] Assuming, of course, that it can be defined as food to begin with.

client will be legally determined to be a vulnerable person, in need of the Court's protection. And, if that happens, then all of Linda's personal rights and her own decision-making authority will be shifted to her daughter, Rich Bit… I mean, Rhonda the Rich. Wow, and yikes to boot! Things should never have gotten this far.

Musing, I understood that if my client were fat, it would be <u>enormously</u> easier (pun) to argue that edible food-like products are OK. Unfortunately, my client is slender, and the law apparently requires her to have "nutritious" food in her refrigerator in order to be considered "normal."[28] Who would have guessed that the law is more likely to allow a fat person to retain their legal rights than a slender person?[29] Huh? Do I smell a class action here? Probably not. Maybe I can make an equal protection argument? You know, "Your Honor, it is unfair

---

[28] Reading between the lines: "Presumed to either be on a successful diet and not suffering from some kind of mental illness related to food consumption." There's no doubt in my mind that by now psychologists have come up with sort of weird classification (with a compelling catalog of symptoms and a whole body of "treatment modalities") for allegedly self-abusive behavior for persons who are underweight.

[29] Underweight people have the same rights as fat people to be frightened into self-diagnoses by television ads and magazine advertising, don't they? Like a computer virus, it just goes on and on. It was so much easier when skinny people could just be skinny.

for the Court to treat my slender client differently than if she were a fat person. She is in a protected class, after all. You know, the class of slender people in the United States... BLAH... BLAh... BLah... Blah... bla...." My own eyes glaze over. Boring myself to death and still grasping for straws, I am forced to take a "zen" moment.[30]

... I am at the cabin again. My cabin in the woods. I stride across the oaken floors to the closet door with the little round window in it; still dirty, still mocking me. I turn the doorknob. What! It easily moves! I step forward into the tiny room where all secrets are revealed; where all the answers are given. Look! Look over there! There in the corner... why, it's a...

My head jerks up. I instinctively reach for the nylon stocking covering my curls. Then I remember. No, thank God, I don't have to do that anymore.

"Natalie," I work the intercom, "did you ever get a copy of Linda Jorgensen's Trust?" I ask.

"Sure. It's in her scanned file. Oh, by the way, her lawyer - you know, the guy from Oregon - left a message for you. Saturday, when he got back from China. You know, when you were in Duluth with the longshoreman and I was having a nervous breakdown trying to find you?

---

[30] Actually, to anyone else in the world, it might appear as if I had nodded off.

Yeah. That Saturday. He said he was flying in for the hearing tomorrow. Get this. He's flying in on his own private jet. How cool is that? And, he even gave me his private cell number!"

"Oh really?" I reply. This is nothing unusual for Natalie. She probably has the President's private cell number too.

"Natalie. Tell me the truth," I apprehensively ask, "did you give him your roller derby name?"

"Of course I did. He googled me while we were talking."

"No doubt." I say.

"Oh, by the way, Johnny said he wants you to call him asap." Natalie continued.

"Johnny? Johnny who?"

"God, you're dense today, Gracie. You know, Johnny, the lawyer we are talking about. Linda's attorney." Natalie tersely replied.

"Oh, yeah. Sure." Suspicious, I ask. "Hey Nat, you didn't somehow give him the idea that I was a roller girl too, did you?"

"No." There is a slight pause. "Of course not. He just thinks you are one of the weird lawyers that I work for." Um. Another slightly longer pause. I sense that maybe Natalie isn't telling me the whole truth. Perhaps a little white lie by omission. She continues, "He said something about wanting to talk to you about Linda's Trust. You know, some kind of trigger thing if Linda is declared incompetent. He said the kids had tried something like this before when Linda was visiting her other daughter last year. In North Carolina; or was it South Carolina? Oh hell, one of those southern states, you know. Where Dolly Parton comes from. I'm not sure."

"You mean, Pigeon Forge, Tennessee?" I ask. "Stop." I hurriedly say. "It really doesn't matter." Better and better yet. "Isn't that just predictable?" I say rhetorically. "Thanks, Nat." I power up my Mac and disconnect the intercom before Natalie can reveal any more secrets. The machine hums like the little white miracle machine it is. Low and behold. I discover the nice words, "Irrevocable Trust of Linda Jorgensen" on the file menu. Come to mama, I repeat to myself. I'll bet you $1,000 big ones that if Linda is determined to be incapacitated, then Rich Bit... her daughter, I mean, gets control of all of the dough. Twenty minutes later, I complete my phone conference with Attorney "Johnny" Johnson of Portland, Oregon, print out his emailed copy of Linda Jorgensen's Health Care Directive, and, with an appropriately-sized black skirt barely skimming my knees, I head to the Courthouse with a big smile on my face. Once "Johnny" had understood that not all Minnesota women are roller girls, it was easy. Well, to be honest, maybe the two free tickets to Natalie's next roller derby bout helped make "Johnny" a little more willing to get me what I needed in a hurry.

"Back before 9:00 a.m.," I holler as I hurry past Natalie's desk where she is filing her nails and reading the latest pin-up girl magazine.

"Better the hell be," she says. "Can't entertain all the boys in blue by myself now, can I?" She winks at me, "but I'll give it a go if I must."

"Always willing to sacrifice yourself for the greater good, aren't you, Nat? Such a saint!" I mutter on my way out of the office. Hurrying in the skyway again, I notice the sky color is changing, from dark to more dark. I briefly wonder how Quinn is doing at the lab.... and whether or not he's figured it all out yet. And, if he has, I wonder if he'll tell me. And, if he does, I wonder if I'll believe it.

Chapter 23

Lab Work

"Of course! Brilliant! She knew! She knew the answer all along!" He jumped up from his chair. Quinn's excitement reverberated around the room interrupting Feynman and Dirk who were troubleshooting the wavelength controller across the room. They watched in surprise as Quinn bounded across the room in three giant strides and began reaching past them, adjusting the dials purposefully.

Feynman and Dirk stepped away from the control console to give Quinn more room. "What do you mean, Quinn? Who knew? The answer to what?" Dirk asked.

"Anna. Anna knew. She must have unconsciously known that the energy has to be just slightly above the infrared." Quinn replied.

When Dirk looked perplexed, Quinn offered an explanation, of sorts. "Our mathematical calculations," he nodded at Feynman, "came up with a much higher energy input level. That's why it wasn't working. We were off by a magnitude. That's why it was always wonky. It would have fried the circuits each and every time! Why it might even have fried us. That's what must have happened the first time - when Gracie was born. Nobody died, thankfully, but Anna emerged. She knew! She kept trying to tell us." Quinn had an intense look on his face as he continued to adjust the wavelength generator. The oscillations seemed to be less erratic, slowing down. A pattern began to emerge on the screen. An almost recognizable pattern. A few more adjustments. And, voila!

"Anna? You mean's Grace's double?" Feynman asked.

Again, Dirk looked perplexed. This time, no one attempted to help him understand, as usual. He was just the lab's genius post-doc after all. Nothing special.

"Yeah. Anna." Quinn answered Feynman. "The old lady who died in Gracie's office last Thursday night, remember? She was fixated on the color orange. Her orange candies; her orange clothing; and, finally, her orange hair. She couldn't express it in language, so she communicated it by surrounding herself with the color. The color 'orange.' It was a clue."

"A clue? A clue for what? What does the color orange have to do with anything?" Dirk stuttered and began to sweat.

Ignoring Dirk's question, Feynman considered the significance of colors as clues. Specifically, color with respect to energy outputs. Thinking out loud, Feynman considered the questions. "What unconscious knowledge could Anna convey by using color? Particularly the color 'orange?' Let me see... unless..." Feynman's eyes were twinkling when he met Quinn's. Quinn nodded.

They looked down at the screen, now stabilized and showing the oscillations of a well-tuned engine. "Of course. The electromagnetic spectrum." Feynman answered Dirk. "Isn't that just the prettiest girl you've ever seen?"

Dirk was shaking his head. Quinn picked up the thread. "Dirk - don't you remember? In the electro-magnetic spectrum, the color 'orange' is a lower-level energy vibration, almost outside of the visible range."

Dirk still looked perplexed, so Feynman jumped in, "Some electromagnetic energy can't be seen at all. You know, infrared, ultraviolet, x-rays. Take a rainbow, for example. Some colors in a rainbow can be seen, vivid and bright. Others, are just a shimmer. Kind of like a shadow. Hardly visible, or not visible at all. Orange is one of the colors in the visible range, just barely. It has very specific electromagnetic..."

"Sure, whatever." Dirk replied. "Since you two seem to have figured it all out, and the world apparently is no longer teetering on the verge of destruction, I'm getting a coke." He walked out of the lab shaking his head, muttering under his breath, "...ego maniacs ...tired of this shit... tired of being a post-doc... gotta get a real life..."

Feynman and Quinn winced, remembering what it had been like to be a post-doc for just a moment. Then, out of habit, they refocused their attention, glancing down at the screen again, mesmerized. The oscillations had settled down into a repeating pattern. Beautiful smooth waves. They grinned at each other.

"This is great." Quinn began. "Now that we have the energy tuned in, I wonder if..." he hesitated.

"Wonder, what?" Feynman prodded him on with an exasperated look. "No time to hold back. Spit it out, Quinn. You've learned to trust your instincts. So, what have you got simmering up there now? And, how the hell did you figure out the 'orange' thing?" He tapped Quinn's forehead.

Quinn nodded, exhaling. "Yeah. OK. Well, I've been thinking about this time thing, you know, for a little while - for some 'time', actually." He grinned sheepishly. "Oddly enough, I knew this had to fit into the equation, somewhere." Quinn quickly pulled out a folded paper from his pocket and handed it to Feynman. "Here. Take a look at this." Feynman unfolded the paper, and began to study the diagram. Quinn continued, "I had a dream Saturday night about this pattern," he pointed to the diagram, "about an eight-pointed star burning brightly. See here?" He gestured. "Each point is linked by four golden ropes, bound together. It felt like energy circuits to me." He scratched the stubble already growing on his chin at 9:00

a.m. in the morning. "And then Gracie drew this last Sunday morning after we..." He paused again and cleared his throat.

Feynman glanced up smiling, quirking his eyebrows in interest. No statement ever escaped Feynman's attention, especially if it concerned behaviors of the opposite sex. Quinn started again, "I went to get coffee and Gracie started doodling. She added this lacy stuff around my original drawing. At first I thought it was a girl thing. You know, like lacy underwear, or something like that. But, she said the pattern was familiar somehow. And it seemed familiar to me at the time too, but I couldn't place it just then. Later, I realized that it matched the pattern on the tiles in my shower. For God's sake, Richard, my shower. At my Cottage. Hillside Cottage. The Cottage I bought just a few months ago. Coincidence, I guess." He looked balefully at Feynman challenging him to say something, anything. Neither man believed in coincidences.

"Connections." Feynman said. "It's all about connections."

Quinn nodded and took a deep breath. His words came out in a rush as if they could no longer be held back. "What if Gracie's drawing represents the people involved in the transference? You know, paired-off. Kind of like energy twins, positive and negative attractors. Each pair a syzygy. The energy would have to flow though the pair, the couple, then through all the couples, to complete the circuit. Eight points of connection."

Feynman quirked his eyebrows.

"I know this sounds far out, but like you said; it's all about connections, isn't it?" Quinn asked.

"I got you on the 'connections' part. But eight?" Feynman raised his eyebrows even more. "I understand what you are saying - at least conceptually. But eight people? More precisely, how do we wind up with eight people, intimately connected to each other by tomorrow night? The connections would have to be very strong for it to have even have half a chance of working right."

"Well, we can account for seven right off." Quinn elaborated.

"We can?" Feymann grimaced. "How so?"

"Thinking out loud, here... Well, it seems the main actors are Gracie and I, one pair; her parents, Harvey and Grace #1; the second pair. Then there's Carnegie and Anna."

"Stop. Wait." Feynman started shaking his head. "Why does Carnegie get paired up with Anna?" Why don't I get Anna?"

"Believe me, you don't want Anna. Anna's not right for you. We'll have to find someone else for you. Someone younger, and more in tune with your... proclivities."

With a falsely innocent expression on his face, Feynman grunted, "My... proclivities, you say? Whatever could you mean?" The innocence was gone now, the true Feynman, amused and mischievous was revealed. Quinn replied with a shrug of his shoulders.

"OK. Let's assume for a moment that your theory is correct. We're talking about syzygies aren't we?" Those relationships are quite significant. You know they're not easy to achieve, don't you? Rare, in fact." Feynman looked at Quinn who nodded in agreement.

"So, how in the hell can I find someone... significant, not to mention arrange for a..." he cleared his throat, "biological connection by tomorrow night?" Feynman questioned. "It's quite impossible." Feynman said.

Quinn made a face at Feynman. "Really, Richard, all of this is so far-fetched how can any of it be possible? Yet it is. If I'm right, it's at least one possible way. There may be other possible physical connections that could work, things we haven't considered yet - that nobody's considered yet, but we're running out of time. The energy, the connections, all have to line up by tomorrow night."

Right on cue, as if the universe wanted to add emphasis to Quinn's line of thinking, Quinn's cell phone began ringing. "Hi, Gracie. Sure. I'm at the lab. Feynman's here with me."

He nodded, responding to Gracie's question. "Yeah. We got the energy connections figured out, I think. I'll tell you about it later. Sure. We can take a break. OK." Quinn wrote down an address and hung up. Twenty minutes later, Quinn and Feynman were on their way to meet Gracie at Anna's home in Stillwater, an old river town about twenty-five miles east of Saint Paul, on the St. Croix River.

Chapter 24

The Government Man

"Howdy, boys." Natalie said as Sergeant Sean Donahue of the Saint Paul Police Department stepped into the lobby of the law office. Natalie looked appraisingly at Donahue: a tall, handsome, and predictably Irish cop who had worked with Gracie a time or two before. In Natalie's opinion, he was pretty fair-minded and mostly harmless as far as cops go, and, unfortunately, married. The guy with him, however, looked different. Not harmless. Probably not married. Black suit. Black tie. A Government Man. The kind of guy who slaved away, night and day, at a high-tech ergonomic keyboard somewhere, attempting to siphon out all the mysteries of the American people. Slime. High cheek bones; emaciated; little round glasses just like a Nazi interrogator in a Spielberg movie. Basically, creepy. "Can I get you some coffee?" She asked. Both men declined.

"Not a social visit, eh? Oh. That's right, you're here to see Gracie aren't you?" She batted her eyelashes seductively.

Sergeant Donahue nodded in assent. Natalie sat up straighter, threw her shoulders back and inhaled, displaying the "girls" in all their glory. Natalie understood that any red-blooded male would appreciate the view, and it always worked to stall for time. Sergeant Donahue appeared dumbstruck. The Government man appeared unaffected, remaining silent, his eyes staring soullessly into space.

Natalie spontaneously hiccuped, a small nervous habit, breaking the spell. "Gracie... I mean... Ms. Swan had to make a quick stop at the Courthouse this morning, but she should be back any minute." Natalie prayed she was telling the truth.

With some effort, Sergeant Donahue tore his eyes away from the "girls" and managed to squeak, "Oh, sure. Good morning, Natalie. This is Agent Cruz from the NSA. He has a few questions about Anna Strong."

"Anna Strong?" Natalie asked. "Oh yeah, the old lady who died here on Thursday night. Well, I'm sure Gracie never met her before that night. Even though they are related. Well, at least she said they were. Related. Gracie, I mean." Natalie felt like an idiot, but blundered on. "Gracie told me, just this morning, that she and Anna, were related."

"Related?" The creep began.

"What? They were related? Related to who... whom... whatever!" Officer Donahue spurted.

Exasperated with herself and with the whole situation, Natalie summarized succinctly, "Gracie said that Anna Strong was her aunt."

Officer Donahue looked startled, then astonished.

"Well, some kind of relation anyway, I guess. That's all I know." Trying to change the subject, and praying to the Goddess that Gracie would get her ass back soon, Natalie attempted some further small talk. "Snow coming?" She began and then stopped. Something about the vibes. Something felt wrong, terribly wrong. "Blizzard, I hear. Duluth got plastered last weekend." She prattled on, with little hope.

"Yeah. Feels like it. Right time of the year." Officer Donahue replied.

With a silent glare, the Government Man started down the hall to Gracie's office. Natalie rose to follow him. As if on cue, Tom stepped into the hallway, blocking the creep's path. Tom looked past the little creep, directly at Natalie. Natalie shrugged her shoulders as if to say, "I did my best, now it's your turn."

"Can I help you?" Tom said, directing the Government Man and Officer Donahue into his office, just like they were old friends, or as if he had been expecting them. "Bring us some coffee, would you, Natalie?" He said. Natalie replied, "Sure, boss." Tom shut the door.

"Well, gentlemen," he started, gesturing to chairs in front of his massive desk, "what can we do for you?"

"A few questions about Anna Strong's relationship with Ms. Swan, if you please," the Government Man said in a clipped voice.

"Yes?" Tom began encouragingly, and they all sat down.

"Well, apparently Gracie was related to Anna Strong in some way. I didn't know this before. I thought Gracie had no relatives. But Natalie just told us that Ms. Strong was Gracie's aunt. Or, at least, I think that's what she tried to say. The NSA believes that the old lady gave Gracie something..." Officer Donahue began.

"Anna Strong was doing preliminary work on a specific prototype for us." Agent Cruz said. "The project is classified."

"Are you serious? Let me get this straight." Tom reiterated. "Anna Strong is the old lady who died in Gracie's office last Thursday night, right? And Ms. Strong was working for the NSA, the government, on some secret project? Have I got that right?"

After a long pause with a pained look on his face, Cruz replied, "Basically."

"OK. But what has Gracie got to do with that? Gracie works for me, not for the 'government'." Despite what she might let her neighbors believe, Tom muttered under his breath. "I'm sure Gracie never met Ms. Strong before last Thursday."

"The old lady may have given Gracie something that she shouldn't have. Something that belongs to the project - to the Government." Sergeant Donahue interjected. "I have been assigned to assist Agent Cruz in recovering the object."

"What kind of object?" Tom asked in a reasonable tone.

Cruz just glared. "We need to find it now."

"Or?"

"Or else it's very bad for Ms. Swan; for everyone." Agent Cruz answered.

"I thought you were here about Anna Strong's Will." He paused. "Let me be sure I've got the picture straight here. You think that the old lady had some secret 'object' and she passed 'it' along to Gracie the night she died? But why would she do that?" Tom challenged.

Before Cruz could answer, there was a knock on the door, and Gracie's curly mane appeared. "Natalie says you're looking for me?" She peeked in.

"Come on in, Gracie," Tom said. "Take a seat."

Gracie flowed into the room, a triumphant gleam in her eye, and took a seat next to Sergeant Donahue. "How's it hanging, Sean?" Gracie asked as she settled into her seat. "You wanted to see me about Anna Strong, I guess? Or is it about Jimmy?"

"No, Gracie, it's about Anna Strong. Your Aunt? Jimmy's doing just fine. He and his mom are living pretty well, now that the grandmother's Estate is settled. I heard the ring was sold and the funds put in trust for Jimmy, for his college."

"Yeah, at least we could do that for Jimmy."

"Well, the scum bag's finally been sentenced. He won't be killing anyone else or bothering Jimmy and his mom for a very long time. So, all in all, Jimmy doing just fine." Officer Donahue updated Gracie.

"Jimmy?" Tom said. Who is Jimmy?"

Gracie replied, "You remember, Tom. I was Court-appointed to represent Jimmy last year. Jimmy should be about nine years old now, right Sean?"

Gracie looked at Sergeant Donahue, who nodded in agreement. "It turns out that Jimmy's father murdered Jimmy's grandmother." He said.

At Tom's blank look, Gracie explained. "Jimmy's father killed his own mother - to speed up the inheritance, I guess. But, when you kill someone, you can't inherit from them. You're 'disqualified.' So, Jimmy inherited in his father's place. What's more, Jimmy's grandmother was wearing this gigantic diamond ring when she was murdered. The police found the ring in Jimmy's father's possession when they arrested him. Evidence. So, I had the privilege of figuring out a way to get the ring released from impound so it could be sold and used to fund a trust for Jimmy. It was good."

"Yeah. It turned out good for Jimmy, at least." Sergeant Donahue nodded in agreement.

Exasperated, Cruz cut in, "This isn't about any kid named Jimmy or any diamond ring released from impound. This is about Anna Strong, and what she gave you the night she died." Cruz was looking straight at Gracie now. His gaze cut through her like knife.

"What! Who?" Gracie began.

"Gracie, this is Agent Cruz from the NSA. He wants to ask you a few questions about what Ms. Strong gave you the night she died." Tom explained.

Uh-oh! The shit was about to hit the fan. Gracie swallowed. What Anna gave me? He wants what Anna gave me. What the hell did she give me? She gave me nothing! She shocked me. She scared me. But she gave me something... important? Something important enough for the NSA to want? Out of the corner of her eye, Gracie thought she saw sparks, and a black cloud descending over the top of the Government Man's head. What's happening? Who's doing that? Am I doing that? Gracie wondered. She shook her head; no cloud, no sparks. Holy cow! Now I'm beginning to see things too. Seriously, if things get any weirder, she thought, I'll have no choice but to check myself into Regions Hospital for an electroshock session. Maybe two.

Noticing that Gracie didn't appear to be able to answer Agent Cruz, Tom summed up the conversation so far, for

Gracie's benefit, "This isn't about the old lady's Will at all. Gracie's not in trouble because she inherited from Anna. You're just looking for something that Anna 'may have' given Gracie the night she died. Am I correct?" He glared at Cruz, waiting for an answer.

Gracie looked like a zombie now, with a vacant uncomprehending look in her eyes.

"The NSA doesn't care about Anna's Will. She could leave everything to the Cat Society if she wanted to. We want to know what Anna Strong gave Ms. Swan the night she died." Agent Cruz glared back at Tom and then immediately shifted his gaze to Gracie. "Young Woman. Listen to me! You would be wise to cooperate. What did she give you?" Agent Cruz demanded a response.

"You know about the Cat Society?" Gracie considered, astonished, "But the Will's OK, see, since Anna's my aunt." Gracie tried to clarify for everyone's (mostly Tom's) benefit. "I just found out last weekend, in Duluth. I didn't know she was my aunt when I met her, and then she died right away before she was able to tell me anything. Oh, God, it was awful." Gracie was beginning to get hysterical, short of breath even. She felt like chanting something in Latin, and she didn't even know Latin.

"No, that's not the point. Listen, idiot." Cruz snapped. "Anna Strong gave you something. Something that she shouldn't have given to anyone. You need to produce that item. Now." His words were spoken, quietly, ominously, with a cold resolve. Gracie looked over at Sergeant Donahue and then back at the Government Man. Donahue's face had begun to redden. Tom came around from behind his desk. Gracie shivered. All she needed now was another mystery! What in the world does the NSA think that Anna gave me? She didn't give me anything, other than the weirdest day of my life. Instinctively, Gracie knew that this part of the problem would not go away. She only hoped that she could come up with some satisfactory explanation for the NSA. Barring that, she needed to find the thing that the NSA wanted, and turn it over to them right away.

"Wait. Wait a minute! Anna's Cub bag. Maybe there was something in the bag. She didn't actually give the Cub bag to me, you understand, she just left it in my office when she left... died, I mean! Maybe what you are looking for is in the bag. There were some keys in there too; but I think they were just house keys."

Gracie wanted this guy gone. It was imperative that she stay under the radar. Especially now. Now with Quinn and his thingy-machiney on the verge of some psychic/ unknowable/scientific/multi-dimensional episode of some sort. She simply couldn't tolerate having an administrative agency rulemaking at her. It was too scary. Never-ending, eternal litigation. Secret tribunals. No constitutional protections. Heaven forbid and Aunt Jemima to boot! It would be worse than law school. Gracie knew she was teetering on the brink of... disaster. If she couldn't come up with something, anything, she would wind up in the cross-hairs of the NSA for a long, long time. Gracie unconsciously began to stare out into space, chewing on her lower lip. She wondered if she would soon be targeted by other 'initialed' agencies. As a comfortable exercise in futility, Gracie began to compile a list in her head, chanting: NSA... FBI... CIA... IRS... KGB... CBS... NPR... The initials were quite calming actually, kind of like playing hopscotch. And, it never hurt to be prepared. Extra initials or extra tossing rocks? Either one could be quite valuable under the right circumstances.

"Get the bag." Cruz snapped.

"Sure thing. It's in my office. I'll get it." Gracie stuttered.

"Now. Right now."

"OK. Back in a minute," Gracie replied as she raced out of Tom's office. She reappeared in less than two minutes with the Cub bag. She dumped it on Tom's desk. All four of them, Cruz, Tom, Gracie, and Officer Donahue looked down at the mess. Cruz sifted through the grocery receipts, stock certificates, bank books, coupons, orange candies, more orange candies, and looked up, enraged. "There's nothing here!" he shrieked. "You have twenty-four hours to come up with the item, or there will be severe consequences." Cruz declared. "I'll be back here tomorrow morning at 9:00 a.m. sharp, and you'd better be ready to turn it over." Cruz turned on his heel and exited the room, like a man on a mission, though no one could comprehend what the mission could possibly be or, alternatively, what the apparently dire consequences would be if Gracie wasn't able to surrender the "item" by tomorrow morning.

Gracie looked at Tom and Officer Donahue, grabbed a handful of orange candies from Anna's Cub bag, and exclaimed, "Gotta go. Things to do; places to go. You know - situations; circumstances; shoes." And, before either Tom or Officer Donahue could respond, Gracie was gone. Gone like the wind. It was almost as if a purple cloud of energy swirled around her as she rapidly exited the room before either man had a chance to speak. They looked at each other, still dazed at Gracie's abrupt departure. Speechless.

Gracie swept through the receptionist area, pulling out her cell phone and speed-dialing Quinn as she flew. Her gaze swept by Natalie and she halted. She remembered that Natalie had grown up in Stillwater; she also remembered how Natalie had kicked ass at Whistle Binkies last year. Natalie was her closest friend. "Hey, Nat, you wouldn't know how to find 303 North 4th Street in Stillwater would you?" Gracie asked.

"Of course I would." Natalie replied. "That's the house next door to the old Carnegie library." She answered.

Gracie shook her head in utter disbelief. "Of course it is." Nothing could possibly surprise her anymore.

"Something tells me that we need to take a little field trip to Stillwater. I might need your help. Can you come?"

"Like last time, at Whistle Binkies?" Natalie queried.

"Maybe." Gracie replied.

There was a sudden gleam in Natalie's eye. "Nothing to do here anyways." Natalie said. "Let's hit the road. I'll drive."

"Good idea. Thanks." Gracie replied as she grabbed her warmest coat and mittens. Never know when you might need your best friend, protection from the elements, or some combination of both.

"Got anything to eat?" Natalie asked as she put on her man-killer four-inch spike-heeled boots and fur-trimmed leather coat. Together, the pair looked like a Japanese geisha spy-girl and a curly-haired eskimo.

"Sure." Gracie pulled out two orange candies from her coat pocket and threw one to Natalie as they hurried out of the building.

About time, Natalie was thinking. It's been far too long since Whistle Binkies, and this show was getting kinda boring.

Chapter 25

The House Outside of Time

Thirty minutes later, Natalie swerved right and turned down the hill onto Myrtle Street in Stillwater, a gut-wrentchingly, seriously steep, almost vertical hill ending at the St. Croix River.

The car lost all traction immediately.

With a mere ten blocks to go before the pavilion at river's edge, Natalie shouted, "Hold onto something!" Horrified, Gracie recognized the look in Natalie's eyes. Oh no! Just like that time at Whistle Binkies!

The car continued picking up speed in its uncontrolled slide. Then, without another word, Natalie floored it! What the hell? Within seconds, the car was moving even faster - and now sideways - careening wildly out of control on a direct path toward a huge oak tree on the corner of Fourth Street.

Gracie gripped Natalie's arm and shouted back, "Watch out!" Gracie wasn't clear why they were shouting, or what exact plan Natalie had in mind, but at least Natalie had a plan. Thank God! Natalie always had a plan.

... Plan? What plan? What was Natalie up to? ...

Losing hope, only seconds before impact, Gracie shut her eyes. She loosened her belt and covered her face with her hands. She desperately searched her intellect for steps in any rational plan that contained the elements of an impact with a gigantic, immovable oak tree and an out-of control car swerving toward the St. Croix River and oblivion. No way there could be a satisfactory outcome to Natalie's plan! Had Natalie finally gone mental?

Gracie visualized Quinn finding her body, all bloodied and smashed up, in a car wrapped around a tree.[31] She wondered how he would feel. Sad? Desperate? Desperately sad? Would she become the lost Gracie of his dreams; his one regret in life? And then, would she... die? Or would she just be paralyzed for life? Would Natalie survive? Would Natalie receive a full personal injury settlement and would it all be eaten up by subrogation interests? Geez. Where did that come from? Gracie thought. Alas, thinking like a lawyer to the very end.

... Wait. Wait a minute. A Plan? Why do we need a plan? In a flash of insight I knew the answer to my own question. We don't need a plan at all ... because ... because I trust Natalie, and I know things

---

[31] Actually she visualized a hopelessly deflated hot air balloon. Maybe there was some subliminal stuff going on here.

will work out just right. Quinn said I needed to have "blind faith,"
just like kids have. How simple. And, how very wise. In this moment,
I understood that Natalie could drive her car right off a cliff into the
ocean -- or even into an erupting volcano, and still everything would be
alright. I can't explain how I knew, or even where that certain
knowledge came from, but I knew it was an absolute fact. We were
going to be just fine. Here goes -- OK universe -- deliver up!

Then Gracie heard it - a low, primal growl. Where was that sound coming from? Still fighting her instincts, on the verge of hysteria, Gracie tore her hands away from her eyes, just in time to see the enormous oak tree sweep past. The sound was coming from Natalie! Natalie was growling and grinning at the same time! It was brilliant! Natalie was using the momentum of the slide and the speed of the car to make a sharp left turn uphill onto Fourth Street at exactly the right moment, strategically planting her car into the largest snow bank she could find, and magically arriving in front of 303 North 4th Street. Wow. Impossible! But rationality be damned! This could be nothing less than pure and simple synchronicity,[32] with a healthy serving of blind faith thrown in.

---

[32] Being in just the right place, at just the right moment, with just the right person! How often does that happen, I wonder? Or maybe it happens all the time, and I just forget to notice.

Natalie shut off the engine, turned to Gracie, and nodded with satisfaction. And, maybe there was just a slight smirk on her face, as if to announce, "Wow. Am I good or what?"

Gracie could not argue, squeak or respond in any way. She desperately hoped she had not wet her pants, but she couldn't tell. She suspected that it would take her a solid week just to unclench her sphincter muscles. In response, Gracie simply threw her arms around Natalie's shoulders and embraced her friend in relief and gratitude.

Even though Natalie worked out, and I was passingly strong, it took all of our combined strength to shove the car doors open just enough to exit without slipping and smashing our faces into the tall walls of snow surrounding the car. We climbed to the top of the snowbank and stood silently staring at what I hoped was Anna's house.

Wiping snowflakes from my eyes with a mitten, I tore my gaze away. So, here we are, in Stillwater, the oldest town in Minnesota. I searched my memory for details. Ah, yes, the town was founded by lumber barons. These particular lumber barons had no apparent leanings toward acrophobia however,[33] since they built many of their most magnificent homes on the bluffs high above the river.

Now ice particles were landing on our cheeks. The wind was gusting to a gale level. I looked up at the

---

[33] And must have had nice strong thigh muscles to boot.

darkening sky and knew there was no chance in hell that it would stop snowing within the next few minutes. In fact, it likely would be a miracle if it stopped snowing before February. It really doesn't matter though, I thought, since it will probably take at least that long to dig Natalie's car out of the snow bank anyhow. Time to take cover.

I turned my gaze back to look at the enormous house on the other side of the snowbank. Wait. Am I certain this is Anna's house? Um. The house was closely aligned to the stereotype, but it was not quite situated high enough on the bluff to be an authentic lumber baron's mansion. Still, the house was impressive and something... else. Yes. Orange. It was orange. Or, some kind of peachy-orangey kind of blended color. Huh? Ruminating on the Sherwin-Williams color palate, it was easy to speculate that the color was probably listed as "desert dust."[34] It was also abundantly clear that the house could have served as a castle, the local bordello, or a gambling hall from the 1880s. It must have taken a full-time staff person just to wash the windows.

As the ice particles began hardening on our coats and faces, Natalie and I continued to stare, mesmerized. The single most prominent feature of the house was its square

---

[34] Naturally, it had to have a unique color name. It was imperative that the color could be duplicated for any other brave soul who is either color blind or who desires to paint their house like a popsicle. Speaking from experience, I knew this to be true, but we won't go into that right now.

turret three stories up, at the very front. The turret held double-arched windows facing the street with two more sets of arched windows symmetrically facing north and south. The ornate turret rose imposingly above the first balcony on the second floor, which was directly above the entrance. The entrance was at a slight diagonal to the sidewalk, angling up six steps to an elaborately carved front door. The wood on the door looked as if it had been carved by elves on a drunken holiday. But that wasn't the end of it all. Just to the left and slightly behind the square turret was an onion-shaped dome atop twelve arched windows in a two-story bay. Finally, at a nod to convention, I suppose, a grand porch wrapped around the entire front and north side of the house. Really, it was hard to take it all in.

The weak sun glinted on some windows at the rear, probably a greenhouse or a small conservatory facing the river on the bluff side. Hum. I finally managed to tear my gaze away from the house and looked at Natalie to gauge her reaction. Natalie's victory face had been replaced with a look of awe, and Natalie said, with a small quiver in her voice, "Queen Anne. Orange."

"Yup," I say. Then, with enormous effort, we began to trudge our way through the deep snow toward the front door of the house.

While in transit, I had attempted to explain to Natalie my relationship with Quinn. Although she still had a hard time distinguishing him from her fantasy longshoreman, she had no difficulty with the rich part. I had also attempted to explain to Natalie that I had to find whatever the NSA was looking for by tomorrow morning, or else. "Or else what?" She had asked. Since there was no adequate answer to that question, my simple response was that I didn't have a bat-shit clue as to what the NSA was looking for, or even what they could or would do to me if I couldn't produce it. But we still had to find IT. And, IT didn't appear to be in the Cub bag that Anna had inadvertently left in my keeping. So, IT had to be somewhere else - most probably at Anna's house. So that's why we were here. In Stillwater. At this magnificent old house on the hill.

I looked down at the key in my hand. I knew this was Anna's key, but the key to what? Or to where? The orange Tweety Bird key was the one I had plucked out of Anna's Cub bag just before I emptied its contents onto Tom's desk in front of the NSA guy. I did the analysis: this was the only address listed on Anna's bank statements and investment accounts, not to mention quite a few of her stock certificates - apparently now my stock certificates. And, if Anna's Will was valid, this was now my house anyway because I had inherited it from her. I still felt vaguely uneasy about the whole Will thing, but I couldn't think about that now. I had to stay focused. I needed to find IT!

So, my best guess was that this was Anna's house and I had every right to enter and take possession of it. But, no matter who the hell the owner of this house was, I knew for certain that all of my earthly possessions could easily fit into the foyer!

I wondered if the key I was holding would unlock the front door or the back door. For all I knew, this key might be the only key to Governor Dayton's private bathroom! Well. No more stalling. (Oops. Pun.) There was only one way to find out, and I was no where near the Governor's mansion.

Still worried, and chewing on my lower lip, I knew there had to be a security system on this kind of house. Wait a minute. It was Anna's house. It had to be. And, Anna was weird enough not to need or want a security system. OK, then. So, if I had made a mistake in my analysis and this wasn't Anna's house, I would certainly be charged with breaking and entering once the security alarm went off. Another sure way to get disbarred. Then, my problem would be solved easily enough - I would find myself in the custody of the Stillwater Police within the next twenty minutes or so, and thus I wouldn't be able to deliver IT to the NSA guy tomorrow morning. Either way, I'd end up in a much warmer place. So… here goes…

… Natalie saw Gracie take a deep breath, and then began slowly treading through the deep snow. Natalie tried to follow in Gracie's footsteps as much as possible. She did not want to ruin her Fluevog boots. There had been that incident in Uptown last year, when she'd

zealously put her life on the line to acquire them! No way she wanted
to go through all that again! Gracie's path led them directly to the front
door of the Queen Anne Victorian house that belonged to the perhaps
dear, but mostly dead old lady - Gracie's aunt, Anna ...

They arrived on the porch stoop. Gracie and Natalie
looked at each other. Gracie stepped forward. She rang the
doorbell. Natalie almost hoped that Lurch the Butler would
answer, but she didn't really expect anyone to answer at all.
Nobody did. Natalie noticed that Gracie's hands were
shaking when she inserted the Tweety Bird key into the
front door lock. Nothing happened. Gracie jiggled the key
in the lock; still nothing happened.

Natalie said, "Let me try. It's probably frozen." Natalie
stepped forward and took the key from Gracie's hand.
Gracie stepped aside and Natalie moved to the door. She
jiggled the key in the lock more vigorously than Gracie.
Still nothing happened. Losing patience, Natalie cursed.
Then as an added incentive, she swung her hip in a wide
arc as the tip of one of her gorgeous boots made contact
with the door. Ow! Immediately, Natalie and Gracie heard
a click, and the ornately-decorated door swung open wide.
Natalie took a moment to revel in the power of her
Fluevogs, not to mention her hips!

Just about this time, however, Natalie's "weird"
barometer - Gracie called it her "spidey-sense" - kicked in.
Ignoring it, Natalie concluded that there must be some

kind of release mechanism built into the door, to make it open so widely on its own.

Natalie looked over at Gracie. They surveyed the expansive space before them. Gracie motioned for her to follow and then Gracie stepped over the threshold into the foyer. Natalie followed. The weak wintry light floated down from the square turret three stories up. Wow. All of Gracie's stuff would fit into the foyer, Natalie thought, and mine would fit into the foyer closet!

Glancing around, Natalie noted that a massive carved fireplace, serving two rooms and big enough to walk through, stood to their left. She wouldn't have been surprised to see the ghost of a woman in a cool négligée float into the room at any time. Egad! Natalie and Gracie turned back to the still wide-open door. The snow was drifting in. It took the strength of both of them to push the heavy door shut and latch it against the howling wind.

Gracie walked around the fireplace into the next room. Again, Natalie followed. They had entered what appeared to be a gigantic library, with floor to ceiling bookcases on their right. Thousands of volumes. On their left was the two story bay, filled with light from the arched windows above. Natalie noticed a large painting of an old fellow on a ladder, reading a book, with a carved sign on the top of the bookcase labeled "Metaphysics." Of course, Natalie thought, what else? This house was just simply over the top.

It would have made a wonderful backdrop for a horror movie, she thought.

She stepped back a few feet to get a better look at the scale of the room and bumped into something hard. Normally, bumping into something hard as she was backing up was a little bit of a turn-on for Natalie. But this was a slightly different situation. Turning around, there was no cute guy who was happy to see her, but a cold, hard statue of some sentry goddess holding an open scroll at the foot of the staircase. Whoa. How did I miss that? Natalie wondered. Looking closer, it appeared as if the goddess was checking her guest list before allowing visitors to ascend. Natalie was 100% sure she was not on the goddess' guest list. Um. Things are getting a bit weirder now, Natalie thought. More tingle. No doubt about it, the barometric pressure was definitely dropping.

Gracie was on the other side of the room, looking at book titles. Natalie caught Gracie's eye and she glanced upward as of to say, "Well, shall we?" Gracie nodded and wordlessly moved toward the staircase, letting Natalie take the lead. They began to climb the stairs in syncopated motion. First right; then left; breathing slowly. When they reached the top they paused.

In the middle of the circular room sat a substantial library table with leather chairs around it. Kind of like King Arthur's table, Natalie postulated. The table was piled high with books and other paraphernalia; lots of pens, paper folded into odd shapes, and, of course, many pieces of those orange candies were scattered about, just like the ones Gracie had shared with her on the way to Stillwater. But, wow, what a place to read! Not to mention… eat. Natalie couldn't imagine that reading a book under the Eiffel Tower could be any better. She also wondered if there was any real food around. You know, food that wasn't orange candies? She was beginning to get hungry. The orange candies just hadn't done the job. It had been a long, long morning, not to mention the white-knuckle drive with the icy road conditions and the wind gusts blowing the car all over the road. She wondered if they would be able to get back to Saint Paul, or if they would end up stranded here overnight. Natalie wandered over to the table, hoping for food and instead noticed a strange looking instrument clamped to the side of the table.

"Hey Gracie, look at this." Natalie pointed. Gracie stepped closer to stand alongside a steam-punk machine-type of contraption.

Natalie moved closer to the object and Gracie, and then said, "It looks like an instrument of torture, doesn't it? See those spikey things in the middle?" When Natalie touched the handle, her "tingle" turned into a buzzing in her ears.

"What the heck!" Gracie exclaimed. Even though Gracie had not touched the object herself, they both had shared Natalie's 'buzz' shock, probably because they were standing so close together. They looked at each other. Whatever this object was, it mattered.

Cautiously, without any further touching, they scrutinized the object more carefully. In the center, there was an articulated piece that moved in an arc around the top of a turning disk with spikes. There were clamps to hold a blade, and some kind of hand-crank attached to the whole works. The buzzing in Natalie's ears had subsided, but she wasn't willing to touch the handle again, just yet.

Probably gears and pinions attached somewhere too, Gracie mused, but she was not sure she could actually explain to any other living creature what a gear or a pinion was. Natalie would know. Maybe they were in that little black box attached to the underside of the table. Wait! There's a little black box attached underneath the table?

"Look, Nat, maybe that's where the shock came from." Gracie pointed, but she didn't touch the box to confirm her theory. Natalie moved closer to get a better look at the underside of the table.

It could be a mouse-trap, Gracie thought. Then again, no, it couldn't be. But it was obviously designed to hold something. Maybe some type of an apple peeler? Heavens, no! Why would Anna be working on an apple peeler? It was clear that this object was still under construction though. It had to be, since the orange paint can was sitting next to it on the desk. It was a work in progress. It couldn't possibly be finished. Otherwise it would have been painted orange already. But the design made no sense.

Finally, Gracie squatted to look under the table again where Natalie was still poking around. She finally stood up and said, "Well, the only thing I can think of is that it could be a re-design of an old-style apple peeler, but why in the world would Anna want to design a new, improved apple-peeler? Nobody peels apples today anyway. They just eat the skin and all - you know, health food."

"OK, I get that," Natalie replied, "but what's with the electrical cord? If you have a crank, why do you need a cord? And look at the size of the plug. It has to carry 220."

"Good question." Gracie replied. Gracie hadn't even noticed the cord. And she sure didn't know what a '220' was. But, Natalie was an astute observer and full of surprises, Gracie knew. Her skills were legendary, and almost spooky. Natalie's hidden talents had come in handy on several other occasions, most notably at Whistle Binkies. But, before they could brainstorm further as to the exact purpose of the object, the doorbell rang. Well, bring it on, Gracie thought.

"It's either the police or Quinn," Gracie announced. Then, Gracie squared up her shoulders and with a strangled voice said, "I'll get that."

"Sure thing, boss," Natalie said sarcastically, still under the table. She rolled her eyes and continued to fool around with the wires attached to the contraption on the table.

"Nat, be careful with that," Gracie said. "Who knows what it might do? Touch the wrong thing and you could end up creating some kind of time paradox or a wormhole! In my world, right now, anything is possible."

"You betcha. Maybe I could send us back to last Thursday, eh?" She quipped.

"No! Not Thursday! Try for Tuesday!" Gracie squeaked in a panic. Too many weird machines in my life lately, she muttered to herself as she hurried down the spiral stair.

Gracie knew that she, of course, was the main reason why all this bizarre stuff was happening anyway. Didn't Quinn say, only a few short days ago, that the machine - his time-traveling machine, the inter-dimensional doohickey - was somehow "personal" to her? Whatever the hell that meant! So it was her responsibility to open the goddamn door wasn't it? And Natalie knew it. Gracie growled with worry and frustration. Anyway, Natalie was her best friend. If somebody was going to jail, it wouldn't be Natalie, she vowed. Gracie crossed her fingers for good luck, hurried down the spiral staircase and sprinted for the door, just as it swung wide open again. It was Quinn. Wow! How'd he do that? Gracie wondered.

"Thank, God," Gracie spurted, "it's you."

"Sure it's me," Quinn answered. "You asked me to come, remember? Were you expecting someone else?" Quinn looked at Gracie appreciatively, noticing her tousled hair and the fuzzy sweater that reminded him of how soft she had been earlier in the day.

"No, no. I wasn't expecting anyone else." Gracie told a small white lie. "Just an old habit; worrying about everything as usual," Gracie chided herself. She gave herself an internal lecture: Today's the new day, remember, Gracie? And it's a good day.

Quinn said nothing, but his blue, blue eyes were registering concern, and a question.

Still unwilling to respond to the unspoken question, Gracie touched Quinn's cheek gently and changed the subject. "You said Feynman was coming with you? Is he here?"

"He's here, but it may take him a few minutes to come inside. He's trying to find a place to park the cab without ending up in the St. Croix River. It's pretty slippery out there. Somebody rammed their car into the snow bank blocking the street out front."

"Right. I know. It's Natalie's car. The roads were pretty bad on the way down the hill, so Nat's only choice was to do a controlled slide to avoid the oak tree on the corner. She managed to plant the car pretty well, though, didn't she? Probably have to wait till spring to dig it out."

Quinn grinned. "Yeah. The roads are getting pretty nasty, and the wind is picking up. I think another Alberta clipper's coming in."

"It felt like it earlier this morning." Gracie answered.

"Wait. Who's Natalie?" Quinn asked.

"Oh. I forgot to tell you about Natalie. She's my friend, ah, my assistant. Actually, Natalie's just... Nat. Who knows what else? Hey, come on in. Let's find the kitchen and see if we can get some coffee going. We've got to find the thing the NSA is looking for."

"The NSA? What thing?" For once Quinn was the one who looked baffled. He thought that more confusion was just impossible at this juncture. But, heh. It was Gracie's life. So, he just smiled and followed Gracie down the hallway. As they passed a spiral staircase, Gracie called up, "Hey, Natalie. Quinn's here. We're going to try and find the kitchen to make coffee."

"Sure. Good. Make some tea too, would you? And, look for some food, OK? Some interesting stuff here. I'll catch up in a minute." Natalie replied.

Quinn and Gracie moved down an elaborate corridor, opening mahogany doors as they headed toward the back of the house. "Wow, what a place," Quinn said. "This was Anna's house?" He asked. "It's more like a gambling house or a bordello." At Gracie's quick look, Quinn restated, "I mean, there are enough rooms for many different... activities."

Gracie chortled, "OK, big guy, good save. This has to be Anna's house. It's the only address listed on all of her papers. Plus, have you noticed? It's orange. I guess Anna was fixated on orange stuff. Remember, I told you about all those orange candies, her hair, her clothes - you know, all orange."

"Yeah. It all makes sense now. Anna figured it out. She tried to tell us by surrounding herself with the color orange - because of the energy signature, you know..." Now it was Gracie's turn to look baffled. Quinn stopped. He said, "I'll explain later when Feynman gets here. It'll be easier."

"OK," Gracie replied, "but I thought you said we would be meeting Feynman tomorrow night at your lab, not today."

"Well, I needed his help," Quinn replied, "so he 'popped in' a day early."

"What do you mean 'popped in'?" Gracie asked.

Quinn had a pained expression on his face. "I know you're cutting me some slack here, and I appreciate it." He said.

"You think?"

Quinn paused. "The way I understand it, Gracie, is that when my super-conducting synchrotron created that voltage surge I told you about - well, it somehow punched a hole in the space∞time continuum."

"A hole? What do you mean?" Gracie asked.

"Yeah, well. Richard likes to call it a 'portal'. It loops backward and forward in time and space. Like I told you before, right now it seems to be stuck between last Thursday and our present; between the Carnegie building in Duluth and my lab - I think. There seem to be intervals where it's possible, just barely possible, for inter-dimensional travel to occur - or time travel if you want to call it that. Feynman seems to have figured out a way to 'ride the tide' for now. I'm not sure exactly how. We'll ask him about it when he gets done parking the cab."

"OK then." Gracie was sorry she had asked.

They found the kitchen. It was at the back of the house, in the space that Gracie had thought was a greenhouse or conservatory. The whole east wall was glass. Plants were hanging everywhere, trailing over the tops of the windows, many blooming in the middle of winter. Must have good vibes here. Thankfully that, at least, was something she could understand.

It wasn't too hard to locate an orange coffee pot, some coffee beans and the grinder. Gracie set up the coffee pot and waited for it to drip. Then she found some loose tea and an orange teapot and put the water on the ancient orange gas stove to boil. She even figured out how to turn it on!

Quinn found some chocolate chip cookies in the orange cookie jar and was placing them on a flowery plate. Watching the swirls of snow out the window, Gracie noticed the solidly built brick building next door to Anna's house. It must be the Carnegie library, Natalie had mentioned... Natalie had said something about Anna's house being next to the library, Gracie remembered. Hmm. They had just seated themselves at the gigantic butcher block table when the doorbell rang.

"Your turn," Gracie nodded to Quinn.

"I hope I can find my way back to the front door. Hey, save me some cookies," he said as he slid off the chair and headed for the other part of the building.

"I'll try," Gracie said, "However, its the first non-orange food I've had all day. Hurry back."

Quinn left the room and Gracie bit into her first cookie. It was delicious. She looked around as she chewed. She noticed the flowered wallpaper, orange flowers, of course, and the old-fashioned refrigerator with rounded edges. No dishwasher. A couple of cat food dishes, but no cats. They'd probably be orange tabbies, no doubt. I wonder where they are? She swiveled on her stool and noticed a door directly behind her; probably the door to the basement. She took her cookie with her, and moved toward the purported basement door.

Gracie opened the door with a jerk, prepared to find anything. Two tabby cats with cobwebs on their whiskers came sprinting out, dancing to their dish, meowing. They had smiling green eyes. "Well, hello," she said as the larger tabby unexpectedly rubbed up against her leg. Friendly.

Hopefully, they were not as strange as Anna, their recently-deceased owner.

Oh poor demented, dead Anna, Gracie remembered. So much has changed in the last few days - for everyone. Gracie suddenly realized that she had also inherited two cats. OK, then. Many new considerations, as it turns out.

"You guys must be thirsty," Gracie said as she stepped over to the refrigerator to look for milk. She hesitated only momentarily, slightly concerned about opening the refrigerator door, and wondering if she might somehow be required to inventory it at a later date. Yet, despite her apprehension and hoping for the best, she opened the refrigerator door. Wow. Only one kind of milk! Whole milk. And it wasn't even past its expiration date. Small miracles are the best, she mused. She poured milk for the cats. It looked like their little brains were burbling, almost bursting, with joy. Then she realized that they must have been locked in the basement since last Thursday when Anna died. Ouch.

"Well, let's find out where you guys have been, and what you've been up to," she said to the cats.

Just as she was about to explore the stairway where the cats had come from, she heard footsteps. The tea kettle began to whistle, and Gracie stepped over to the stove. Quinn and Feynman entered the room.

Chapter 26

NATALIE and RICHARD Sitting in a Tree, K*I*S*S*I*N*G*. First comes love, then comes....

Feynman. Cute. Middle 40s. He was wearing white pants. A boyish - no, rakish - grin on his face as he took her hand in greeting. He even kissed it. A charmer certainly; very gallant in any case. But white pants? A little odd looking for a person of his age. Not hip at all. How 1970s. He asked me to call him "Richard."

I was handing him a cup of tea just as Natalie bounded into the kitchen with her normal exuberance. Distracted, he turned to greet my rather stunning compatriot, and I watched in horror as the glue on the tea cup handle (obviously one of Anna's favorite mugs which had been glued in an attempt to save it) disintegrated. Oh, no! Not again! Oh, the look on his face when the hot tea hit his tender thighs (only his thighs, I hoped)! Oh my. What a way to begin a friendship/collaboration/relationship! He will either think I am a nut case who can never throw anything away[35], or he will think I gave him the uncertain cup with the hope that he would scald himself. Which shall it be? Bag lady or assassin?

Natalie obviously witnessed the disaster, and immediately took control of the situation. She rushed over to Feynman, elbowing me aside and, grabbing, one of the cotton towels neatly stacked on a nearby end table (ready to be put away, I assume) she immediately began rubbing Feynman's lap (and his lower parts) vigorously. It was apparent that Natalie's rubbing was having a very obvious effect on Mr. Feynman. He looked up with a giant grin on his face. I guess you could say, it was a warm welcome after all.

Quinn cleared his throat and, using his professorial voice, introduced himself. Then he said, "Richard, I would like you to meet my... ah... friend, Gracie." He gave Richard that certain look which conveyed in 'man talk', as far as I can tell, of course, 'if you touch her - you're a dead man.' Apparently some things never change. Then he looked over at me, smiling that devilish smile that I was so getting used to. I gave him a sweet, sunny smile.

"Yes," I continued the introductions. "And this is my... ah... friend, Natalie." Natalie did a sort of curtsy/bow, with

---

[35] NOTE: Sadly, true in some instances. I glue my coffee cups all the time as you know.

317

her cheeks heightening in color, just a bit. Why, I've never seen Natalie... blush before! Was that a blush? No. Couldn't be. I reassured myself. "Natalie," I forged on, "this is Richard Feynman, Quinn's... ah... friend." So many, many things unspoken.

Natalie looked at me curiously. Then she turned and said, "Richard Feynman? Are you related to the genius physicist, Richard Feynman? You know, the professor at Cal Tech - the one who worked on the Manhattan project?"

Without a beat Richard replied, "You could say that. You say he was a genius?" There was an even wider grin on his face now. "Was he good-looking too?" Too bad Carnegie's not around to hear this, Feynman muttered under his breath, not loud enough for Natalie to hear, I hoped.

Natalie wrinkled her brow, "As a matter of fact, you do look like him, a little. Maybe in his younger years. I reviewed some of his recorded lectures while I was at Yale. He was quite probably the best scientist the United States has ever produced. He was able to convey conceptual physics with so much clarity that I understood even some of the most complex concepts. I heard that some of the other physics professors even tried to sneak into his lectures from time to time." Natalie replied.

"True, oh so, true." Feynman muttered, a little louder this time. "They were a bunch of..." Quinn gave him a slight nudge, and Richard went silent.

"You studied physics?" I asked, astonished.

"Sure. Before I started working for Tom. I did my dissertation on the color spectrum and particle energy emissions." Natalie said, glancing back at Feynman and Quinn.

My mouth was hanging open now. Natalie had never talked about going to college before, or mentioned that she had any kind of post-graduate degree at all. "You studied what? And then you went to work for Tom - at the law office?" I asked.

"Energy and particle physics. Theoretical stuff. But, it never went anywhere, and I didn't want to work as a post-doc in some tyrannical geek's research lab." Quinn and Feynman both flinched and an incomprehensible look passed between them. Natalie continued, "A girl's gotta make a living, as you know. And, unfortunately, physics is still controlled by the good ole boys who wanted me to work on refining their zippers, rather than on refining their antiquated theories. They knew exactly what they wanted me to do," she rolled her eyes, "and how I should do it." Then, she winked at Feynman. "But, I had my own ideas." She walked over to the table, smoothed her skirt and sat down, crossing her gorgeously shaped legs. With deliberation, she picked up a chocolate chip cookie and took a big bite, looking directly at Feynman. "Mmm, good. Really yummy." She sighed orgasmically.

... Well that explains it. Natalie would never have allowed any man to tell her what to do, unless she wanted to do it herself. In fact, it was clear from the way that both Quinn and Feynman were fixated on Natalie's gams, that Nat did not have to pay attention to what any man wanted. She controlled them all. But, I knew that already. Natalie called the shots, and she always had. She would do the research that she wanted to do; in the way she wanted to do it. That made her dangerous to any well-funded project with a standardized or political agenda. Natalie was definitely not your standardized sort of girl, nor did she give a hoot about politics. She was a bona fide renegade. A renegade in killer boots, I amended. I wonder where she picked them up? Macy's? I'll have to ask her later, I vowed. Then I tuned back into the conversation ..

"So, you're a scientist too?" Natalie was asking Feynman.

"Yes, I've been helping Quinn in his lab. We've made substantial progress in the last twenty-four hours, but we still have a few bugs to work out before tomorrow night." Feynman answered.

"What happens tomorrow night?" Natalie innocently asked.

Uh-oh. Here it comes, I thought.

"Well, in simple terms, we're planning to open an inter-dimensional portal, and send Gracie's mother and father back to their own dimensional space."

"Oh you are, are you?" Natalie replied, making a face at me. As if to say, 'one of your lunatics again, ha, Gracie!'

I shrugged.

Feynman continued as if he had said something totally normal, rational even. "We were having some trouble with energy fluctuations, but we finally figured out that if we can tune the energy to stay within the orange-colored energy signature, it'll probably work." There was an incomprehensible look on Natalie's face now.

I was stunned. "Orange?" I questioned. "It has to be orange?"

"Sure, it makes sense because of the energy signature. If you were going to open a portal, a mini-black hole, you could say, it would have to be contained within that framework. Otherwise, you could end up with some awful strange results - in theory, of course." Natalie replied.

Everyone's attention was riveted on Natalie now. She noticed the intensity of our gazes and said, "Wha??"

"I have to sit down." I said and took another cookie.

"Sitting sounds good." Quinn said. He took the chair next to me.

Feynman had a devilish smile on his face as he stepped over to Natalie, took her hand, and kissed it. "I pronounce you the inter-dimensional Queen of Today," he said, offering her a another cookie. "Natalie," he said, "I'd like to know a little more about your dissertation - your thesis about particle energy emissions - especially the orange ones. By the way, in your research, have you ever considered the existence of initiation points? Uh. I mean, coordinate points?"

Richard glanced over at Quinn and winked. "I think that Natalie and I should start a fire in the library. Perhaps you would care to join us a little later?" He asked. "It's a bit chilly in here, isn't it, with all this glass?" Then he winked at Natalie and, offering his hand, said, "shall we?" Natalie looked up at him and blinked, twice. Then, of course, she placed her arm in the crook of his and they both swaggered out of the room.

Meanwhile, Quinn and I were riveted in place. All of a sudden I started laughing. "What the heck was that all about?" I asked. The spell broke. "They seem to have a certain... chemistry, don't they?" I commented.

Quinn replied, shaking his head, "It never ceases to amaze me how things can just... fall into place. How one moment leads to the next, most perfect moment, without much effort. It's almost as if there's an underlying structure to the universe, a structure that gently moves us in the direction that is the most beneficial to us no matter how messed up we get or how hard we try to resist... whatever 'it' is though, it's not random, that's for sure."

"Wow." I answered, "that's a hell of a statement for a scientist."

"What do you mean?"

"Well, science is so sure that everything is provable and rational and well... evolutionary. How can there be room for 'an underlying structure' or an 'it' holding us up, and then turning us in the 'right' direction - for our own good? Almost sounds like a god-thing or predestination."

"I told you before, I don't believe in destiny. There are too many choices out there and too many screw-ups to believe we are predestined to do anything. There's just a lot we don't know. I think it's safer to conclude that we simply don't have the whole picture - yet."

"Well, I'm in 100% agreement on that! So, are you finished with your cookies?"

"Yep."

"Well, let's check out the basement."

"What basement?"

"The door over there. It's where the cats came from. Let me show you." I glanced around the room; the cats were nowhere to be seen.

"What cats?" Quinn stood up and looked around as Gracie eagerly snatched his hand, leading him across the room to the door where the cats had come from. He wondered if the whole rest of his life would be spent following Gracie around, and always wondering what the hell she was talking about. They descended.

"My, this is cozy." Natalie said, looking over at Richard and patting the seat next to her on the sofa in front of the now-roaring fire.

He banked the fire and took the proffered seat, placing his arm around the back of the sofa, lightly skimming Natalie's shoulders. "Ah. Yes. Cozy here - in front of the fireplace." He started to trace a light line from Natalie's left earlobe down her right arm, with a slight detour along the way. "It's... the... fire. It's a good place to be," he shook his head, "The fire - in the fireplace, I mean. Yes. Cozy." Richard foolishly replied, feeling his brains turn to mush as he began to nuzzle Natalie's ear.

"Ah. Fire. Yes. Good." Natalie shivered, and, for once, was silent, as the roar of the fire and Richard's hands began to explore her entire body, one inch at a time. It all felt so right and good.

"Ah. Fire. Yes. Mmm. Good," Richard agreed, and he, too, was silent (and busy), for quite a long while.

Chapter 27

Down the Rabbit Hole

Descending the narrow, uneven wooden staircase wasn't as hard as it had seemed at first. Quinn had almost managed to attain zen mode. You know - one foot in front of the other, mindlessly, slowly, almost casually moving downward. His mind was clear. He wondered how Richard and Natalie were doing with "the fire." Glancing behind him, he noticed that Gracie was shivering. It was understandably quite chilly below ground, and they had left their winter gear upstairs. He slowed even more, trying to close the gap between them in an attempt to heat the air and transmit some of his body heat to her. If only it were that simple! Yes, indeed. If everything could be resolved by physical action alone, it would be so much simpler. Then, eventually, it would be possible to explain everything objectively. On inner levels he understood that "the real world" was anything but purely physical, anything but simple, and certainly not explainable in objective terms alone. There was so much more that needed explaining. And, to top it all off, he was stuck with all this emotional stuff. It would be the challenge of his life, along with Gracie.

Without warning, the stairs ended abruptly. It was good to finally walk on a flat surface. He noted that the passage forward seemed to curve up ahead to the right. Curiously, the passage was better lit than the stairs had been. There were small wall sconces about every twenty-five feet or so, reminding him of the tunnels - the underground passages at the University - well travelled passages - as this one seemed to be.

...Either skyways or tunnels, that seems to be the way we manage everything in Minnesota, Gracie mused. Cut off from everything and everyone. Insulated from each other in general and the universe in particular. Our skins never touch the air. Our minds never acknowledge our connections. Maybe it has to do with low levels of Vitamin D? Some kind of mole instinct? ... So, not only am I Vitamin D deprived, she acknowledged, but quite naturally I find myself here, 100 feet underground in some kind of tunnel; cold and worried.[36]

Gracie grabbed onto the back of Quinn's T-shirt for reassurance. She said, "It seems like we've been down here

---

[36] Yipes! I just realized that I'm turning in to a curmudgeon - as in a bad-tempered or surly person. A grouch!

an awful long time. I wonder how Natalie and Richard are doing? Maybe we should go back up?"

"I have to admit, this is a mighty peculiar basement," Quinn responded. He touched the wall. "It appears to be carved out of some kind of rock. It has the feel of a labyrinth, with all the twists and turns. I'm not sure the GPS unit on my cell will work down here either." He started trying to access the app that would tell them their exact location underground.

"Look. Over there." Gracie pointed.

Quinn looked up. "Ah. A door," he said. But, a door to where? He wondered. When he stopped and turned back to glance at Gracie, she was so close she plowed right into him.

"Oh, sorry," she said. She looked a little worried, and slightly pale. He noticed that she had grabbed onto the back of his T-shirt. Funny, he hadn't felt her grab onto his shirt at all. It was kind of cute. She obviously needed some reassurance, or something else. The path had widened, so he pulled her beside him, and gave her a sweet little kiss. She tasted like oranges and chocolate chip cookies. "Maybe we'll find the rabbit hole shortly." He said jokingly.

"Great. But, I think we've already gone down one." Gracie replied.

Not exactly the light-hearted note he had hoped for.

"Oops." She stumbled over something. She bent down to get a closer look. "Why, I'll be darned! Look at this." She stooped to pick up a small, intricately carved object. "It's a tiny key." She examined it and, after a moment, handed it to Quinn. "Odd-looking isn't it? I wonder where it came from. Looks like some kind of bronze. Is it?" She inquired. "Bronze, I mean."

Quinn's face changed as he took the key from Gracie. He became quite still, either excited or aggravated, Gracie couldn't tell. She had never seen this exact expression on his face before.

Quinn examined the key. It was old. A skeleton key - but not exactly. And it was articulated. He had only seen a few of those before, mostly in medieval museums. As he turned it over, it seemed to shimmer, almost a reflective surface - but there was no light - nothing for it to reflect off of. Curious. "I wonder…" his voice trailed off. "It's a strange kind of metal for sure," he answered Gracie's question, "but I don't know exactly what kind of metal it contains without testing it. One thing for sure," he said.

"What's that? And don't tell me that this tiny key will unlock that door over there - it's massive." Gracie responded.

"At least it's not 'the key that rules them all'." He gave her a lopsided grin.

"Oh for heaven's sake," Gracie groaned.

He pocketed the key.

Quinn moved ahead in the tunnel and reached the door. He beckoned for Gracie to come nearer. "Look." He said gesturing to the door. "See the carving - the motif? It reminds me of the drawing you made last Sunday at my Cottage in Duluth."

"You're right." Gracie said, startled.

Suddenly Quinn knew that Richard and Natalie needed to be here. Now. Right now. Making a snap decision, he said, "Richard needs to see this," and he turned back toward the stairs. Before he could take Gracie's hand to retrace their steps back upstairs together, she moved forward and grasped the knob. It would not budge. "Well, so much for that." Gracie groaned in frustration. "It's the story of my life. First the closet door at the cabin up north. Now... this. It's just too much. I'm either going to take a course on locksmithing or larceny. Maybe both. You pick." At Quinn's pained expression, Gracie paused, "Oh. Right. Pun. Bad choice of words again." She shrugged. "I wonder why it's locked?"

"If I were to speculate..." Quinn started.

"Please do." Gracie urged.

"I would guess this is an underground passage to the building next door."

"To the Carnegie library, you mean?"

"What?" Now Quinn looked startled.

"Well, Natalie told me that Anna's house was next door to the Carnegie library. So, if there's an underground passage, it probably goes to the library, right? Anyway, it makes a weird kind of sense."

"What do you mean?" Quinn asked.

"Two Carnegie libraries in about that many days." Gracie replied.

"I don't believe in coincidences."

"Neither do I." Gracie continued to study the pattern on the door. "But why is it locked?" They looked at each other, knowing instinctively what needed to be done.

"We need to get the door open." Quinn said.

"I agree."

"I have a feeling we need Richard... and Natalie... right now." Quinn said.

"Why Natalie?"

"Well, we need four pairs, four syzygies. And, it appears that Richard and Natalie, well... you know." He wiggled his eyebrows like Groucho Marx.

"Don't wiggle those eyebrows at me! Listen. I know that Natalie can sometimes have... a little fun. But she just met him a few hours ago. I'm not sure even Natalie moves THAT fast!"

"But, where a syzygy is implicated, and I think it is - I would expect that the normal rules wouldn't necessarily apply."

"You mean, like with us?"

"Huh?"

"Like, whatever happened between us, you mean?" Gracie repeated.

They exchanged a long gaze.

"It was pretty significant and unexpected wasn't it?" Quinn asked.

"Definitely out of the blue - not normal - I'd say." Gracie answered.

"Is that a problem?"

"I didn't say that. In fact, I would never have said that." Gracie replied. "But, what do you mean?"

"What do YOU mean, 'what do I mean?' About what, exactly?" Quinn answered. He had a confused look on his face. When Gracie didn't answer, he continued, "I thought it was pretty plainly stated. I was asking you about what happened between us. Whether it was significant for you too? Or was it just me? And..." What the hell am I saying? Quinn gulped. Too much information too fast. And do I really want to know?

"Are you always going to be like that?" Gracie asked.

"Like what?" Quinn replied.

"Like asking me questions about what I mean - especially when I don't know what I mean! I'm just too hard to understand, even for myself most of the time."

"No shit." Quinn replied.

"What if we were married for forty years and, all of a sudden you say, 'I don't understand you,' and you leave. How would I feel then?"

"What in the hell are you talking about? I just asked a simple question. I just wanted to know - a very simple question by the way - if you felt - that if what occurred between us - was more than just an... easy thing...?"

"Stop. You're getting me scared now. And, you made me say the "M" word. I'm really confused." Gracie responded.

Quinn inhaled sharply, and then broke into a sunny smile, "Oh, Gracie. You worry too much, and I'm an idiot." Then he pulled her close for a deep, lasting, breathless kiss.

"Oh, my." Gracie said. She felt much warmer.

"Yeah." Quinn answered.

"It's just that simple?" Gracie asked.

"I think so," Quinn replied, not letting go.

They sensed movement behind them in the passage and they heard Natalie's voice saying, "Looks like you two are getting pretty cozy over there. They make such a pretty couple don't they, Richard?"

"Natalie, behave yourself," Feynman's voice cautioned. He nipped at Natalie's ear; well, maybe he licked it.

"We were just coming to get you," Quinn said.

"Looks like you were trying to get something else," Natalie teased.

Gracie finally broke away from Quinn and turned to look over at Natalie and Richard. She studied them for a moment. Something felt different. Sure, they were holding hands but, it wasn't just that. They felt like - and they looked like they were together! They looked like a couple! Like they had known each other for a long time, and were involved in a comfortable, loving relationship with one another. Well, maybe a little sizzle too. How could that possibly be? Gracie wondered. They had know each other only a very short time. "Had they 'known each other,' in the biblical sense, maybe? As in carnal knowledge? In the library? As in syzygy? Could it be? Gracie turned back to Quinn and said, "syzygy?"

"Could be," Quinn replied. "They sure look... contented. And we need four pairs."

"Four pairs? Four pairs of what?" Natalie asked.

"Four syzygies." Richard replied. "Quinn and I worked it out at the lab. The energy will only work if we have four syzygies. It's critical."

"Huh?" Gracie asked.

"For the transference to work, we need four matched pairs. Just like in your drawing, Gracie. Quinn showed it to me."

"My drawing?" Gracie asked. "What drawing?"

Quinn pulled Gracie's drawing out of the pocket in his jeans. He unfolded it and showed it to her. "Remember the pattern, Gracie? I drew the basic pattern and you drew the connections, the energy signature."

"What energy signature?" Gracie was baffled.

"Let me see that!" Natalie examined the drawing.

"The syzygies around the pattern - the lacy parts." Quinn explained.

"Sure, I remember adding that part. But..."

Gracie was interrupted by Natalie's voice saying, "C'mon, Gracie. This is just the best adventure yet. Even better than Whistle Binkies! Let's just run with it, OK?" Natalie handed the drawing back to Quinn with a nod of approval.

"Whistle Binkies?" Richard asked.

"Isn't that a sports bar in Rochester?" Quinn asked.

"Sure is." Natalie replied. "And Gracie and I..."

"We'll talk about it later." Gracie hurriedly interrupted, changing the subject. "Well, as long as we're all here, let's look at the door."

"What door?" Richard asked.

"It's down the passage a little way. We were headed back to get you, to look at the carving -- the pattern's on the door. Gracie's pattern!" Quinn hurried down the hallway.

"We think it's the door to the Carnegie library next door." Gracie said.

"Duh." Natalie replied. "Of course it is. I bet it's a coordinate point too! Let's go see this great door!"

"What do you mean, 'it's a coordinate point too?'" Gracie sputtered, looking at the three persons standing in front of her. And, remember, I'm a lawyer, not a scientist! Give me a simple answer in plain language." She commanded.

Feynman, Quinn, and Natalie all looked at each other. Natalie shrugged.

"You give it a go, Richard, " Quinn said, "you're better at explaining things."

"OK. I'll attempt it." He paused. "I've always thought of a coordinate point as a physical place that contains great energy potential. Theoretically. A point of power. You could call it raw, untamed, uncontrolled power." Richard answered. "Because of its wild-card power, it has the potential to become an initiation point."

"You've heard of ley lines or vortexes haven't you, Gracie?" Natalie questioned. "It's the same concept, actually."

At the astonished look on Gracie's face, Quinn chimed in, also in 'professor mode,' "Coordinate points are almost pure points of energy. They would be sources of fantastic energy actually. 'Wow' kinds of energy. We can prove they exist mathematically, but no one's actually found one physically - yet."

"I had a hunch one was located in the Twin Cities, but I wasn't quite sure exactly where to look." Natalie added. "I was looking for places where plants grew with wild abandon; where a person always felt more alive; neighborhoods where houses were..."

"Natalie!" Gracie exclaimed. "What the hell? How do you know all this stuff?"

"Hobby, you know. Have to keep my brain alive. Can't do it just working for Tom. It's a little better working for you, but not much."

Gracie was unable to formulate an adequate response.

Richard tried to re-direct the conversation. "You could think of coordinate points as points or 'places' where realities can merge. Where time and space are able to impinge on each other."

"Places of double reality, in other words." Quinn said, adding his two cents.

"My work led me to believe that there were four absolute coordinate points - where ALL realities merge. That's what my unpublished work is all about." Richard added.

"So, your unpublished work - those were the books that Quinn was studying in Harvey's office, right?" Gracie asked.

"Yes," Quinn answered, "using Richard's model, I determined that we could use a coordinate point as a channel through which energy can flow, inter-dimensionally. Kind of like a transformer. A transformer that converts thoughts and emotions into physical matter." He paused. "Are you following me?"

"Oh yeah. Sure thing." Gracie replied.

"It's not that difficult of a concept, actually." Quinn took Gracie's hand. "Think of it this way: when a thought or emotion attains a certain intensity, it attracts the energy of a coordinate point and becomes highly charged. That's you, Gracie, highly charged. And, don't try to deny it. It's always been that way for you, hasn't it?"

Gracie nodded, acknowledging that weird things always seemed to happen to her or around her, and this was certainly no exception. But it had never occurred to her that she was literally a magnet! Why couldn't she be something sexy, you know, like a 'lodestone' or 'solenoid' she wondered?

"So, you were attracted here. You sensed where the coordinate point was. That means that this place is important." He kissed her hand. "You… are important. But I knew that from the beginning." Quinn said.

"There's just one itty, bitty little thing, isn't there?" Natalie said, looking directly at Richard. "I can always tell when a man is holding something back. You'd better spit it out."

"OK. OK." With a resigned sign, Richard said irritably, then, looking directly at Gracie, "I think that Natalie wants me to tell you that coordinate points alter physical laws to a certain extent."

"And…" Natalie prompted.

"Oh for crying out loud." Richard said.

Natalie blurted out, "Get it over with. Just tell her," she said, "it's the only way."

"Tell me what?" Gracie asked.

Richard sighed again, looking directly at Gracie and at Natalie, now standing shoulder to shoulder like two soldiers in arms, "But, the energy is dormant until it is activated. And, it cannot be activated physically."

"So... you mean...?" Gracie started.

"You can't just plug the cord in." Natalie said bluntly.

"So, how is the energy in this coordinate point thingy activated then, if not physically, and you can't plug it in?" Gracie asked reasonably.

"Mental images, accompanied by a strong emotional connection will usually do it." Richard replied.

"Do what?" Gracie replied. "What the hell am I asking anyway?"

"Well, you could say it would create a blueprint. A physical model for an object or a condition to occur - to cause it to 'appear' if you will - in this dimensional space. Our inter-dimensional bridge, in other words."

"Well, your theory fails right there." Gracie said. "I have often visualized something I wanted quite badly, with a great deal of emotional energy, and nothing happens. I visualize donuts all the time, and they don't miraculously appear on my desk, do they? Of course not! Why just last Friday morning, as I was leaving for work, my jeep tire was hopelessly flat. So, I visualized a perfectly intact, round tire and nothing happened! You know, the morning I met Quinn... when he pulled up in his cab... and... then... we met... and... started on this whole crazy business... oh, oh. You don't mean that...?"

"Exactly. If you had been able to fix your own tire by visualization, you wouldn't have meet Quinn. We are all cooperatively connected to each other. So what one person wants - or visualizes in your case - may not always be the ultimate solution to the problem. The lyrics to that old song, 'You can't always get what you want... but you get what you need' - it was right on point." Richard replied.

"But what about the donuts?" Gracie asked.

Richard made a face at her. "You weren't meant to be fat anyway, Gracie. Quinn likes slender women. The bottom line is that we're all connected to each other, so just visualizing what you want isn't always enough - at least not unless others are also cooperatively involved and tuned into what you want. Sometimes it takes something a little 'extra'. We don't always see the whole picture, you know."

"Something a little 'extra'." Gracie repeated. "That sounds vaguely familiar. I'll think about the 'fat' part later." She made a face at Quinn.

"What the hell!" Natalie interjected. "I liked your story until it got to this part. Now, I'm not so sure."

"What do you mean, Natalie?" Gracie asked.

"It sounds dangerous to me. And, it's Gracie isn't it? Am I right, Richard?" Natalie asked. "Don't lie to me. I'll know it if you're lying. Gracie is the bridge, isn't she?"

"Partially right, Natalie." Quinn jumped in. "I think it will actually take all four syzygy's, all four pairs, to open the portal to sustain the inter-dimensional bridge. But Gracie is the key. She's the initiation point - the focus."

Gracie's head was spinning. Wild, uncontrolled power? Oh no! Me, an initiation point?

"So, is it dangerous or not? Answer the question!" Natalie asked.

"Yeah, will I turn into a pumpkin or something?" Gracie asked.

"I hope not. We'll see." Richard replied.

They all looked at each other, a little overwhelmed by the implications of what lay before them. At least two out of the four persons standing in a tunnel 100 feet below ground, with a blizzard raging above, wondered if they had all been drugged by Anna's chocolate chip cookies or, alternatively, if they had all been affected by some kind of hallucinogenic underground gas pocket. The other two knew the absolute truth; that the connections were vital; that it was dangerous; and that they might be in for a rough ride if they had failed to take into account even one small vital detail. Like Mark Twain said, "it ain't what you don't know that gets you into trouble, it's what you know for certain that just ain't so."

"Well, what now?" Natalie asked. Gracie noticed that Richard had moved to Natalie's side, taking her hand in his own. One syzygy.

Gracie looked down at Quinn's hand, snugly holding onto hers. The second syzygy. They needed two more.

Gracie turned around and headed back down the tunnel toward the carved wooden door. She drew in a deep breath. "OK. So, follow me," she said. And they all did.

Chapter 28

The Infinite Loop

~Part I~

Anna had been observing it all. It had taken her a bit of time to get used to her "new" body. All in all, she felt wonderful - vibrating with energy. She hadn't understood that it would be like this. That she would be so amazingly full of energy and, yes, life. It felt like she had opened a door to full spring - with all the colors of the spectrum singing a tune in her ear. Her skin felt soft. Did she have skin, she wondered? She looked down, and indeed she "saw" her hand. A very lovely hand - without the brown age spots! She swung her head and the long, glistening copper-colored hair moved from side to side. She didn't need a mirror to know she was beautiful.

Looking around, she lovingly "touched" every object she encountered, glorying in the shared energy, the connectedness of everything. She was home at last. And, it felt good to be home. It had been so long. It was like she had finally awakened from a very long, sad dream. If she had known it would feel this good to be dead, she would have passed over much sooner. But, if she had known all of this beforehand, would it have given her a more meaningful life? Maybe. She had to think about that. But, for now, there was still Gracie to think about; to look after.

She had watched over Gracie her whole lifetime, from the very beginning to the very end. And, recollecting that first (and last) very short and abrupt meeting in Gracie's office, she knew there were a few things she needed to finish before she could move on. First of all, she needed to share with Gracie the simple truth that they were connected to each other in a bridge across time and space. Gracie was always pondering the great truths, and she needed a little help and encouragement. Gracie felt all alone. Not so. Gracie needed a reminder that her world was filled with MAGIC AND HOPE.

Of course, Anna realized she still had some other, more personal concerns... the never-ending concerns. And, unfortunately, the concerns hadn't changed all that much. But she would deal with it. One thing though - she did miss her orange candies. It was hard to get to work without them melting in her mouth. Did she have a mouth? Hurriedly, she pursed her "lips" together. Sure enough. The real deal. She could still recall the exquisite taste of her orange candies. She knew she could get orange candies anytime here, simply by "thinking" of them, but it wasn't quite the same as unwrapping one of her strangely beautiful orange candies in her orange house, with her orange tabbies close by, in the middle of a stormy night, with all of her books and plants nestled about her. She signed a small sigh. And, she hadn't been able to finish her final masterpiece either, the apple peeler that the NSA wanted so badly. Well, actually, the NSA didn't know it was an apple peeler. It was sort of a joke after all; but they'd wanted a surveillance device so badly. She could have given them anything - but she'd decided to have some fun with it. There were still a few simple adjustments to be made, and then it would be done. She wondered how she would be able to accomplish that.

Ah. More unfinished business: her research - the white hole stuff. She and Quinn had really had some lively discussions on that topic. Well, thinking back, maybe she had gone a bit overboard in her assertions. She felt ever so slightly embarrassed because now she realized that the whole concept was a bit ludicrous. It was all so simple and now crystal clear. Quinn had been right all along. She understood that Quinn would eventually figure it out all on his own, but she wanted to wish him luck, and give him one small clue just for fun. Maybe the cats could help with that? Hum. He was particularly fond of cats, she knew. All in all, she guessed this particular dimensional space wasn't so much different from what she had experienced before, when she was "so-called" living!

Well, enough settling in. For now. Time to get to work. She'd do without her orange candies. Yes. She needed to work on the Bridge. The Bridge through time and space. It will be so easy now! Let's see, what was that formula again? Ah yes. 1 TBSP. of time = 3 tsp. of space. Simple as baking a batch of chocolate chip cookies - but ever so much more satisfying!

~Part II~

"Harvey, we need to get to the rotunda now! Right now! Gracie needs us, I know it." Grace #1 shouted. "And, where's Carnegie?" With remarkable strength, she grabbed Harvey's hand and pulled him to his feet - up from the sofa where they had been snuggling.

"Darling," Harvey said, "what's going on? Gracie's with Quinn in the Twin Cities. They're in the middle of a blizzard. We couldn't get there right now even if we wanted to! Anyway, we don't have to be there until tomorrow night - at Quinn's lab."

"No, there's something... I feel it... it's now. It's not tomorrow, it's today! Right now!" Grace #1 gasped and began to run up the stairs toward the rotunda, carpeted in red. She started pulling up the edges of the carpet, just as Carnegie came around the corner.

"What's going on? What's all the ruckus about?" Carnegie said with a concerned look on his face.

Harvey answered, "Grace says the transference event is now. I don't understand how she knows, but she..."

They both glanced down at the pattern that Grace had revealed under the carpet. Then they looked at each other. Harvey scowled at Carnegie. It looked like Roger Penrose's pattern - a Penrose tiling.

It was a quasi-crystalline tessellation.[37] It could only be described as a non-pattern, pattern. As soon as your eyes recognize and focus on a pattern with a clear boundary, the pattern changes or dissolves. The pattern coalesces into... chaos.

Had Carnegie been messing around with Penrose too? Harvey wondered, astonished. He pointed to the Penrose tiles and shouted at Carnegie, "What did you do?"

"Oh, yes, that's right, I remember now. Roger and I had a few whiskeys, figuratively, of course, the night he came up with that idea - you know - his tiles." Carnegie said.

"You actually helped Penrose with this tessellation?" Harvey asked.

---

[37] A tessellation is the tiling of a plane using one or more geometric shapes, called tiles, with no overlaps and no gaps. In theoretical mathematics, tessellations can be used to represent a fourth dimensional object in a three-dimensional space. From wikipedia, the Dictionary of our times.

"Apparently. I seem to be getting pretty good at this inspiration thing. Had to do something while I was waiting for you and Gracie to get back. Roger was quite easy to inspire, brilliant actually."

"You simply haven't a clue, have you?" He asked Carnegie. "Sometimes things are better left alone - to be figured out in their own time - without our help! You may have royally fucked things up - again."

"Why do you say that? What do you mean?" Carnegie glared at Harvey.

"The pattern that you so 'artfully' shared with Penrose contains so much energy - in this dimension - that most of us have stopped fooling around with it until we are better able to work out the energy fluctuations - too many variables - unforeseen consequences."

Shaking his head and groaning, Harvey stepped over to the rug to help his wife reveal the last part of the pattern. "So, what's next?" He asked. "Do you understand any of this?"

"Well, I'm not absolutely certain, but I think we have to stand on the right tiles. The ones that connect with our personal energy." Grace said.

"OK. Which tile do I stand on?" Harvey asked.

"Your own tile, of course, the one that matches your own energy signature." Carnegie replied.

"So, how do I know which one is mine?" Harvey was getting flustered and glanced, concerned, at his wife.

Grace motioned to the Penrose tiles at the far edge of the pattern. "Why don't you start over there." She gestured. "Try stepping on the tiles, one at a time. You're supposed to definitely know which one 'belongs' to you when you step on it. There should be no doubt. Everyone's experience is said to be slightly different."

"How do you know all this?" Harvey asked.

"Well, I've been trying to figure it out for awhile. Since you've been gone, actually. I thought it might come in handy if someone tried to wrench me away from my family again." She frowned and took a deep breath. "But, remember. Once you've found your tile, you can't step off of it until we're done, otherwise..."

"Otherwise, what?" Harvey questioned.

"Otherwise, old man, you'll just go..." Carnegie started to reply.

"Go where?" Harvey persisted.

"Go pfssst." He held his arms aloft as he turned full circle, his gesture encompassing the entire room. "You'll end up somewhere, in hell maybe, but not here! So, be careful."

Harvey looked over at Grace, then back at Carnegie. He swallowed. Sweat had begun to bead up on his forehead and his face seemed to be getting redder and redder by the moment. "OK. OK. I'll go first! Carnegie... you, you... you're such an idiot! Assuming I 'find' the correct tile - my tile - what do we do then? How do we connect with Gracie, Quinn and Feynman? Don't we need them too?"

"This transference thing - I'm not quite sure. I thought we would all be in the same room and able to speak to one another - but apparently not. Remember, Richard tried to explain..." Carnegie began.

"If we are all standing where we're meant to be, wouldn't the energy circuit be completed? Wouldn't we at least be able to talk to one another then?" Grace said.

"Well. Why not? We're not in the same room with the others, it's true. But heh, maybe we're all where we're supposed to be - somehow. Besides, we have to run with it if this is the right time. We have no choice. Let's give it a try." Harvey replied, considering. "It's highly unlikely that we're traveling anywhere tonight, anyway. Unless, of course, these tiles work the way Grace said. Then, who knows?"

Harvey took a cautious step forward, gingerly, as if he expected a static charge to give him a zap. He shrugged his shoulders. "Nothing," he said as he began to slowly circle the edge of the pattern. He saw a curious yellow-gold colored tile and stepped on it. With startling speed, he received a small jolt of energy, almost like an electric shock, but not quite. He heard Grace's short intake of breath. He looked down at himself, and, although his feet were there, and they appeared to be firmly planted on the tile, he felt like he was floating. He looked at Grace and smiled.

"Ah, found yours, did you?" Grace smiled back. She blew him a kiss. Then, with the pattern totally revealed now, she instinctively moved toward the outer boundary of the pattern until she was one step away from a slightly reddish colored tile. She knew then. The moment she stepped on the tile, she felt as if her hair were on fire - in a good way, and she looked directly across the Penrose tiles to smile at her mate and partner. Their eyes met, and it felt as if their bodies were touching, even though they were at opposite ends of the Penrose circle. They smiled, realizing that there was a chance; that there was some hope that things would turn out all right this time. They grasped onto that hope, and in some unexplainable way, they held each other too.

"Your turn," Harvey said to Carnegie. Carnegie moved fast, surprisingly agile for a man of his age, heading straight toward Grace. When he got about half way, it looked like his hair and beard had begun to glow. He stopped and cleared his throat, with a startled expression on his face. "Well, it seems I've found my place as well. What's next?" He asked generally looking first to Grace and then to Harvey.

"Well, we've each found our tile. So far, so good. But..." Grace began, and Harvey's voice joined hers, "But... where are the others?"

Part III

"Christ," Natalie exclaimed. "Doesn't anybody ever dust down here? Ick. Yuck. I've got spider webs in my hair. How gross!"

"Here, let me help." Feynman began gently removing the silken webs from Natalie's hair.

"Thank you." Natalie said. "Spiders give me the creeps. I can't even watch a Spiderman movie."

"You're joking," Feynman said. "Spidey's the best. You know, the metamorphosis, and then the way he..."

She placed her small hand gently across his mouth. "C'mon, hon. Let's just get the damn door open and blow this popsicle joint. I'd like to take this discussion back upstairs... you know, where the spiders can't find me - to the warm place. I'm so much more interesting - and entertaining - without spiders in my hair." She winked at Richard. "Besides, we have numerous superhero stories to share - among other things."

Gracie glanced at Feynman, who seemed to suddenly perk up. He was grinning, adoringly, at Natalie. Gracie had seen men stare adoringly at Natalie before. In fact, Natalie could bring tears of lust to a deadman's eyes. But this was different. Gracie considered. Was Richard actually smitten? Were he and Natalie really "a thing?" Gracie tore her eyes away from whatever was going on between Natalie and Richard, and forced her attention back to Quinn who was crouched down, inspecting the door for the third time. "Anything?" she asked.

Quinn was running his fingers over the perimeter of the door, nearer to the floor, searching for... anything. A hidden catch, maybe. No. The door was solidly in its frame, and it wouldn't budge. There were no hinges showing either, so the door had to open inward. No help there.

Quinn shook his head. "At least we don't have to deal with a wormhole or energy surges. Although it might be easier."

"At least not yet." Richard said.

"What? What do you mean?" Quinn asked sharply, standing up and turning to face Feynman.

"Quinn," Gracie said. "We need to hurry."

He glanced back at her. "Why?" He asked.

"I have a feeling we need to be on the other side of that door." She pointed. "Now."

"OK, then. So, you're pretty sure about that are you? You have a feeling?" He asked.

"More like a hunch actually," Gracie replied in a low, husky voice.

"Uh-oh. Gracie's in Schizophrenistan." Natalie said.

"Schizophrenistan?" Quinn and Richard echoed.

"Yeah. You know, not a real country - one of those 'mental states'." Richard and Quinn looked confused; Gracie was staring off into space. Natalie tried to explain.

"Geez, Louise. It's a pun - a joke. Listen up you guys. You're really both pretty smart, so I know you can handle it. But, I'll try to explain using small words anyway. Gracie's in a totally different place - again. I call it Schizophrenistan. The place where all the mental cases go." She shrugged her shoulders.

"You're kidding, right?" Quinn asked.

Natalie shook her head. "No. No joke. You'd better learn to pay attention," Natalie continued, "to Gracie's hunches, especially if you plan on hanging out with her. Believe me, I know. Eeek." She suddenly hollered. "Another goddamn spider." She kicked at a moving spot a few inches to the right of the door. The spider scurried away into the darkness, out of harm's way. As Natalie's stylishly-booted foot made contact with the wall, the massive door swung open wide. Everyone turned to look at her in astonishment. Natalie had a smug look on her face...

...Yeah, man! Natalie gave a mental whoop. I love my kick-ass Fluevogs...

"Well. Naturally." Natalie said with a toss of her head. "No big deal. Like I was saying - if you have enough snus to hang out with Gracie, you'll understand what I mean about her being in Schizophrenistan. And, if you have enough snus to hang out with me, not only will you learn that Gracie always has these hunches, but that I always deal with the doors. Just like at Whistle Binkies." She threw her dreads back, shrugged her shoulders, and nodded toward the open door. "You first, Gracie, it's your show."

Quinn was speechless. Feynman recovered first. "That's my girl. Good job. But, better let me go first." Richard said as he moved through the entrance ahead of the others. He immediately stopped, in stunned silence.

Natalie and Gracie followed closely on Richard's heels, with Quinn entering the room last. They all stood, mesmerized.

Chapter 29

Through the Veil

The room was large and circular, with a domed roof at least thirty feet overhead. The floor appeared to have a pattern emblazoned upon it, a strangely repeating, almost geometric pattern. The pattern was surging and swelling in a dance-like wave motion. Poppin the quiff?[38]

What kind of independent energy source could produce this effect? Feynman wondered. While he watched, the pattern changed again. Now it appeared to be floating, moving, glowing, and pulsating at the same time. My god, Feynman realized, it was Penrose's pattern! Yes. It was Penrose's pattern all right, but it was multi-phasic, fluctuating between dimensions! Within seconds, the floor

---

[38] "Poppin the quiff" is a physics term that implies a shift in a quantum wave function that allows it to change from the gooey 'stuff' to prickly 'stuff.' The idea here is that consciousness may be key in creating or initiating the change in the quantum wave function. Who ever said physics was dull? See the work of Fred Alan Wolf, Ph.D, Professor of Physics at UCLA.

began climbing on top of itself! He could see Harvey on one tile; and Harvey's wife - Grace #1 - on a tile directly across from him. He could see Carnegie riding a wild tile, tilting and galloping in midair. Despite all the mathematics and even with the wildest theoretical physics he could imagine, he had never expected to see this. But what? Was that shimmer an energy fluctuation? And then, another change in the pattern - more symmetry this time! The pulsating slowed. Gracie pushed ahead of him. As she stepped farther into the room, the pattern dissolved again, destabilizing, shifting into another entirely different form. Now asymmetric. She was affecting the pattern somehow. Of course, Gracie was the bridge.

The transference event was in progress. No stopping it now. The whole scene unfolding was surreal. Quinn was following closely behind Gracie. Feynman tried to call out to him to wait; to make Gracie understand that she had to slow down; that they had to stop until the pattern was more stable. Then, startled, he saw Gracie break into a run, if you could call it that, staggering forward while the pattern was shifting and swaying. She was moving swiftly away from Quinn and safety, toward the other end of the room.

"No." Feynman and Quinn shouted in unison. "Gracie, wait!" Gracie did not stop but kept moving unsteadily forward. She appeared to be moving toward one of the shimmering lights... toward Harvey, or was it Harvey's wife? Feynman couldn't tell. The figures seemed to be blinking on and off, interchanging. He had to close his eyes. He reached for Natalie to be sure she was safe, but… she was gone! She wasn't behind him! Where had she gone? Oh God, no! He searched the room and found that Natalie had climbed onto a black tile to his right. The tile was pulsating. She was blinking on and off now too. This was happening too fast! He had to slow it down.

"Richard. Hurry!" Natalie shouted. "You need to find your tile. Now."

"What do you mean," Richard said, "my tile?"

"I'm not sure, but at Whistle Binkies, I just knew what to do. Same here. You need to be across from me - over there." She pointed to a glowing red tile directly to his left, across from her. "Trust me. I know this is right." She had a brave, shit-kicking grin on her face, but her voice was unsteady, quivering slightly. She was scared. "It's OK." She said with a sheepish grin, "I love you!"

Richard looked at Natalie, really looked at her, and he knew it was true. He felt her - near him, and in him, and touching him, somehow. He knew he needed to be near her, joining her, in an age old dance. The noise in the room was deafening. It felt like there was a hurricane wind howling in his ears. Debris was rising upward; the air felt heavy. The instant he stepped onto the red tile he knew it was right. Natalie reached for him across time and space and they were joined, as one.

Gracie kept moving, steadily, oblivious, toward the far end of the room. She could hear Quinn shouting something, but she could not make out his words. It was all gibberish. She was moving toward her mother and her father; she needed to reach her place in the pattern - the eye of the tornado, the center of the chaos. She was the bridge. They needed her! She was moving through mud; her arms were heavy; her legs were leaden. As she neared the center of the room, she was blocked by an obstacle directly in her path. She tried to push it aside. She had to keep going. It was important! She had to reach the other side. But it was useless, the object was too large and heavy. Trying as hard as she could, she couldn't get the object to budge. She had to find another way! She looked up in frustration at the immovable obstacle in her path. Why it was Quinn! What was he doing here? Why wouldn't he move aside? He was trying to tell her something. With all of the noise, she couldn't understand what he was saying. The air was swirling and spinning around him. How could he stand? How could he breathe? She finally heard his words reverberate, as if they were both deep, deep inside an echo chamber. She stopped then. Right where she was, in the path of the tornado. She heard him say, "You don't have to do this, Gracie. Gracie, don't do this alone. Please, Gracie. Wait. Wait for me." He begged. "We'll do this together - if we must."

"But I can't! This is crazy!"

"Sure it is," Quinn replied. "But, Gracie, it's all crazy. It's your story, and you're at the center of it. It's up to you now."

"Quinn, how can all of this crazy stuff be true?"

"Have faith. Trust what you know."

"You're sure?"

"You know I am, Babe."

She felt a touch - a movement behind her. She shifted and turned away from Quinn, gazing in awe at a blue, tubular whirlwind. It could have been inches away or it could have been thirty feet across the room; there was no way to judge the distance. Quinn reached for Gracie, to pull her to safety, but before he could reach her, time slowed down, and then stopped altogether. A moment in time, frozen and separate from all others. Then Gracie saw her. She saw Anna, emerging from the whirlwind. She had reached the center of the storm.

Seeing the shocked look on Gracie's face, Anna smiled broadly, as if she were presenting Gracie with a present at a surprise birthday party!

... No! It can't be Anna! But it has to be Anna! It feels like Anna, but this youthful, beautiful woman looks nothing like the weird old lady who died in my office! But I know it's Anna all the same, there is no doubt!

I opened my mouth to speak, but nothing came out at first. I took a deep breath, closed my eyes for a brief moment and then opened my eyes again. No change. Anna was still standing right in front of me. Anna, as in "dead-as-a-doorknob" Anna.

"But, but, you're… dead! I saw you die in my office! There was no mistake. The paramedics took your body out of my office on a stretcher… I have your bag. You… signed a Will leaving everything to... me!" I began to ramble on like an idiot. "I was in your house. I pet your cats." I shook my head trying to find some clarity. "I must be hallucinating. Harvey must have put something in my water. I've been set up, brainwashed…"

Anna said, "Well, I have to admit, this wouldn't be a typical day for you would it? Or would it? Um. Actually, Gracie, I'd think by now, that you'd have a better grasp of how it all works."

My mouth fell open in astonishment. Not only was she dead, but she could talk too! And she was sassy!

Anna continued in a matter-of-fact tone, "It's all a matter of perception, actually. You are way more than what you were taught - more than you think you are! Wake up, girl! As you expand your consciousness, things begin to change, don't they? It's useless to deny it. At the very core of your being you know this is true. Why, you've seen it happen in your own life, for goodness sakes, haven't you? It is one of the primary rules - and you're very, very good at rules. Remember, that's why you're a probate lawyer!"

Wow. Ouch! This lady really knew how to hit where it hurt!

"Gracie... Believe your own eyes! Obviously, I'm not dead. It's true that my physical body, in your space∞time may be categorized as 'dead,' but that's only part of me. And, actually, it was only a very small, old, and as you know, somewhat weird part anyway."

"It sure was." I said. "You gave me the creeps, you know..." I've had many challenges in my life, and at this point, I was clamoring for some way, any possible way, to make sense of how I could be in this place, taking to a dead person who was really alive. Despite what Anna had said about perception, this was beyond the pale; beyond anything I had ever experienced before. All I could do was look at her and try to understand.

"My dear child." Anna sighed. "Let me try to explain - in your terms. When Quinn's machine opened up the black hole that allowed your mother to travel back to find Harvey and you, I knew my time was running out. You are so dear. Nothing could stop me then! I could not pass up the chance to see you... to help you understand... to meet you in person, as I've wanted to for your entire life. I've always felt you near to me. We are connected, you and I, through all of time and all of the universes. I am you; you are me; we are one."

"But this can't be real." I blurted. "How can it be? It doesn't make sense."

"Ah. Yes. The rational approach. OK." Anna seemed to ponder her response for a moment. "Listen up. The best way that I can put it is that it's all fake. A veneer. Yes. That's a good word, 'veneer.' Your accepted rationality is a thin, fake veneer. It covers up a more full, spontaneous and magical reality - where all the facts actually come from."

"Huh?"

At the blank look on my face, Anna rephrased, "Try to think of it this way. Your life has always been full of strange stuff, in your terms, because you are simply dealing with a 'larger' version of facts than most people do. You are more open. You believe in everything. Because of your openness, you have been able to tune into those extraneous bits and pieces, those odds and ends of the 'real' reality because of who you are - how you look at the world. Never stop looking at life that way, Gracie!"

"But it doesn't make things simpler. It makes everything so much more complicated." I wailed. "And people think I'm nuts!"

"Does it really make things more complicated, or more clear? And, do you really care if people think you're nuts?" Anna replied. "If you hold onto the so-called 'rational' approach - the accepted approach to life - in some misguided effort to maintain a balanced viewpoint and an open mind - you will miss out on all the good stuff. Why do you think I operated 'off-the-deep-end?' Duh. It was a lot more fun! You know this."

By now, panic was written all over my face.

"Listen! Pay attention. You are who you are. I'm not saying you have to be like me. Heavens, no! True, the good stuff may be the odd stuff, but it's also the really amazing, insightful, and interesting stuff! Not to mention, amusing. You've always tried to limit your 'factual' world because you have been trained to limit yourself to a very narrow reality. They bludgeoned that way of thinking into your brain in law school, remember? And, in your world, if you step out of the very narrow, accepted reality, then you will be called irrational, fanatic, mentally ill... whatever. You know you are none of these things. You are ever so much more. Darling, just make your life what you want it to be. You know how!"

It made sense. But it was hard to take it all in. I wanted my life to be magical. In fact, I think it has been. Especially now. Especially since last Thursday. Especially since Quinn.

"So, here I am now, seeing you, finally meeting you in person, and saying goodbye - again. This time deliberately. We both lose - but only a little, and we both gain - quite a bit."

"But..." I started to say.

"Gracie, you know this - things always change. Nothing stays the same. In fact, you could say that change is what you ordered up for yourself! It's what you bargained and paid for in this dimension! Except for one thing..." she grinned and winked at the same time (if that is possible)... "except for love - that never changes - that's our connection. And it always will be."

Anna must have sensed what I was feeling. A sense of what - loss? Of... understanding? Or, maybe... of wonderment?

"Now don't start worrying again Gracie! Everything always shows on your face," she grumbled. "Oh for heaven's sake! Think of me as your aunt, your angel, or, if it pleases you, your old, dead, weird client. It doesn't matter. But Gracie, remember this... you won't be alone. You will never be alone." With that, Anna turned and began walking back toward the blue whirlwind, still suspended in time. "Oh, one more thing." She said.

"What is it?" I stammered.

"You're not the bridge. I am."

"What do you mean?" I asked, my voice steadying.

"You must take your place on the tile next to Harvey. Quinn needs to take his place across the room from you. Then..."

"Then... what? And, what about Quinn? How does he fit into all of this?"

"Too many questions. You are so curious!" Anna sighed.

"Well?"

"Then your time line will be restored, and Harvey and your mother will be able to go back."

"Go back to where?"

"To their own 'time', dimension or whatever you want to call it, of course."

"What about me?"

"What about you?"

"Where do I belong? Am I supposed to go with them, or stay here - with Quinn?"

"It's up to you."

"Me? Why me?"

"Well, it's your life isn't it?"

"Sure, but isn't there some kind of rule or order that I'm supposed to follow - you know - like the Minnesota Rules of Court - the Universal Rules of the... Universe?" I swallowed, a little worried about the answer I might get.

Anna made some kind of choking noise. What? Why, it was a chortle! Was she laughing at me? Are ghosts or angels supposed to laugh at humans? Was I even human?

"You are so funny." Anna didn't even try to hide her laughter now. "You make the rules, Gracie. It's your story, remember? Oh, by the way, give this to Natalie for me. This will help her finish the apple peeler for the NSA." Anna handed me a folded paper.

"Aha! I was right! It is an apple peeler!" I said.

"Why, of course it is."

"Wait, won't the NSA be pissed when I give them an apple peeler, even if Natalie completes it? Did they hire you to make an apple peeler?" I asked.

"No, of course not. They asked me to build them a white hole electromagnetic spying device. But, don't worry. The NSA are morons. And, who knows? If they peel enough apples maybe they will eventually get the device to work the way they want it to! Besides, I loaded the device with enough 'extra' stuff to give them something to think about for the next 100 years or so anyway."

My mouth was hanging open in frank astonishment now. I didn't know what to say.

"Oh." Anna paused. "One more thing."

Oh no! "What else?" I asked apprehensively.

"My journal."

"Your journal?"

"Yes. It's in the wall safe behind the Mucha painting in my bedroom. Gracie, use the information wisely," she commanded, "and don't fool around with my Apple stock! Steve and I worked really hard on that one!" Then, her face filled with an expression conveying both amusement and mischievousness. She laughed out loud and turned back toward the center of the room. When she reached the blue whirlwind, time began again.

I turned back to Quinn. He grabbed me and held me tight to his chest. "Oh, Gracie. I thought for a moment .."

"C'mon." I said. "No time. I need to get over there. Next to Harvey." I pointed to a shimmering blue tile that I knew was mine. "And you need to be directly across from me." We both looked across the room, to a vivid green, glowing tile."

"I do?" Quinn said. "How do you know I need to be over there?"

"Remember the pattern I drew Quinn? Each pair, each part of the syzygy - you and I - need to be standing opposite each other. Besides, Anna told me."

"Anna told you? How could..." He started to say.

"I'll explain later. I have a feeling we don't have much time."

"OK then. Let's do it!" And with a warm reassuring squeeze, Quinn, my hero, bravely moved to his tile as I moved swiftly toward mine. We stepped onto our tiles at the exact same moment. A jolt of a new kind of energy flowed through my body; holding me, surrounding me - Quinn's energy - as my energy joined and flowed into his. I knew then, without a doubt, that Quinn was mine, and I was his, and that it would always be that way.

I tore my eyes away from Quinn, and gazed into the room, now beginning to spin slowly. The room had taken on a pinkish glow. I saw Harvey standing next to me, and directly across from him, his wife, Grace... my mother. One syzygy. I looked at Natalie standing next to my mother. And, across from Natalie, I saw Richard. The second syzygy. Quinn was standing next to Natalie, directly across from me. The third syzygy. Then, on my other side, there was an odd-looking older man, wearing a funny necktie. He was riding a wild tile. Who was he? And, more importantly, where was his partner? We needed a fourth syzygy. And, in a flash of insight I knew. Of course, it was so obvious. It was Anna, it had to be! It was no surprise to me then, that within moments, Anna, still encapsulated in her blue whirlwind, reappeared at the center of the room.

I heard Quinn's quick intake of breath. "Anna," he exclaimed. "Thank God! Do you know how to modulate this energy? Is it safe for Gracie to...?"

"Now, dear boy, don't worry about the energy modulations. You and that handsome fellow over there, she pointed at Feynman, already worked that part out, pretty much anyways. So you did good. And, I'm so proud of you, you figured out the orange part! Such a bright boy! We had so much fun, didn't we? Ah, well. And, you finally met Gracie too. Isn't it wonderful? And, Gracie? Well, she'll be fine. She's the focus, it's true, but I am the bridge." Anna said.

"But we need another syzygy! See Carnegie over there?" Quinn pointed at Carnegie on his wildly bucking tile. "The energy isn't balanced unless..."

"You mean that funny-looking old guy over there? He's kinda cute isn't he?" She winked at Carnegie and blew him a kiss. You didn't think I invented the recipe for those outstanding chocolate chip cookies all on my own, did you?" Anna asked. She gave Carnegie a brilliant smile as she stepped onto the tile directly across from his, and said, "So glad to finally meet you - ah - in person, Andrew," she said, "I've been looking forward to this day for a very, very long time."

"The pleasure is most assuredly mine," Carnegie said in a very formal, gallant tone, as his tile began to stabilize, "and I think it's not a moment too soon."

"My timing has always been exemplary," Anna said, with a coy smile filled with innuendo. "By the way, do you like orange candies?"

"Um, orange? Well, it's always been my favorite color. Orange candies, eh? Perhaps we'll be able to come up with a recipe that pleasures us both?" Carnegie suggested.

The humming became louder; the pinkish hue intensified to a siren red. Suddenly, there was a loud cracking sound, a thunderclap, and the portal appeared. The portal was in the center of the room, where the blue whirlwind had been. The light was too bright to penetrate, too bright to see anything on the other side of the portal. Each syzygy acted like a path, one of the spokes of a gigantic wheel, leading directly to the center of the hub, the portal. The time had come. Harvey and Grace, Anna and Carnegie had their bridge. It was solid and real. It was time to go home.

"Shall we?" Anna said to Carnegie. Both Anna and Carnegie stepped off their separate tile, and began walking toward the portal; walking toward each other.

As the energy surged through my body, my eyes began to glaze over. From what seemed like a far distance, I heard Anna's command, "Gracie! Gracie. Open your eyes. Look at me!"

Obediently, I opened my eyes.

"You'll be all right. In fact, everything is good. You will continue this life, and all these sensations, both old and new, will remain yours, until the end of your years."

"The end of my years? Is that soon?" I gasped, my mind reeling from all the implications.

"No. Not soon. You and Quinn, and all your kidlets have a lot to accomplish yet."

"Quinn... our 'kidlets?' What the hell is a 'kidlet?'"

"Oh, Gracie, use your very wondrous imagination. You figure it out! But remember, Gracie, you won't be alone. You will never be alone."

And with that statement and my exhaled breath, Anna reached the center of the hub; took Carnegie's proffered hand, and was gone... again.

Next, Harvey and Grace#1 began walking slowly toward each other - toward the portal.

I was in a panic. This couldn't be happening. It was too soon; too fast. I needed more time with them! There was so much I wanted to say, to ask, to know. "Wait! Stop!"

Grasping for any reason at all to delay their departure, I stumbled on. "Can I ask a question - before you go?" I pleaded.

"Sure." Harvey said.

"Are there more like me? You know, weird people?"

"Well, you're not exactly one of the 'X-men,' but, yes, there are plenty of others who think like you; who understand that we are all connected to each other, and that our observable universe, in this dimension, is very limited. They're still working out the 'consciousness' piece, though. That's why your mother and I were here in the first place - to experience and to try to understand how things are changing here - in this dimension." Harvey responded.

"OK. But how... how can I find them?" I asked

"Find who?" Harvey asked.

"The others. You know; the ones like me."

"Don't worry, Gracie," Harvey's wife said. "Just look around this chamber." She nodded at Quinn, Natalie, and Richard. "They'll have a way of finding you."

Harvey and Grace#1 nodded at each other in agreement. They had arrived at the hub, and, as they reached for each other, I exploded, "Wait. Just one more question?" I begged.

Harvey wrinkled up his face. "Sure, Gracie, but make it snappy." He answered, "The portal won't stay open forever!"

"It may sound silly." I said.

"It's a silly universe." Grace#1 said.

"Well, here goes." I had to think fast. "Are vampires sparkly where you come from?"

Harvey looked at Grace#1, and shook his head with a 'I should have guessed' expression his face. Grace#1 answered for them both. "You still have a bit to learn, Gracie. Here's the very simple answer: Vampires can be sparkly in any of your universes - if you decide you want them to be sparkly."

"OK then; I'll have to think about that."

"You do that." Grace#1 replied.

"Please... I just wanted to say... I want to say... that I love you, and... thank you - Mom." Gracie's eyes locked onto her mother's face.

Grace#1 answered her daughter, with a small sigh and human tears in her eyes. "Oh my daughter. Be well and happy. Understand this, even if you understand nothing else - love never dies, no matter what, and no matter what world you're in." She wiped the tears from her eyes and deliberately turned back to face the portal. She held out her hand to Harvey.

"Goodbye, Harvey. I love you too." I said.

"I know." He responded with all the love he'd ever had for this wayward, challenging daughter showing in his misty eyes. "It's been a wild ride, hasn't it?" Harvey said, clearing the lump in his throat. "Remember - don't stick any peanuts up your nose and pay your Bar dues on time!" He commanded. And then, with resolve, he turned to face his wife and took her hand.

I nodded in acceptance. I had only stuck peanuts up my nose one time, but it had been pretty traumatic event for both Harvey and for me. Actually, come to think of it, forgetting to pay my Bar dues on time was actually much worse!

"Oh. One more thing - just because you don't see us, doesn't mean that we're not there rooting for you and watching over you, little Grace." My mother said.

"Yeah. Remember that too." Harvey said.

Then, with a wink and a smile, Harvey and Grace#1 were gone too.

Well, so much for privacy, I thought. But, suddenly, the day felt sunnier.

The pulsating movement of the room subsided. The portal disintegrated as if it had never existed. Quinn and I, Natalie and Richard found ourselves standing at opposite corners of a large room containing a pop machine at one end and a cafeteria counter at the other. A lunchroom? The massively carved door was now a steel door with a metal push bar on it. I staggered toward Quinn with a question in my eyes. Had I dreamed it all? He drew me close and said, "Let's go back Gracie, back upstairs. It's been a long, long day. It's time to go home."

I looked down at the folded paper I was grasping firmly in my left hand. I opened it up. It was a drawing of the apple peeler - the NSA super secret electromagnetic thingamajiggee. I gave the paper to Natalie just as Richard reached her side. They looked over the schematic briefly, and Natalie said, "No problem-o."

Richard nodded. "Eminently do-able."

Quinn suddenly exploded, "Richard! Why are you still here? Weren't you supposed to go back too?"

"Quinn," Richard said quizzically, "I thought you understood... four go; four stay. We have to maintain the balance. Besides, you still have some important work to do, and perhaps I could possibly be of some assistance to you?" He winked at Quinn then. He still had that same mischievous look in his eyes as he examined Natalie's hand securely nestled in his. "Besides, I think this cute little firecracker here can... be of assistance as well. At least, I hope so." At which point Natalie stepped forward, grabbed Richard's butt, and kissed him fiercely.

"Well then," Richard coughed, "It's settled then?"

"You betcha." Natalie replied, her eyes shining.

There was a lump in my throat. "Good," I said. Then I took Quinn's outstretched hand gratefully.

Together we pushed the metal bar on the door exiting the cafeteria and starting back down the tunnel, toward the life we knew. Back to the warm, snug, orange kitchen directly above us - with a blizzard raging outside. But now we understood that we made the rules, and that it was all up to us. Our life was our own, in every possible way. It was our story. I grinned widely and finally understood. It was all good.

Chapter 30

Marvelous Mediocrity

"Mr. Rigby, Ms. Swan, note your appearances for the record." Judge Henderson commands.

Rigby and I make our appearances. I also introduce my client, Linda Jorsensen, seated next to me.

I address the Court, "Your Honor, the Court record should reflect that Attorney John Johnson is present in the Courtroom this morning as well. Mr. Johnson is my client's long time friend. He is also her legal counsel in the State of Oregon, where Ms. Jorgensen resides."

"If Ms. Jorgensen is a resident of the State of Oregon, what are we doing here today?" Judge Henderson inquired, somewhat testily.

Without thinking I retorted, "Because you ordered Mr. Rigby and I to inventory Ms. Jorgensen's refrigerator last week, your Honor." Then I winced. Judge Henderson's face reddened. He glared at me dismissively.

"Mr. Johnson, would you care to explain why you are here?"

"Of course. However, as a preliminary matter, I do have some documents to file. If I may approach?"

Judge Henderson asked, "Do Mr. Rigby and Ms. Swan have copies of these documents?"

"They sure do, your Honor," Attorney Johnson replied.

"Any objections?" The Judge needed to know if either Rigby or I objected to Attorney Johnson's documents being presented to the Court. In other words, did Rigby and I want to argue about the documents before the Judge looked at them? I wanted the documents to be admitted into evidence, so, of course, I didn't object. And Rigby wouldn't dare object, so he didn't.

With only a small hope of enlightenment and a now resigned look on his face, Judge Henderson nodded, "You may approach the bench, Mr. Johnson." Attorney Johnson confidently walked to the front of the courtroom, handed Judge Henderson a sheaf of papers which the Judge started rapidly reading.

After a few minutes of silence, thinking I might be of assistance, I asked, "If I may clarify, your Honor?"

Judge Henderson looked up and responded, "Please do, Ms. Swan. But keep it short." Judge Henderson's face was not quite so red now, and, from the look he gave me, he seemed to be catching the general drift of the maneuvering.

I nodded. "To summarize, after the emergency hearing last week I was able to reach Attorney Johnson who had

returned from China. You know, after I inventoried..."
Judge Henderson looked up, daring me to continue. I knew
better. "Since then, I've been able to provide Mr. Rigby
with a copy of Ms. Jorgensen's voter registration card, a
copy of the Lease Agreement on her apartment in
Portland, and other evidence of Ms. Jorgensen's status as a
resident of Oregon."

I glanced over at Attorney Rigby. His face was
reddening and his fists were clenched. He looked
exceedingly uncomfortable, but he didn't say a word.

So far, so good. I continued to address the Court, "Your
Honor, as you can see, my client was never a resident of
Minnesota. She's just here visiting her daughter for a short
time. Proof of those facts are included in the documents
Mr. Johnson just handed to you." The judge looked up
from his reading. He got it. Now I could continue, setting
the stage for the Judge to make a ruling based on my
version of the facts.

I continued, "The bottom line is that Minnesota
doesn't have jurisdiction over Ms. Jorgensen. Since my
client is a resident of Oregon and since she is only visiting
her daughter here in the Twin Cities, any Petition for
Emergency Guardianship brought here, in Minnesota, is
improper. Furthermore, even if Ms. Jorgensen wasn't a
resident of Oregon, she has a valid Health Care Directive.
Minnesota law requires that lesser restrictive alternatives be
applied before guardianship can even be considered, and

my client's Health Care Directive is a valid lesser restrictive alternative. Simply put, the Court doesn't even need to be involved. No subject matter jurisdiction. Besides, Attorney Johnson - who is Ms. Jorgensen's Health Care Agent by the way - has personally flown here to escort Ms. Jorgensen back home to Oregon."

Attorney Johnson jumped in and continued the explanation. "It seems like every time I try to get away on vacation, one of Linda's children - I mean Ms. Jorgensen's children - whomever she happens to be visiting at the time actually, attempts to put her under guardianship. They've tried this same stunt on at least two other occasions in the last five years; the last time in Illinois; the time before that in Nebraska."

Rigby was sweating profusely but still he didn't utter a sound. So I seized the opportunity. "Just one more thing." I paused for emphasis. "I filed a copy of my client's Trust with the Court yesterday, your Honor. It clearly shows that if there is a legal finding that Ms. Jorgensen is incapacitated - for any reason whatsoever - then she can no longer serve as Trustee of her own Trust! In other words, her kids take over management of the Trust. And, since her Trust contains 'sprinkling powers,' the children would then would have the legal power to 'sprinkle' assets to themselves." More like 'pissing powers' than 'sprinkling powers,' I thought to myself. But I didn't share that insight with the Court.

"It's like a hostile take-over, your Honor. The kids could effectively take all of Ms. Jorgensen's money and use it for themselves - perfectly legal of course, but terribly wrong." I finished.

Mr. Rigby finally found his words and jumped to his feet. "I object, your Honor." He sputtered. "This is all speculation. Plaintiff is just trying to help her mother with her eating problem!"

"Oh yes. The eating problem." I responded before the Judge could rule. I didn't want to antagonize the Judge anymore than I already had, but I needed to make some kind of legal argument, even a shaky one. So I bravely proceeded, "It's true that Mr. Rigby and I completed an inventory of my client's refrigerator last week as the Court ordered; however, it appears that, lacking in rem jurisdiction over Ms. Jorgensen's refrigerator or even possibly in personam jurisdiction over Ms. Jorgensen, the Court should simply dismiss the Petition and allow Ms. Jorgensen to return home to Oregon with Mr. Johnson this afternoon. Actually, the plane tickets are in his briefcase. He showed them to me just before the hearing. Let Oregon deal with the 'eating problem' if there actually is one. Minnesota doesn't have a public policy of taking hostages from the State of Oregon or any other state, as far as I know, and my client feels like she has overstayed her welcome here anyway. And, seriously," I winked at the

Judge, "the Court of Appeals would probably agree with her." Then, I held my breath, waiting for the Judge's ruling.

"Objection overruled." Judge Henderson's face was livid. He turned to Rhonda the Rich's attorney, glowering. "Mr. Rigby?" he said, almost in a whisper. Rigby's body went rigid. "Did your *Emergency* Petition note Ms. Jorgensen's residence as the State of Oregon?" Judge Henderson emphasized the word 'Emergency' as if it were a dirty word. Everyone cringed. I knew what was coming.

"Well, not exactly, your Honor. She was present within the borders of the State of Minnesota so I thought - I didn't think it was important."

"Did your '*Emergency*' Petition disclose that Ms. Jorgensen had a valid Health Care Directive?"

"Well, no. I didn't know. That is, I didn't find out until Gracie - I mean, Ms. Swan, served me with a copy of the Health Care Directive yesterday." Oh, God! I thought. Rigby was doomed to purgatory for the next 100 years or so in Judge Henderson's Court. He had lost all credibility. I almost felt sorry for him.

Without pause, Judge Henderson then turned his controlled, but furious gaze upon Rhonda the Rich, "Ms. Albertson, did you know your mother was a resident of Oregon? That she was just temporarily in Minnesota to visit you? And that she had a valid Health Care Directive?" Oh God, three questions in rapid fire order. Rhonda the Rich's case was in its death throes!

"Well, sure, I guess." Rhonda the Rich glanced nervously at her attorney, "But I didn't think that it mattered! She's so skinny, you know. I was just so worried!" Rhonda the Rich was much too scared to cry this time.

No longer fooled, Judge Henderson's brows were meeting in the middle of his forehead. He had reached a new state of calm. He had one final question for Rhonda the Rich. The Courtroom was deathly silent. "Did you know that your mother would lose control of her Trust if a Guardian was appointed for her?"

"Well, I guess so, but she doesn't need all that money anyway..."

Wrong answer! No Judge likes to be manipulated. And, no person, living or dead, wanted to be on the receiving end of that Judge's gaze just now.

The Judge surveyed the attorneys in his Courtroom, then he looked directly at me! Yikes! Calm down, Gracie, I said to myself. I knew that look. It wasn't deja vu exactly, but close.

"Ms. Swan." He said.

"Yes, your Honor." I stood, bravely squaring off my shoulders.

"Did you wish to file a motion to dismiss, with prejudice, and ask for an award of attorney's fees for your client?"

"I most certainly do, your Honor. As it happens... If I may approach?" He nodded at me.

And so I did. I walked slowly up to the front of the Courtroom and handed the Judge a second sheaf of papers, which he briefly reviewed and - almost - eagerly signed. One lesson I learned long ago. It's always easier for a Judge to sign an Order drafted by me than for the Judge to write the Order himself. It's almost like writing a Christmas wish list and handing it to a Santa Claus who really loves you - at least in that moment.

"Oh, by the way, Ms. Swan," the Judge said with a wink, "Orders in emergency proceedings are non-appealable." Oops.

As I left the Courtroom, I could hear Rhonda the Rich furiously reaming out her lawyer, "You said this was a slam dunk, especially after the inventory... what did she mean, no jurisdiction? My mother was standing right there! What do you mean I have to pay my mom's attorney's fees!" Rhonda the Rich was glaring at me now. "She's got all the money. She should pay." Not only was Rhonda the Rich confused about what had happened in her moment of triumph, but she was even more confused about the Armani skirt, just skimming my knees. And she surely would have been surprised to know that my bank account far exceeded her own - well, probably. At least it was far in excess of the $10.57 balance of just one week ago! Anyhow, I was feeling quite magnanimous at that particular moment, so I gave her my sunniest smile. Just another day in the life of... a Winner!

Epilogue

The Closet Door

Well here I am again - at the cabin.

Looking back, it was no surprise to anyone (especially not the IRS) that Anna left me quite a bundle, even after all of her special gifts and the death tax bill. So much extra dough, in fact, that I've felt some responsibility to fund various other charitable institutions in addition to Anna's favored charities, for example: The Cat Society, Doctors Without Borders, and the Minnesota Rollergirls, just to mention a few. However, this cabin was the only material thing I ever really wanted. So I did it! I finally bought the cabin! It's my cabin now, and there's no dispute about it. The closet door is mine, all mine. Yipee!

The realtor's eyes had nearly popped out of her head when I made the offer. I suppose $500,000 was a bit excessive, but what else is excessive money good for anyway? I have no regrets. To be fair, the realtor made a half-hearted attempt to talk me into reducing my initial offer, but the fact was, her commission on this transaction alone was greater than the average annual income of most Americans. So, ultimately, she didn't argue too much. And, it got results! I had a firm deal the very next afternoon.

So now, more than ever, I wanted to share the cabin with someone special - I wanted to share it with Quinn! I wanted to prove to him that some things never change - and hopefully last forever. Maybe even us.

Things have been fairly tame since all that crazy stuff happened last November. At times, it still feels like it all had been a wild drug or alcohol-induced dream. That is, until I roll over and bump into Quinn's warm body in our bed, in the gigantic orange master bedroom at the house in Stillwater. It seems like we never really left Anna's house last November. Somehow we just started filling it up - with ourselves, our books and our lives.

Not that things have been dull since then, to be sure. Natalie and Richard easily finished Anna's 'apple peeler" for the NSA. They had made such an impression upon our main spy agency that at least Natalie and Richard could honestly tell their neighbors that they "work for the government." Anna would have been so proud! Furthermore, there is no doubt in my mind that our world is now a safer place with Natalie and Richard running the show (whether "the government" knows it or not)! And, as if that wasn't enough, as soon as they knew "Little Richard" was on the way, they tied the knot. As in the "M" word, for real. Again, choices. They needed to do something! They decided they wanted each other, and they wanted the little guy, so heh. Bed of Roses, and all that. They sure seem happy together. And, despite Natalie's big, big belly, she still turns heads. Thankfully, she hasn't demanded that I take her back to Whistle Binkies in quite some time. My only complaint is that she has stalwartly refused to tell me where she got her cool boots from! No fair.

Although Quinn makes the commute from Stillwater to his lab most days, he drives the cab less. For whatever reason, time seems to "stretch out" when we're at home together, and we spend quite a bit of that "extra" time discovering and exploring all the new rooms we seem to be constantly finding in the Stillwater house. It seems like there's always another door that we haven't opened, down a corridor that we don't remember having traversed before! It's kind of like being on a perpetual tour of House on the Rock in Spring Green, Wisconsin.

Quinn has decided that there is some underlying transcendental - no - intercontinental - no - transducive - deal going on at our house. Yeah, that's the word he and Richard have been bandying about lately - transducive - whatever the hell that means! I think it has something to do with the orange tabbies blinking "off" and "on" every now and then or maybe it's because the cookie jar is always filled with chocolate chip cookies. Also, no surprise, our supply of orange candies never seems to run out!

I've been studying Anna's journal, as she demanded in our last meeting, so I think I've got most things figured out pretty well. And, by the way, I haven't touched her Apple stock. Despite my new knowledge, it sure was entertaining to listen to Quinn, Richard and Natalie as they were brainstorming in front of the fireplace last Winter. So much so that I'm almost - I repeat ALMOST - looking forward to cold weather for the simple pleasure of sitting with my friends in front of the fireplace again, enjoying those long discussions and quiet moments of friendship.

Oh, yeah. Quinn and I've gone down the tunnel to the Carnegie library several times since last November, but all we've ever seen at the end of the tunnel is a locked metal door. No rumblings from 'the other side', so to speak. I guess Quinn and Richard truly and securely shut the portal during the transference event - at least so far as I can tell.

Quinn's new SUV (with a hemi) pulls up on the gravel drive next to the cabin. I rush out to meet him and hug him fiercely. He says, "Gee. I just saw you this morning, Gracie. Is everything OK?"

"Everything is amazingly good!" I say. "Quick, come inside. I want to show you something!" I pull him inside and march him over to the kitchen cabinet with the twin wine glasses. "See - I told you - no dust!" I pull out a small cup at the back of the second shelf, the cup with the paper clip in it. "Look! Here it is. I put this exact paperclip in this exact cup more than two years ago and it's still here! Quinn, it's like I told you, nothing ever changes up here!"

"Are you sure you're OK?" He asks again, almost making 'that' face at me.

"Sure. I'm good. I just wanted you to know that there are some things in life that don't change; that don't go away. There are some things that last forever. I swear it's true!"

"I believe you, Gracie." He paused, "But, to be honest, I always told the caretaker to keep everything the way it was. Just like it was when my grandmother lived here. I liked it that way. I wanted it to stay the same forever!" Quinn answered.

"What...? You... told the caretaker... to leave everything just the way it was... not to change anything in... your grandmother's cabin?" It felt like the top of my head was coming off. "You, you owned this place? And, you sold this cabin to me... ?"

"I wouldn't have sold it to anyone else..."

"For $500,000?"

"...for any amount of money. But, the money was nice. A good incentive. Now we can broaden the research, maybe really get a good start on..."

"Why didn't you tell me?"

"Tell you what?"

"That you owned this cabin?" I asked, astonished.

"Oh. That. Well, to begin with, I wasn't absolutely sure that this cabin, my grandmother's cabin, was the one you were buying for that ridiculous sum of money! And once I figured it out, I honestly didn't know how to tell you." He shrugged his shoulders and grinned a little sheepishly. "It didn't seem that important at the time. You were having so much fun with it! I would have sold the cabin to you for 25 cents. But it really doesn't matter now anyway."

"Wow," was all I could think to say in my stunned state. Then, "For 25 cents, you say?"

"Yeah. Well, maybe 50 cents since I drive a hard bargain!"

"Ah, shit." I said. "I told you I was never any good at bargaining!" I took a few deep breaths. "Oh well. You have all the money now. Better that way."

"Yep. I'm totally in control now. I've got the power..."

"You know I don't care about money. But, there's just this one little thing..." and I stepped closer.

"What now? I thought it was all settled!"

"Quinn, are you always going to be a contrarian?"

"A contrarian? What's a contrarian?"

"You know, whenever I say one thing, you take up an equal and, perhaps, opposite position."

"You mean, like positive and negative charges - equal, but opposite. Matter and anti-matter and..."

"Stop. Stop, right now. You know what I mean and..."

He stepped forward and kissed me. Then he kissed me again. "First things first." Quinn said.

"What now?" I asked apprehensively. "I thought it was all settled!"

Quinn pulled out a small articulated key from his pocket. Seeing it, I realized he held the tiny key we had discovered in the tunnel under Anna's house on the night of the transference event. "Remember this key, Gracie?" He said.

"Yeah. It's the one we found in the tunnel, right?" I had forgotten about it, till just now.

"When I was a small child, my grandmother told me a story about how she had lost a special key, a magic key, a long, long time ago. She described it as a small articulated key just like this one." He paused. "She told me some other things too."

"Oh?"

"She said that when I found it - she was certain that I would find it some day - that I could easily open that door over there." He pointed to the small closet door to the right of the fireplace - at the warped door with the curiously small round window in it. A seriously dirty window. "She said she had left a special surprise in there for me. She also told me she had a vision that I would be standing right here next to someone, and that someone would be the most important person in my life."

I gulped, but said nothing.

"She said I had to wait for the right moment, the right person, and the right occasion before I attempted to open the door. She made me promise my most solemn promise." Then, he stepped over to the closet door with the articulated key, and held out his hand to me.

"Oh! Oh my! Does this mean..." I moved to Quinn's side. He took my hand in his; he inserted the small key into the lock, and we turned the key together. The lock clicked easily. He pushed the door open and drew me into the small, dusty room. The room was empty. We looked at each other. Quinn said nothing.

"It was a sweet imaginative story for a small boy," I said as a small tear slid down my cheek. "She probably understood your temperament even then - trying to encourage your mad scientist tendencies!" I forced a laugh as I tried to comfort him. Turning to leave, my shoe bumped into something metallic near the side of the room. I hadn't noticed it before. Quinn bent down and picked up the tarnished object, covered in dust, and handed it to me.

Why, it was one of my antique spoons, with floral embellishments! How did it get here? No. Wait. My five antique spoons were back at home, at the house in Stillwater. I had moved them from my old apartment to Anna's kitchen just a few weeks ago. This had to be the missing spoon! The long lost Sixth Spoon! How could this be? I looked at Quinn again, not with tears now, but with joy and wonder! It made such perfect sense.

Quinn knew. He cleared his throat. There was a twinkle in his eye, and something else. An unspoken question. This time I wasn't afraid to look, and I was ready to answer.

"Knowing all this... and now even a bit more, why don't we just give it a try, Gracie? For now; for forever; and maybe even if things change sometimes?"

"Works for me."

"It's settled then?"

"Yes." I said to Quinn - to the handsome and totally unexpected Quinn of my dreams - and then some.

Om Mani Padme Hum .... Om Mani Padme Hum ...
This little light of mine, I'm going to let it shine ...

Author's Note

Passing the Torch On

I went to a seminar once, where a highly successful woman lawyer had left the practice of law to form a business to advise women how to live their lives without chaos. I can't recall too many details of that day, or even what she offered as a remedy to a high-stress life, but I do remember a few comments she made. She said that when she left the practice of law, the only papers she kept were the "thank you" notes, which she had shoved into her desk over many years; some notes she hadn't even read until she was closing her law practice. She said that lawyers in general never stop to reflect when one case ends; they just plough through to the next, and the next, and the next, without ever looking back. She said she was tired of not looking back. She needed closure.

A truly wise woman.

Ever since that seminar, I have saved, read and treasured each and every one of my "thank you's." I received a globe of precious metals from a client's family once, and even an authentic warrior's eagle feather for bravery. I try never to forget those sincere moments, squeezed into a day, when a client reflects that I have actually helped, rather than just bothered them, and then takes the time to remember me with a "thank you." Maybe my clients really are angels after all.

And I will always remember my law professors with fondness - even the especially tough ones. They honed my skills and my spirit until I was ready, and able, to practice law as a profession, not as a business. For this, I will be forever grateful.

So, this book is a sincere and heart-felt "thank you" to my family, friends, clients, and colleagues, and especially to all the persons, both living and dead, who have inspired, encouraged and supported me in the writing of this crazy book. You know who you are!

Finally, while writing this book, I realized that not one part of my story has to be "real," "true," or even firmly based in reality. What I know is that anything and every-thing is possible. And, in its simplest terms, at least in this dimension, that's what life is all about.

Wishing you MAGIC AND HOPE,
C.

About the Author . . .

Carelle Jean Muellner Stein was born in Duluth, Minnesota. She graduated from the University of Minnesota Law School in 1993.

Carelle likes to travel, enjoys music, art, architecture and design, and is an avid reader. She practices yoga and dances as often as she can. She has also attained 4th Rank in Shorin Ryu Karate.

Carelle has a healthy, maladjusted family (a pack of ring-leaders). She can usually be found somewhere in the midwest with her husband, Ted, where she is famous for not answering her cell phone.

This is her first book.

About the Artist...

Though a soft spoken child, Susan Mrosek
could often be seen traipsing through the house
waving a ten foot needle, determined to sew
her creative oats. And over the past 35 years
she has - via paintings, sculptures, cards, posters,
a book, videos, etc. All, at times, have been her favorite,
yet writing, she says, is by far the most freeing.
It's what inspired her to create Pondering Pool...
a place where truth and humor unite,
forming a cast of sweetly odd, outspoken
characters who graciously show us that
being different isn't a flaw, but a blessing.

Susan lives and creates in her tiny Tucson AZ studio –
she, herself, is bite-size.

To see more of her work, visit:
www.ponderingpool.com

About the Shoes . . .

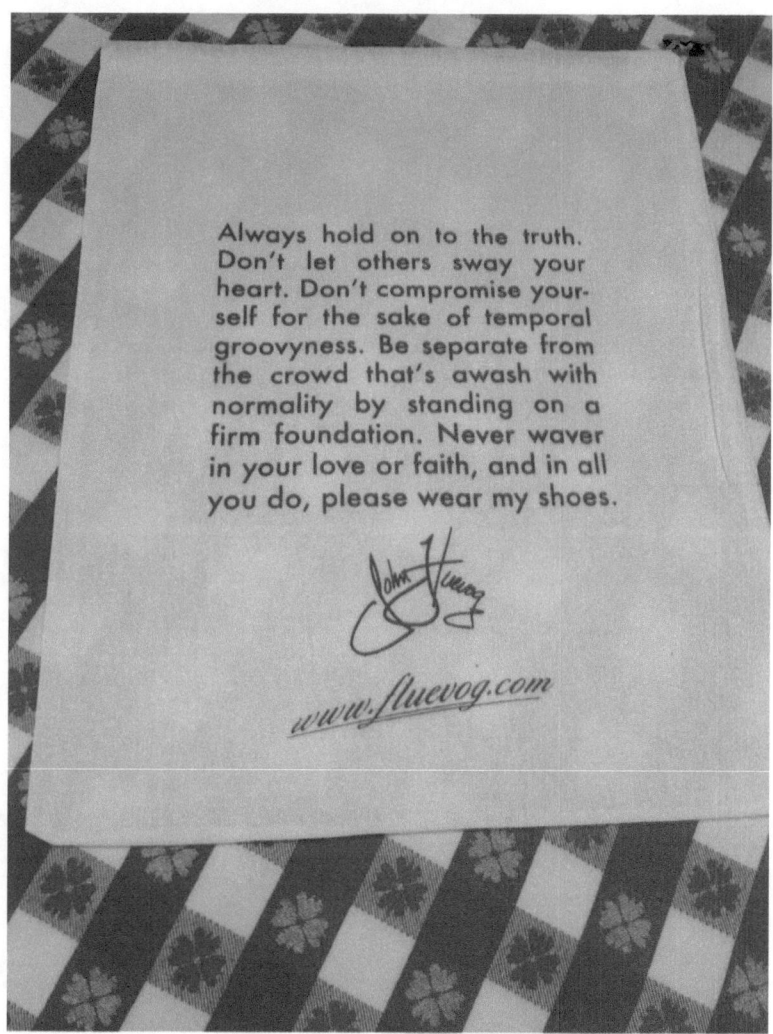

Always hold on to the truth. Don't let others sway your heart. Don't compromise yourself for the sake of temporal groovyness. Be separate from the crowd that's awash with normality by standing on a firm foundation. Never waver in your love or faith, and in all you do, please wear my shoes.

John Fluevog

www.fluevog.com

www.ingramcontent.com/pod-product-compliance
Lightning Source LLC
Chambersburg PA
CBHW051518250626
47156CB00001B/138